The Concept of Islamic International Criminal Law
A Comparative Study

Farhad Malekian

Graham & Trotman/Martinus Nijhoff
Members of the Kluwer Academic Publishers Group
LONDON/DORDRECHT/BOSTON

Graham & Trotman Limited
Sterling House
66 Wilton Road
London SW1V 1DE
UK

Kluwer Academic Publishers Group
101 Philip Drive
Assinippi Park
Norwell, MA 02061
USA

© Farhad Malekian, 1994
First published 1994

ISBN: 1 85966 085 1

British Library Cataloguing in Publication Data and Library of Congress Cataloging-in-Publication Data is available

Printed and bound in Great Britain by Hartnolls Ltd, Bodmin, Cornwall.

In the Name of the Lord
the Most Merciful, the Most Compassionate

For my mother—the core principle of human morality

Table of Contents

Preface   xiii
Glossary   xv

Chapter One
A Preliminary Examination of the
Characterization of the Islamic
International Criminal Law   1

1. Overview   1
2. Islamic International Law   3
3. Legal Dimension   6
4. Practical Implementation   8
5. Universality Principle   10
6. Legal Characterization of Islamic Obligations   12
   6.1. *Pacta Sunt Servanda*   12
   6.2. *De Lege Lata*   13
   6.3. *Jus Cogens*   14

Chapter Two
The Basic Elements of Both Systems of
International Criminal Law   17

1. The Purposes of International Criminal Law   17
2. Definitions   18
   2.1. Definition of International Criminal Law   18
   2.2. Definition of Islamic International Criminal Law   20
   2.3. A Comparative Definition of Both Systems   23
3. Sources of Both Systems   25
   3.1. Sources of International Criminal Law   25
      3.1.1. Conventions   25
      3.1.2. Customs   26
      3.1.3. Decisions   27
      3.1.4. Publicists   28
   3.2. Sources of Islamic International Criminal Law   28
      3.2.1. The Qur'an   30

3.2.2. Sunnah   31
3.2.3. Consensus   32
3.2.4. Juridical Analogy   34
3.3. A Comparative Examination of Sources of Both Systems   36
4. Subjects of Both Systems   36
5. The Concept of Crime in Both Systems   38
5.1. The List of Crimes   39
5.2. Differences   40
6. Punishment   41
6.1. Lack of Methods in International Criminal Law   41
6.2. Flexibility of Punishment in Islamic International Criminal Law 43
6.3. Comparative Conclusions   44

Chapter Three
Aggression   45

1. Aggression in International Criminal Law   45
2. Aggression in Islamic International Criminal Law   48
2.1. Definition   48
2.2. Prohibitions   49
2.3. Peaceful Settlement of Disputes   50
2.4. Inevitable Situations   51
2.4.1. Defensive War   52
2.4.2. Assisting Victims   52
2.4.3. Protection of Fundamental Rights   53
2.4.4. Fulfilment of Serious Obligations   54
2.5. Jihad   55
2.5.1. Definition   55
2.5.2. *Jihad* as a Means of Defeating Aggressors   58
2.6. Acts Constituting Aggression   62

Chapter Four
War Crimes   63

1. War Crimes in International Criminal Law   63
1.1. The First Development   63
1.2. The Second Development   64
1.3. The Third Development   65
1.4. The Fourth Development   66
1.5. The Fifth Development   68
2. War Crimes in Islamic International Criminal Law   70

2.1. Codification   70
2.2. Acts Constituting War Crimes   72

Chapter Five
Poisonous Weapons   74

Chapter Six
Crimes Against Humanity   76

1. Criminalization in International Criminal Law   76
2. Criminalization in Islamic International Criminal Law   77

Chapter Seven
Slavery   79

1. Slavery in International Criminal Law   79
  1.1. Abolition   79
  1.2. Criminalization   80
2. Slavery in Islamic International Criminal Law   83
  2.1. Manumission   83
  2.2. Abolition   84
  2.3. Protection   86
  2.4. Criminalization   88

Chapter Eight
Genocide   90

1. Genocide in International Criminal Law   90
2. Genocide in Islamic International Criminal Law   91
  2.1. Prohibitions   91
  2.2. Classification   92
  2.3. Criminalization in Human Rights   93

Chapter Nine
Discrimination / Apartheid   94

1. Apartheid in International Criminal Law   94
2. Apartheid in Islamic International Criminal Law   96

Chapter Ten
Torture   98

1. Torture in International Criminal Law   98
   1.1. Non-Criminalization   98
   1.2. Criminalization   99
2. Torture in Islamic International Criminal Law   103
   2.1. Definition   103
   2.2. Administration of Justice   104
   2.3. Prohibitions   105
   2.4. Practice   106

Chapter Eleven
Crimes Against Internationally
Protected Persons   107

1. Criminalization in International Criminal Law   107
2. Criminalization in Islamic International Criminal Law   109
   2.1. Immunity   109
   2.2 The Scope of Protection   110
   2.3. Criminalization   110

Chapter Twelve
Taking of Hostages   113

1. International Criminal Law   113
2. Islamic International Criminal Law   114

Chapter Thirteen
Drug Offences   116

1. Criminalization in International Criminal Law   116
2. Prohibitions in Islamic International Criminal Law   119

Chapter Fourteen
Obscene Activities and Publications   121

1. Non-Effective Criminalization in International Criminal Law   121
2. Prohibitions in Islamic International Criminal Law   123

Chapter Fifteen
Crimes Against Natural Environments 126

1. Nature 126
2. Protection of Living Creatures 127
3. A Double Criminalization 127

Chapter Sixteen
Crimes Against Foodstuffs 129

Chapter Seventeen
Criminalization of Alcoholic Drinks 131

Chapter Eighteen
Piracy 132

1. Piracy in International Criminal Law 132
2. Land Piracy in Islamic International Criminal Law 133

Chapter Nineteen
Limitations of Hostilities
in the Conduct of States 135

1. Declaration of War 135
2. Contraband of War and Trade 136
3. Self–Defence 136
4. Reprisals 138
5. The Principle of Proportionality 139
6. Self–determination 141
7. Humanitarian Help 145

Chapter Twenty
Institution of Protections 148

1. Overview 148
2. Refugees 148
3. Extradition 150
4. Quarter 151

Chapter Twenty One
Humanitarian Protections
of Prisoners of War   154

1. Prisoners of War in International Criminal Law   154
2. Prisoners of War in Islamic International Criminal Law   156
   2.1. Definition of Prisoners of War   156
   2.2. Protections of Prisoners of War   157

Chapter Twenty Two
The Principles of Human
Rights in Both Systems   160

1. Human Rights in International Criminal Law   160
2. Human Rights in Islamic International Criminal Law   162
   2.1. Basis   162
   2.2. Functions   163
   2.3. Judicial Criminal Autonomy   165
   2.4. Human Rights within the Sunnah   168

Chapter Twenty Three
International Criminal Responsibility   172
1. The System of International Criminal Law   172
2. Islamic International Criminal Law   174
   2.1. The General Concept   174
   2.2. International Aspects   175
   2.3. Superior Order   177

Chapter Twenty Four
Comparative Conclusions   179

Appendixes   181
Universal Islamic Declaration of Human Rights   183
Bibliography on Islamic Law   192
Bibliography on International Criminal Law   197
Index   211

Preface

If the terminology of Islamic international criminal law seems unfamiliar to some, it is because such terminology is exclusively my own innovation and has not been used previously in the Islamic system of international law. This type of criminal law has existed within Islamic law for a long period of time and has not been previously analyzed within a separate field of law. The purpose of this comparative study between the system of international criminal law and the Islamic concept of international criminal law is to point out that there are principally very minor differences indeed between these two legal systems. The main purpose of this study is to evaluate certain important regulations in both these systems and examine them in the light of the growing development of international criminal law, thereby proving that conflicts and apparent differences between the two systems are not principal but political, ideological, procedural and more importantly as a result of specific interpretations of both legal systems. By this examination we hope to be helpful in resolving a very important issue recently raised in the International Law Commission of the United Nations, on the establishment of an international criminal court in order to prosecute and punish the perpetrators of international crimes.

It is relevant to mention here that both systems have been carefully analyzed side by side in order to ensure that the reader can examine the principles of both systems simultaneously and to also avoid any seperate interpretations of the two systems. The book is simply an introduction to the wide range of instruments, cases and other material to be found in both systems and does not exhaust all the criminal issues which may be found under both systems. It does nevertheless present the basic principles of both systems and their possible cooperation and accommodation in solving the most important questions surrounding the criminality, prosecution and punishment of criminals at an international level.

Obviously the work is written for those who have legal knowledge and are familiar with the various civil and criminal terminologies used. The book also serves as a key principle to the rights of all those who belong to different types of minority groups including those which differ on the basis of race, colour, *religion*, politics or ethnic origin. There should not exist any form of discrimination between different ethnic, political or religious groups. This is a basic principle which should be respected in both Islamic and Non–Islamic societies. This book may thus be judged in the light of any peaceful cooperation between both systems for the settlement of certain seemingly unsolvable international conflicts. I wrote this book because I have worked intensively with the system of international criminal law and am familiar with the legal ethics of Islamic international criminal law. *I am well acquainted with both systems and am therefore objective.* The book purely represents certain basic principles of Islamic law governing the subject and has *nothing* to do with early or contemporary practices of Islamic law in different states. The contents of the book consequently serves as a history of law in general and as an integral part of jurisprudence of law in particular. The pioneer character of this work may be a strong reason for any misintepretation and/or indulgence found by the reader.

It is my hope that this book will create international juridical grounds for all who work with the system of international law in general and the system of international criminal law and the Islamic concept of international criminal law in particular. Governments should understand that to exploit these legal principles does not bring peace and justice since both legal systems presented have similar aims, purposes, functions and present more or less similar conclusions. I believe that to hope rarely ends in happiness but does however create the psychological basis for a writer to live and work with the future.

Uppsala, May 1994
F. Malekian

Glossary

aman	immunity
Asl	original case
bellum justum	law of war
Caliphat	leadership
dar al-'ahd	territories in peaceful relations in accordance with obligations of treaties
dar al-Harb	the realm of war
dar al-Islam	Islamic territories
dar al-sulh	territories in peaceful relations
de facto	by the fact
de jure	by the law
Fatawa	legal decision made by a supreme leader, collections of judicial decisions
fiqh	jurisprudence
hadith	the narrations of the Prophet conveyed to man through revelations or hearing
hudud	fixed penalties
ibadat	ritual
Ijma	consensus of opinion
Ijtihad	individual judgement
Istislah	Public interest
Jihad	struggle
mu'amalat	transactions
nulla poena sine lege or *nullum crimes sine lege*	a maxim embodying the basic principle of the criminal law that conduct cannot be punished as criminal unless some rule of law has already declared conduct of that kind to be criminal and punishable as such
Pacta Sunt Servanda	obligations of a treaty must be respected by the parties
Qadis	judges

Qital	fighting
Qiyas	analogical reasoning
Quesas	crime against a person such as murder, homicide and causing serious bodily or mental harm
Sawa	Equal
siyar	universal law, international law, law among nations
Sunnah	the manner or mode of life of the Prophet during his lifespan.
Ulama	Islamic jurists

Chapter One

A Preliminary Examination of the Characterization of the Islamic International Criminal Law

1. Overview

Islamic law basically has the virtue of internationalizing the conduct of states.[1] It is upon this basic principle that the whole theory of Islamic international law or *siyar* is built and developed with the purpose of creating flexible and acceptable international relations between various nations of the world.[2] Islamic law, in contrast to that which is understood by many writers, is not therefore exclusive to Muslim state conduct. Islamic law not only regulates the conduct of Muslim states[3] but also regulates the rules of conduct between other nations, regardless of the theological attitudes of the relevant nations. It is a law for all nations and is basically applicable at all times, especially during

---

[1] The development and the collections of the rules, provisions, regulations and other cases of the system of Islamic international law has greatly depended on the most significant and valuable labour of Al-Shaybain, Abu Abdallah Muhammad b. al-Hassan b. Farqad (749/750-805 = 312-189 Hejja). His classical work is called al-Siyar al-Kabir which can be translated into one of the following terms; The law of nations, the universal law, international law or to be more precise, Muslim law of nations, Muslim international law and Islamic international law. In any event, the overwhelming majority of Islamic writers are of the view that Al-Shaybani is without doubt the father of Islamic international law. Ghunaimi, M.T.A., The Muslim Conception of International Law and the Western Approach (Netherlands, 1968), p.35.

[2] Islamic international law has been traditionally called *siyar* and has been recognized as an integral part of Islamic law or *fiqh*.

[3] The first Islamic state was established in Medina according to the discussions noted from a conference between Muhammad, the Prophet of Islam, his uncle Abbs and some seventy delegates of Medina, resulting in the Second Pledge of Al-`aqaba in July 622. The Covenant of Medina was signed in the next year. The Covenant consists of 47 Articles. Watt, M.W., Muhammad at Medina (Oxford, 1962), pp.225-6. Hamidullah, Muhammad., Le Prophète de l'Islam (Paris, 1959), Vols.I-II.

the modern conduct of international relations.[4] This means that Islamic law is not a limited or a conservative law, it can coincide with the regulations of other nations in order to achieve peaceful international relations.[5] Moreover, 'Its primary significance is the 'making of peace', and the idea of 'peace is the dominant idea in Islam.'[6] Islamic international law thus promotes reciprocal obligations and duties and due to its philosophy of justice consent constitutes the main principle for obedience to the law. According to this philosophy no force should be employed for the implementation of Islamic law.[7] Rules and obligations must come into existence through authentic consent and not by ideological or military force. Equality between subjects of the law also constitutes one of the main elements of Islamic international law. This original legal theory of Islamic law and Islamic international criminal law has also been greatly effective in the Western concept of international law.[8] Moreover, 'it was the Muslims who have not only developed international law, the first in the world, as a distinct discipline, but also have made it form part of law instead of politics.'[9]

Although the system of Islamic international criminal law has an entirely independent characterization in relation to the system of international criminal law, the majority of principles, rules, provisions, regulations and customary obligations in both legal systems are not only in conformity with one another

---

[4] For views on the modernization of Islamic law see Bonderman, David., Modernization and Changing Perceptions of Islamic Law, 81 Harvard Law Review (1968), pp.1169–93.

[5] Ali, Maulana Muhammad., Muhammad the Prophet (Lahore, 1924), p.275.

[6] Ali, Maulvi Muhammad., Islam The Religion of Humanity (1926), p.4; See also Ali, Maulana Muhammad., Back to the Qur'an, Back to Muhammad, Rise! Advance! (Lahore, 1926), p.19; Ali, Muhammad., Islam or the Natural Religion of Man: A Brief Sketch of Its Principles as given in the Holy Qur'an (Lahore, 1912), p.3–5.

[7] It is a well know fact in the *Qur'an* that 'Let there be no compulsion in religion.'

[8] There are in fact different opinions concerning the legal and political effect of Islamic law on Western international law in general and the Western legal system in particular. On the positive effect of Islamic law in various Western legal systems see Weeramantry, C.G., Islamic Jurisprudence: An International Perspective (1988), pp. 149–58. According to Professor Weeramantry, for example, 'In relation to the vital discipline of international law there was no literature from Greece and Rome comparable to their literature in private law. We do not have treatises dealing with such questions as the binding force and interpretation of treaties, the duties of combatants, the rights of non–combatants or the disposal of enemy property. The only body of literature in this discipline was the Islamic.' Moreover, 'Arabic literature was ... not a great unkown in the days when the first seeds were being sown of what was to become Western international law.' *Id.*, p.150. On the impact of Islamic international law upon Grotius see *id.*, pp.150–8. See also Justice Jackson, foreward to Law in the Middle East, Khadduri, Majid (ed)., 1955).

[9] Publications of Centre Culturel Islamique., Introduction to Islam (Park Lane, Secunderabad, 1376 H/ 1957 A.C.), p.94.

but also have similar purposes and functions for the appropriate prevention and prohibition of international criminal violations. Even in certain procedures such as extradition or the prosecution and punishment of criminals, the system of Islamic international criminal law presents much more significant solutions and legal provisions for settlements than other legal forms.

2. Islamic International Law

Islamic law is indeed a very flexible law. It not only covers the relations between individuals, individuals with organizations and states, but also covers international relations between states.[10] The Islamic law like many other laws consists of different branches. This includes the civil law, the commercial law, taxation law, property law, family law, social law, administrative law, law of contract, criminological law, criminal law, procedural law, and finally international law – which includes human rights, international humanitarian laws and/or international criminal law. For our purpose it is helpful to present several definitions of the Islamic international law which have been ignored in the writings of most publicists.[11]

According to one view Islamic international law may be defined as 'That part of the law and custom of the land and treaty obligations which a Muslim *de facto* or *de jure* State observes in its dealings with other *de facto* or *de jure* States.'[12]

For a clarification of this definition the above source states that 'Muslim International Law depends wholly and solely upon the will of the Muslim State. It derives its authority just as any other Muslim law of the land. Even the obligations imposed by bilateral or multilateral ... treaties have the same basis and unless they are ratified and executed by the contracting Muslim party, they are not binding.' Their 'non-observance does not create any liability against the

---

[10] Khadduri, Majid (translator)., The Islamic Law of Nations: Shaybani's Siyar (Translated with an introduction, notes and appendices, Baltimore, 1966), pp.6–7.

[11] In the system of international law the Hague Peace Conferences of 1899 and 1907 are considered the most important sources of international law, while in Madinah in 973 Hejja a Conference of Muslim leaders from all over the world met and discussed the legal, political, social, moral and economic problems affecting Muslims at that time and decided how to deal with them. The minutes and proceedings of this important conference were published by one of the delegates named Saiyid Abul-Fath alias Shaikh Abd al-Munim al-Baghdadiy under the title Mukhtar al-Kawnain. Hamidullah, Muhammad., Muslim Conduct of State (Lahore – India, 1945), p.26.

[12] *Id.*, pp.1–2.

Muslim State.'[13] The same source also expresses that 'Mutatis mutandis, Muslim International Law would aim at the justest possible conduct of the Muslim ruler in his international intercourse.'[14]

Another opinion compares Islamic international law with European international law.[15] Accordingly, the 'Islamic international law constitutes a vital part of the Islamic legal heritage. This is a discipline which was well developed in Islam, contrary to views which generations of prejudiced writing have instilled in the non–Islamic mind, and requires close attention in any study emphasizing the international importance of Islamic law.'[16] According to this view, the confrontation between the Islam and Christianity is as similar as the confrontation between the two Western and former Communist Worlds.[17] This opinion concludes that 'Western discussions of international law focus sharply on the question whether international law is a system apart from natural law (the dualist view) or whether the two form part of a single fabric of law (the monist view).'[18] He further states that 'If one is a natural lawyer, basing all law upon a set of higher norms or standards, one sees all law, municipal as well as international, as part of a single fabric. If, on the other hand, one takes the view that law owes its validity to state authority, the international legal system rests upon a very different basis from the national.' 'Islamic international law clearly falls into the former, or monist, category. It

---

[13] *Id.*, p.2. This is the same in the system of international law. This is because treaties in the public international law do not create binding force upon signature and therefore the context of most over–whelming treaties require the ratification of the treaties by the national authorities or by the members of parliament.

[14] *Id.*, p.13.

[15] According to another limited definition, 'The Muslim law of nations recognizes no other nation than its own, since the ultimate goal of Islam was the subordination of the whole world to one system of law and religion, to be enforced by the supreme authority of the imam. ... Furthermore, the Muslim law of nations was ordinarily binding upon individuals rather than territorial groups. For Islamic law, like all ancient law, had a personal rather than a territorial character and was obligatory upon the Muslims, as individuals or as a group, regardless of the territory they resided in. ... We may argue, from a philosophical viewpoint, that Islam, as a universal religion, laid emphasis on individual allegiance to a faith which recognized no boundaries for its kingdom: for under a system which claims to be universal territory ceases to be a deciding factor in the intercourse among people. ... Finally, the Muslim law of nations is not a separate body of Muslim law; it is merely an extension of the law designed to govern the relations of the Muslims with non–Muslims, whether inside or outside the world of Islam. ... Analyzed in terms of the modern law of nations, the sources of the Muslim law of nations conform to the same categories defined by modern jurists and the Statute of the International Court of Justice, namely, agreement, custom, reason and authority.' Khadduri, Majid., War and Peace in the Law of Islam (Baltimore, 1955), pp.45–8.

[16] Weeramantry, Islamic Jurisprudence, p.128.

[17] *Id.*

[18] *Id.*, p.131.

depends upon the same sources as national or municipal law – the *Qur'an* and the *Sunna*.'[19]

Another view restricts the scope of Islamic international law and mostly applies it to the conduct of Islamic states. According to this view, Islamic international law is 'l'ensemble des règles dont l'usage est imposé exclusivement aux Musulmans pour régler leurs rapports de guerre et de paix avec les non–Musulmans, individus ou Etats, dans le pays de l'Islam et en dehors de ce pays.'[20]

Another writer states that 'Muslim international law is that which the Islamic State observes towards other States. So far, Islamic States have generally adhered to those established principles of international law which could be said to have gained universal acceptance. Continuous adherence to such principles may have been by virtue of express consent or tacit approval.'[21]

According to my own view, 'The system of international law of Islam rests on two fundamental conceptions, without which its system of international laws would not be fulfilled. First of all, international relations should be based on a principle of legality. Secondly, the practical and philosophical reasons for such international conducts should clearly be set forth. It is obvious that under the former principle international relations come under the union of laws, according to which international consensus should be achieved. According to the latter, international relations should create a permanent international peace within the system of the international legal community.'[22]

Islamic international law means the equal, mutual and reciprocal respect of obligations expressed by rules, norms, regulations, provisions, customs, including moral obligations, which prevail for one reason or another between states, states and organizations, states and groups and states and individuals in order to maintain their universal relations. In contrast to public international law, Muslim international law recognizes individuals as an integral part of its anatomy. This is because in public international law the position of individuals and minor groups is unsettled. Individuals are considered as objects by one

---

[19] *Id.* See also, generally, Abdul Hakim., The Natural Law in the Moslem Tradition, 5 Natural Law Institute Proceedings (1951); Ali, S. A.,The Ethics of Islam (Calcutta, 1893).

[20] Armanazi, Najib., Les Principes Islamiques et les Rapports Internationaux en Temps de Paix et de Guerre (Paris, 1929), p.40.

[21] Moinuddin, Hasan., The Charter of the Islamic Conference and Legal Framework of Economic Co-Operation among its Member States: A study of the Charter, the General Agreement for Economic, Technical and commercial Co-operation and the Agreement for Promotion, Protection and Guarantee of Investments among Member States of the OIC (Oxford, 1987), p.48.

[22] Malekian, Farhad., The System of International Law, Formation, Treaties and Responsibility (Uppsala, 1987), p.8.

group of writers, by another subjects and most recently because of the development of international human rights as beneficiary subjects. Groups in the system of public international law in particular have no independent international legal personality as recognized for other subjects under the system and are therefore not treated equally under its provisions. In contrast, in Muslim international law there is no difference between the international legal characterization of a group and that of a state. They are all considered subjects and are consequently treated equally under the provisions of Islamic law.

3. Legal Dimension

The Islamic philosophy of law is based on *Shari'ah* which essentially contains the basic reasons and elements of obligations. *Shari'ah* is also the source of normative international relations between Muslim states and other states. Islamic law or *Shari'ah* is therefore essentially based on the revealed book of Islam *i.e.* the *Qur'an*. This book was revealed in fragments because of the circumstances at the time to the Prophet of Islam, Muhammad,[23] over a period of twenty three years.[24] *The Qur'an* contains the whole philosophy of Islam and constitutes the main source of Islamic international law and therefore regulates the rules, obligations and duties which must be respected in normative state conduct.[25] Each provision of the *Qur'an* must be examined in relation to their own specific chapters, verses and historical revelation. Thus, this rule for interpreting the *Qur'an* must not be ignored and must be fully respected for the purpose of an authentic interpretation of its provisions. Still, these provisions must be read in conjunction with the whole theory of the *Qur'an* and the *Shari'ah* and *sunnah* as well. *Sunnah* constitutes the second source of Islamic international law and was one of the important reasons for the rapid development of Islamic international relations. In one sense the second source also constitutes a practical interpretation of Islamic law. *Sunnah* also consists

---

[23] For some considerations of the life of Muhammad see Ali, Maulana Muhammad., Muhammad the Prophet (Lahore, 1924); Ali, Muhammad., A Brief Sketch of the Life of the Prophet of Islam (Lahore, 1928); See also Aghnides, Nicolas P., Mohammedan Theories of Finance with an Introduction to Mohammedan Law and a Bibliography (London, 1916).

[24] For statements on the early life of the Prophet see Guillaume, Alfred., New Light on the Life of Muhammad, Monograph 1 Journal of Semitic Studies (Manchester University Press, 1960).

[25] For further consideration and examination see chapter two. For some aspects of the philosophy of Islam see Dominican Pierre Jean De Menasce., Bibliographische Einführungen in das Studium der Philosophie: Arabische Philosophie (Bern, 1948); Watt, W. Montgomery., Islamic Philosophy and Theology (Edinburgh, 1962).

of *hadith* which means the statements of the prophet and also the manner of his life and deeds.[26]

Islamic law is in principle against any type of violations and for this reason it has a large number of rules concerning the prohibition of criminal behaviour. These prohibitions have also been extended and developed in the system of Islamic international criminal law. This system, as will be demonstrated, contains a large number of rules, provisions, customs and moral obligations originally arising from the *Qur'an*. The system is also based on other sources of Islamic law constituting an integral part of the law in the international conduct of Islamic States.[27]

Juridically and theoretically Islamic international criminal law protects all nations. This is because the whole framework of the Islamic system of international criminal law is based on the principle of the protection of mankind and since there is no difference in the creation of men every individual, group or nation can benefit from the provisions of Islamic international criminal law without necessarily being the subject of an Islamic state.[28] This is because according to the theory of Islam all men are the subjects of divine law and in principle every individual must have the respect of other individuals because of the very significant value of the spiritual dignity of man. This principle is extended by the Islamic system of international criminal law, the function of which is to prevent international crimes and to prosecute and punish perpetrators under an appropriate criminal jurisdiction regardless of the nationality of the victim or the accused. In other words Islamic international criminal law protects Muslims and non-Muslims alike and prohibits criminal violations in the system of international relations.[29]

---

[26] For further consideration and examination see chapter two.

[27] *Id.*

[28] See the Universal Islamic Declaration of Human Rights, chapter twenty two.

[29] It contains a large number of provisions governing the humanitarian law of armed conflicts and this law was consolidated fourteen centuries ago when there was scarcely a sign of the humanitarian law of armed conflicts in the practices of most nations. See chapter twenty one. More significantly, 'the twofold division of the world could have factual significance when it relates to reality, that is to say when we want to describe actual war between the Muslim and non-Muslim states. It can have no dogmatic meaning. We object to including this division in the Muslim legal theory as one of its principles. As a matter of fact, this division, under the Abbassids, corresponded to the factual relations between the Islamic state and non-Muslim states. Classical writers only intended to give a legal justification to that institution but in such a way as to corrupt it the conception. Their argumentation is not only unfounded but also introduces two terms which never occurred in the Qur'an or the *hadith*. The terms *dar al-Islam* and *dar al-Harb* are an innovation of the *Abbassid* legists. As their idea on the division of the world is dependent on the notion of constant or aggressive *jihad*, and since this notion is not warranted, inevitably the alleged division should collapse too.' The third division is *dar al-sulh* or *dar al-'ahd*. This division does not either 'cover all the non-Muslim states which are not in

Under Islamic international criminal law protection and respect for the laws of other nations constitutes a legal order and therefore Islamic international criminal law, contrary to what is understood by other writers, strictly prohibits war and aggressive conduct.[30] This means that war is not legitimized under Islamic international criminal law when it is not for the purpose of self-defence.[31] This is not permitted unlimitedly under that system either and must be carried out wholly in accordance with certain regulations in the Islamic humanitarian law of armed conflicts. It must also be based significantly on the principle of proportionality, which constitutes one of the main principles of Islamic international criminal law.

4. Practical Implementation

One important aspects of Islamic international criminal law is that it strongly encourages the principles of forgiveness, amnesty and immediate de-continuation of a defensive war if the aggressive party has desisted actual fighting.[32] These principles are regarded as an integral part of Islamic international criminal law for the purpose of promoting and constantly implementing its humanitarian law of armed conflicts.

More importantly, Islamic international criminal law places great weight on respect for the principles of Islamic human rights within criminal jurisdictions.[33] The respect of such principles are not only necessary on a national level but on an international level also. This means that Islamic law

---

actual war with the Islamic state. For this, and because the tripartite division is generally based on the same philosophy of the tripartite division, we reject it as well.' Ghunaimi, The Muslim Conception of International Law and the Western Approach, p.184.

[30] One Islamic writer drew this conclusion from Muslim jurisprudence, 'the normal relations between Muslim and non Muslim territories are not peaceful, but warlike.' Khadduri, Majid., War and Peace in the Law of Islam (Baltimore, 1955), p.220. This conclusion is surely misleading and is a misinterpretation of the philosophy of Islamic jurisprudence, which is not only based on the practical aspects of the principle of peaceful international relations but is also based on full respect for the rights of those who are non–Muslims and do not wage war against Muslims. Any interpretation that Islam is in a perpetual state of war with non–Muslim nations is obviously without juridical, theological, philosophical or moral grounds and therefore such an opinion expressed by any writer must be considered contradictory to the principles of equality, justice and brotherhood found in *Shari'ah.*

[31] See chapter nineteen.

[32] Hamidullah, Muhammad., The Battlefields of the Prophet Muhammad (England, 1953), p.35.

[33] See, generally, Bassiouni, M. Cherif (ed.), The Islamic Criminal Justice System (London, Rome, New York, 1982).

struggles against any type of violation within its criminal justice system which undermines the dignity of man and jeopardizes an equal application of the principles in the Islamic criminal justice system. For this reason Islamic law emphasizes the principles of brotherhood, justice, equality and respect for the religions of other nations under any domestic jurisdiction. These principles have been especially emphasized within the sources of Islamic international criminal law and have therefore been recognized as chief reasons in the development of Islamic law. Thus, neither the *Qur'an* nor the *Sunnah* limits the application of the principles of Islamic human rights to specific groups. In practice Islamic law should respect all people equally.[34] The same is also true for the whole system of Islamic international criminal law.

Of course we cannot deny that Islamic law,[35] Islamic international law and Islamic international criminal law may be exercised to different degrees because of varied interpretations by different authorities. This is common practice, even in the application of international law and within the system of international criminal law. In this work I do not consequently examine what Islamic law should represent but exclusively the principal spirit of Islamic law as a universal law supporting the constant enforcement and implementation of equal legal principles over all nations. This means that the Islamic law is not a religious law solely allocated to Muslims. It has a broader legal characterization in which several purposes are integrated such as religious duties, public and private laws, commercial law, taxation law, law of contract, family law, human rights and the law of war including the humanitarian law of armed conflicts.[36]

In other words Islam does not necessarily regulate the duties and obligations of mankind towards the creator but regulate the legal relations between individuals, groups and their states. It also regulates the relations between states.[37] This means that Islamic law has a fertile constitution containing the essence of most modern legal systems. The division of Islamic law into the

---

[34] Jafary Langaroody, Muhammad Jafar., Islamic Law (in Persian language, Tehran, 1978), p.202.

[35] *Id.*, pp.202–9.

[36] According to one commentator, 'It would be a mistake to assume that the *Shari'ah* (Islamic law) is a purely 'religious' law such as Canon Law or Kirchenrecht pertaining to Church matters, priesthood, and spiritual affairs. The *Shari'ah* encompasses not only religious duties and obligations but also secular aspects of law (substantive and procedural) regulating human acts; the first class called *Ibadat* (ritual) deals with purely religious matters and the second class called *mu`amalat* (transactions) deals with subjects which normally form the substance of legal systems such as Common Law.' Moinuddin, The Charter of the Islamic Conference and Legal Framework of Economic Co–Operation among its Member States, pp.6–7.

[37] See, generally, Proctor, J.Harris (ed)., Islam and International Relations (New York, 1965).

above legal subjects is for the exclusive purpose of emphasizing that Islamic law deals with various legal systems and it should be noted that we do not necessarily differentiate their sources. This means that Islamic law united legal systems presented fourteen hundred years ago with the purpose of being a core model for a united legal system at an international level.[38]

5. Universality Principle

One of the greatest problems in the system of international criminal law is that it still relys heavily on the territoriality principle, active personality principle, nationality principle, protective principle, passive personality principle, representation principle, distribution and competence principle and some times on the universality principle. States have normally advocated these principles in order to defend their right to implement criminal jurisdiction over an accused. For this reason there has been great confusion in the interpretation of these principles and consequently different arguments presented by states have led to different conclusions.[39]

The variations in these principles themselves and the confusion in their application in given cases have created international and transnational criminal confrontations constituting the most controversial of political and criminal decisions. This problem fortunately does not exist in the legislation of the system of Islamic international criminal law. This is one of the important aspects of the Islamic system which has not, generally speaking, the juridical division of principles advocated under the system of international criminal law. According to Islam, human activities are considered under one jurisdiction and one universal society, although there are many states in practice. This is

---

[38] This basic principal in the Islamic legal system has highly legal value in the development and harmonizing of international criminal procedures including prosecutions, extraditions, jurisdictions and punishments. In a comparative analysis neither the system of international law, the system of international criminal law nor the new regulations of the European Community have been able to create such a united legal system, one which can be enforced under the territorial jurisdictions of their subjects and also be qualified by all legal systems. This lack of unity of laws including their sources, procedures and enforcement measures has led to controversy in the system of international criminal law which has not been resolved; The existence of hundreds of bilateral and multilateral treaties, conventions, arrangements, agreements, pacts and declarations has created complicated situations in relations between contracting parties. The system of international criminal law has for example over three hundred and fifty conventions which do not function appropriately and more importantly fail to regulate relations between contracting parties.

[39] Malekian, International Criminal Law: The Legal and Critical Analysis of International Crimes (Uppsala, 1991), Vol.I, pp.10-19.

because the legal provisions in Islamic law have basically emerged from one constitution and there should not therefore be any difference in the application of the law between different nations.[40]

Islamic law solves confrontations between various legal systems and presents one exclusive legal system. This is also true in the application and implementation of Islamic international criminal law. Consequently, questions of recognition, extradition, prosecution and punishment of criminals are not as complicated in Islamic international criminal law as they are in the system of international criminal law. This is on the grounds that wherever, whenever and to whoever the law is applied it must be to the same degree. It must be emphasized that Islamic criminal jurisdiction does not necessarily rest on the application of old legal punishments applied at the time of its revelation. Punishments must, as we will demonstrate, rest on modern criminal proceedings and prosecutions acceptable in the present development of the international criminal system.[41]

---

[40] The traditional concept of Islamic international criminal law rests however on the universality principle. This does not necessarily mean that the universality principle is employed and applied by modern states which have been affected by Islamic law. This is because, on the ground of international legal and political developments, most states have concluded numerous international criminal conventions which contain in one way or another some regulations concerning the conditions and applications of criminal jurisdictions to the perpetrators of international crimes. These provisions have therefore greatly diminished the validity of the universality principle, which is traditionally supported by the system of Islamic international criminal law. Consequently, in the extradition of criminals to other or third states, most states exercising Islamic legislation in one way or another have not only not applied the provisions of Islamic international criminal law but have also refused to grant the extradition of certain persons to certain countries because of variations in the legal and political aspects of such cases. The basic objections of states having been influenced by Islamic rules are the fundamental legal and political inequalities in the Charter of the United Nations and the non–existence of any practical and enforceable channels for the re–establishment of the rights of oppressed nations. Another strong reason for the non–application of Islamic international criminal law at an international level has been that requesting states have not been recognized as members of the Islamic world and more obviously because Islamic rules and provisions have not been accepted or respected by the requesting state. Due to the above reasons requested states have denied the extradition of accused persons and relied on the application of the territoriality, nationality or active personality principles.

[41] The severe punishments found in the early Islamic criminal justice system have not only been misinterpreted by most Western writers but also by some of the Islamic jurists and in the present practice of many states – the criminal legislations of which is based on the Islamic jurisdiction. It must however be emphasized that early methods of punishment found in the Islamic system are not only opposed to the modern methods of punishment but are also contrary to current interpretations and deductions in the Islamic criminal justice system. The holy *Qur'an* (the chief source of Islamic law) also implicitly denotes the suspension, if not abrogation (the *Qur'an, 2:106*) of its certain provisions which are revealed in connection with certain historical events or the existing understanding and conditions of the antique Arab society. It must however be explained that the provisions of the *Qur'an* are eternal and constantly valid in the context of their historical and contemporary perspectives. This does not necessarily mean that the old

6. Legal Characterization of Islamic Obligations

6.1. Pacta Sunt Servanda

There are certain important legal principles in the system of Islamic law which should be respected at all times. One of the most important of these principles is the well recognized common principle of *pacta sunt servanda* which has long been accepted in the system of international law. This principle denotes the very high respect given to these obligations by the Muslim community. Thus, when Muslims concluded peace or other types of treaties with other communities they were strongly obliged, according to the provisions of *Shari'ah*, to respect their obligations. It was a serious violation of divine law to violate the obligations and duties stated in the provisions of a treaty. The Prophet of Islam also strongly recommended Muslims not to violate treaty obligations.[42]

The term *pacta sunt servanda* in Islamic international law therefore means that the obligations given in a treaty must be fully respected.[43] The *Qur'an* has especially stated the respect due to this important principle. It reads 'And fulfil the covenant of God when you have made a covenant, break not your oaths after you have confirmed them.'[44] Another verse also reads, 'How can there be an agreement between the polytheists and God and His Apostle, except with those you have made a treaty at the Sacred Mosque? Therefore as long as they adhered to their agreement with you, you should also adhere to your agreement with them, surely God loves the righteous.'[45] These provisions of the *Qur'an* are also strengthened by another verse which illustrates that Muslims should not break their agreements and should 'fulfil their agreements to the end of their term.'[46]

One important attitude of Islamic law towards the law of treaties is that a treaty should create equality between contracting parties and moreover duties and obligations must be based on the principle of reciprocity – generally constituting one of the important principles for the conclusion of international treaties. One essential differences between Islamic international criminal law

---

methods of punishment must be implemented but at the same time the non–implementation of old systems of punishment cannot in any way be interpreted to mean that the injunction of new methods of punishment in the Islamic criminal justice system are in contrast to the theological, philosophical and juridical aspirations of Islam.

[42] Khadduri, Majid., War and Peace in the Law of Islam (Baltimore, 1955), p.205.

[43] *Id.*, p.204.

[44] The *Qur'an*, 16:91.

[45] The *Qur'an*, 9:7.

[46] The *Qur'an*, 9:4.

and the system of international criminal law is that the former has juridically and theoretically a much stronger character than the latter. This is because under Islamic international criminal law international provisions must not only be fulfilled by a Muslim community under the system of international law but also under Islamic international criminal law in accordance with Islamic jurisprudence or *Shari'ah*.

6.2. De Lege Lata

Another important characterization of the system of Islamic international criminal law is that its basic provisions and regulations are already fixed and are unalterable. This means that the system heavily relys on the principle of *de lege lata*, which means the law is always in force and cannot be modified by any type of legislation. Although the unchangeable characterization of Islamic law is one of the important elements of the law of *Shari'ah*, new rules and obligations which are not against its fundamental elements can easily be exercised and will not be considered against its eternal characterization. It is for this reason that states which have regulated Islamic provisions into their legislations or definitely implement *Shari'ah* are entered into the ratification of numerous international agreements considered an integral part of the system of international criminal law. In this sense Islamic international criminal law coincides with the system of international criminal law. Although provisions in the former arise from the law of Shari'ah, they do not generally contradict the provisions of the latter and are accordingly able to accommodate the system of international criminal law.[47]

Non-retroactivity of criminal law including punishment is a basic principle of the system of Islamic international criminal law. This principle is supported in the *Qur'an* and consolidated in Islamic law.[48] The *Qur'an* reads that 'We send Apostles as the givers of good news as well as the givers of warnings, so that mankind might not have a plea against God after the coming of the Apostles...'[49] In another verse, the *Qur'an* informs us about the early history

[47] In the system of international and international criminal law there is also the principle of *de lege ferenda*, which means the law which may come into force in the future. This concept does not exist in Islamic law and the Shari'ah always has the characterization of the principle of *de lege lata* which develops by consensus.

[48] For instance, the *Qur'an* states that 'And marry not women whom your fathers married, except what has already passed (no need to divorce such wives, because the past is excusable).' 4:22. This verse denotes the non-retroactivity of Islamic law concerning those acts which were permissable before Islamic law was revealed.

[49] The *Qur'an*, 4:165.

and reads that 'Whoever took the right Path, so he took only the right Path for the benefit of his own soul and whoever had gone astray, then the loss of his going astray only he has to suffer and no bearer of a burden can bear the burden of another, nor it was becoming of Us that We punishing until We raised an Apostle.'[50] It further states that 'And whenever We decided to destroy a town, We first sent Our Commandment to those in authority and rich chiefs who led easy lives in it, but they transgressed in it; so that the word was proved true against them; so We destroyed it with utter destruction.'[51] Thus, Islamic international criminal law rejects the theory of retroactive application of criminal law and punishment. It therefore bases on the principle of *de lege lata*.

6.3. *Jus Cogens*

Islamic law does not have similar legal characterization to the principle of *jus cogens* defined in the system of international law, although it does constitute another type of jus cogens itself. This is because *jus cogens* are certain rules and obligations in international law which cannot be abolished or modified but only reviewed by the expression of a subsequent common consent or consensus through international provisions having a contrary effect. The term *jus cogens* in the system of international law has two basic elements. Firstly, it is unchangeable. Secondly, it can only be modified by an overwhelming majority of consent in contrary effect.[52]

---

[50] The *Qur'an*, 17:15.

[51] The *Qur'an*, 17:16.

[52] The term *jus cogens* in the system of international law is employed to limit the conventional freedom of states in certain important matters which may be against certain international obligations which have broadly been consolidated in the international legal community and are considered as peremptory norms of international law. These obligations are those whose validity are overwhelmingly recognized by the subjects of international law and of substantial importance for the maintenance of collective international legal security which cannot be restricted by the interests of an individual or a group of states. The peremptory norms of international law pertain to independence, equality of states, freedom of the high seas, self-determination, invalidity of unequal treaties, non–intervention, the provisions of the convention of genocide, non–aggression, regulations for prohibition of slave trade or piracy, war crimes, crimes against humanity, the provisions of the humanitarian law of armed conflicts, apartheid, the principles of racial non–discrimination, and many other principles prohibiting violations against individuals.

Jus cogens rules are internationally valid and unalterable as long as the international legal community does not require their modification. The International Law Commission of the United Nations, in its draft proposal on the law of treaties, concluded that the rules of international *jus cogens* are the consequences of international positive law. The Vienna Convention in 1969 refers

Islamic law has the first legal characterization of the principle of *jus cogens* recognized in the system of international law. Its first characterization cannot however be altered by provisions having the expression of contrary effect. This means that Islamic law does not have the second characterization of the principle of *jus cogens* recognized in the system of international law. Consequently any provision, rule, agreement or consensus which is contrary to the basic principal of the law of *Shari'ah* is considered invalid and cannot in any event modify those basic principles. It is in fact a fundamental principle of the law of *Shari'ah* that rules and obligations provided by a national and/or international society should not violate the basic ethics and philosophies of *Shari'ah*.

Islamic international criminal laws arising from the basic sources of Islamic law are therefore based on the peremptory norms of Islamic jurisprudence or *Shari'ah* and cannot be modified by any means.[53] Some of the basic provisions of the *Shari'ah* are equality between all men, brotherhood, justice[54] and the

---

to the term *jus cogens* instead with the phrase 'peremptory norms of general international law.' The Convention reads that "A treaty is void if, at the time of conclusion, it conflicts with a peremptory norm of general international law." (Article 53) The same convention reads that "For the purpose of the present Convention, a peremptory norm of general international law is a norm accepted and recognized by the international community of states as a whole as a norm from which no derogation is permitted and which can be modified only by a subsequent norm of general international law having the same character." (Article 53) The position of the above provisions of the Vienna Convention are also strengthened by other provisions which recognize that provisions of a treaty are invalid when they conflict with a new international legal norm. The Vienna Convention also states that "if a peremptory norm of general international law emerges, any existing treaty which is in conflict with that norm becomes void and terminates." (Article 64) It must however be emphasized that *jus cogens* norms are not retroactive. (Rozakis, Christos.L., The Concept of Jus Cogens in the Law of Treaties (Amsterdam, New York, Oxford, 1976), p.35.) They do not effect the rules period prior to their existence. Nevertheless, new norms of *jus cogens* invalidate the future application of provisions of treaties which have contrary effect. Similarly if the subject matter of a treaty conflicts with a new peremptory norm of general international law the whole future application of the treaty becomes invalid and terminates. Article 4 of the Vienna Convention states that 'Without prejudice to the application of any rules set forth in the present Convention to which treaties would be subject under international law independently of the Convention, the Convention applies only to treaties which are concluded by States after the entry into force of the present Convention with regard to such States.' Malekian, The System of International Law, pp.17–22; Jennings, R.Y., General Course on Principles of International Law, Académie de Droit International, Recueil des Cours (1967–II), pp.323–605, at 563; Brownlie, Ian., Principles of Public International Law (Oxford, 1979) p.513. This footnote is reformulated and quoted from Malekian.

[53] For the sources of Islamic international criminal law see chapter two.

[54] For example, the *Qur'an* emphasises that 'We have revealed the Book to you with the truth that you may judge between people according to the complete Code and knowledge of justice which God has given you, and be not an advocate on behalf of the treacherous who betray their trust.' In another verse the Qur'an reads that 'Shed not blood of your people, nor expel your people from their homes and cities, then you made a firm promise, and you yourselves are

principle of not embracing someone through ideological force. Other basic principles of Islamic jurisprudence or the *Shari'ah* are clearly stated in the verses of the *Qur'an* such as no one is guilty until proven otherwise,[55] equality before the law, prohibition of war of aggression and the protection of the right of self-defence or defensive war.[56]

witness.' 4:105.

[55] This principle is also strengthened by another principle. The *Qur'an* reads that 'And whoever commits a fault or a sin, then accuses of it one innocent, he certainly takes upon himself the burden of calumny and of a manifest sin.' 4:112.

[56] See chapter nineteen. For some other aspects of Islamic jurisprudence see, generally, Coulson, N.J., Conflict and Tensions in Islamic Jurisprudence (University of Chicago Press, 1969); Bryce, J., Studies in History and Jurisprudence, Vol.2 (Oxford, 1901).

Chapter Two

The Basic Elements of Both Systems of International Criminal Law

1. The Purposes of International Criminal Law

The system of international law in general and the system of international criminal law in particular were originally developed from the law of war, or to use modern terminology – the law of armed conflicts.[1] This is because it was normally on the basis of war treaties, agreements and protocols that many principles of international criminal law were originally created. It is however important to mention that the existence of the body of international criminal law has been discussed from various points of view and there are a number of issues which question the nature of its existence.[2]

The concept of international criminal law and its existence was expressed in the early years of twentieth century and the most important reasons for its initial development and the consolidation of its principles were the First and the Second World Wars.[3] The First World War resulted in the creation of the League of Nations and the ratification of a number of international treaties governing the law of armed conflicts and the prevention of states from resorting to unlawful use of force and aggression against one another.[4] It was in fact between the two World Wars that the principles of international criminal law governing the protection of mankind and states from unlawful and illegal acts by one another were primarily regulated in a number of international criminal conventions. This development can also be seen in the international criminal conventions ratified after the establishment of the United Nations.[5]

All these instruments provide substantive protection for their various subjects

---

[1] Malekian, Farhad., International Criminal Responsibility of States (Stockholm, 1985), p.99.

[2] Malekian, International Criminal Law, Vol.I, p.3–10.

[3] Malekian, International Criminal Responsibility of States, pp.55–67.

[4] Id., pp.103–13.

[5] See Malekian, International Criminal Law, Vols.I and II.

terest. Consequently, the varied purposes and functions of international inal law can be seen in the provisions of these instruments, which have strongly prohibited and prevented the commission of certain acts and have recognized their violation as constituting international crimes.[6] Similarly, the purpose of international criminal law is to bring the perpetrators of international crimes before appropriate jurisdiction for prosecution and punishment and it is for this reason that the system of international criminal law contains a wide range of regulations for the extradition of criminals. The purpose and the function of international criminal law is therefore prevention, prohibition, extradition, prosecution and appropriate punishment.[7] To this it must also be added that the system of international criminal law, with its specific purposes and functions, protects and secures the implementation of the international legal system an/or the system of public international law. One cannot deny however that the theory of international criminal law is quite different from its practical enforcement measures.[8]

2. Definitions

2.1. Definition of International Criminal Law

The system of international criminal law has been defined in a number of different ways and in different contexts.[9] This is because, although there are

---

[6] *Id.*

[7] *Id.*, pp.1–53.

[8] *Id.*, pp.49–51.

[9] For the development of international criminal law see Bar, L., Das Internationale Private- und Strafrecht (Hannover, 1862), pp.523–ff; Kohler, Josef., Internationales Strafrecht (Stuttgart, 1917), xii+276; Siegert, K., Grundlinien des Völkerstrafprozessrechts (1953); Glaser, Stefan., Introduction à l'étude du droit international pénal (1954); Glaser, Stefan., Infraction Internationale (1957); Mueller, G.O.W. and Wise, E. M., International Criminal Law (London, 1965); Glaser, Stefan., Droit International Pénal. Son origine, son État Actuel et son développement, L'indice Pénale (1968); Glaser, Stefan., 1 Droit International Pénal Conventionnel (Bruxelles, 1970); Lombois, Claude., Droit Pénal International (France, 1971); Plawski, Stanislaw., Etude des Principes Fondamentaux du Droit International Pénal (Paris, 1972); Donnedieu de Vabres, H., Les Principes Modernes du Droit Pénal International (Paris, 1928); Bassiouni, M. Cherif and Ved P. Nanda., 1 A Treatise on International Criminal Law: Crimes and Punishment (Illinois, 1973); Bassiouni, M. Cherif, International Criminal Law: Crimes (New York, 1986); Bassiouni, M. Cherif, A Draft International Criminal Code and Draft Statute for an International Criminal Tribunal (Netherlands, 1st ed 1981, 2nd ed. 1986); Malekian, Farhad., International Criminal Law: The Legal and Critical Analysis of International Crimes, 2 voles. (Uppsala, 1991). See also Schwarzenberger, Georg., The Frontiers of International Law (London, 1962), pp. 181–209.

a number of international criminal conventions applicable to international crimes, the real nature and the true function of international criminal law is subject to various relevant legal and political discussions between scholars and politicians. According to most definitions international criminal law is that part of international law which applies to serious violations of international law leading to international crimes.[10] According to these definitions international criminal law is that part of international law which prohibits and prevents the commission of international crimes and has certain procedural measures for the extradition, prosecution, and punishment of perpetrators of international crimes. Although these definitions are important in the development of the system of international criminal law, most consider the system an integral part of domestic criminal law and therefore do not give certain necessary independent characterizations to the system.[11] One of the reasons for this is that most relevant writers are of the opinion that the prosecution of most international criminals depends on national criminal systems and since there is no international criminal court to punish the perpetrators of international crimes, the legal characterization of the system of international criminal law largely relys on domestic criminal legislations and cooperations between various legal systems for the effective enforcement of their relevant provisions.

There are however writers who give an independent characterization to the system of international criminal law and are of the view that domestic criminal laws cooperate with international criminal law in the prosecution and punishment of the perpetrators of international crimes.[12] For this reason they do not see the lack of an international criminal court as an essential reason for the independent characterization of the system, but the creation of a criminal court is seen as an essential task for the enforcement of the system of international criminal law.[13] Several opinions have therefore been put forth in the defence of this theory. The system of international criminal law has, in my opinion two clear aims.

---

[10] Malekian, International Criminal Law, Vol.I, p.3–10.

[11] Friedlander, Robert A., The Foundation of International Criminal Law: A Present-Day Inquiry, 15 Case Western Reserve Journal of International Law (1983), pp.13–25.

[12] See, generally, Bassiouni, M. Cherif., A Draft International Criminal Code and Draft Statute for an International Criminal Tribunal (Netherlands, 1st ed 1981, 2nd ed. 1986).

[13] Bassiouni, M. Cherif., The Time Has Come for an International Criminal Court, 1 Indiana International & Comparative Law Review (1991), pp.1–43; Malekian, Farhad., The Principal Function of an International Criminal Tribunal, Paper submitted to the World Conference on the Establishment of an International Criminal Court to enforce International Criminal Law and Human Rights, Associated with the United Nations, International Institute of Higher Studies in Criminal Sciences (Siracusa, Italy, November 2–5, 1992), 16 pp.

The first purpose of international criminal law is to secure the international legal order and therefore to maintain international perpetual peace. Consequently, *international criminal law is a body of law which is attributable to wrongful conduct which violates international public regulation and endangers the maintenance of international legal order and peace.* The second aim of international criminal law is to secure domestic legal systems where they are unable to implement their own legal systems. In this case international criminal law can be defined as *a body of rules cooperating in criminal matters with domestic legal systems for the effective prosecution of criminals.* International criminal law therefore has two characteristics. The first being international criminal laws arising from international criminal conventions having more or less international legal enforceability. The other is to regulate rules between municipal criminal legal systems for the enforcement of national criminal court decisions. Two examples of this are extradition and information gathering. The difference between the former and the latter is that the former is enforceable internationally, while the latter is only enforceable among a certain number of states. The former may, in certain situations be considered as a principle of *jus cogens* and therefore creates obligations for all states regardless of their participation in an international criminal convention – such as the convention on genocide. The latter's enforceability is regional. Nevertheless, both concepts of international criminal law are correlative and have a more or less similar aim in the maintenance of a particular legal system. However, in the final analysis the enforceability of international criminal law of both types depends upon political considerations. This is because the structure of international criminal law depends at present upon national provisions, which means the concept of violation varies from one nation to another.[14]

2.2. Definition of Islamic International Criminal Law

With the Islamic concept of international criminal law, we mean that part of the Islamic law which exclusively relates to certain customs, principles, rules and obligations prohibiting and preventing the commission of certain activities in the relations between individuals and states, the commission of which are extraditable, prosecutable and punishable within the law. Thus, the Islamic international criminal law is that part of the Islamic law which prohibits and prevents the commission of certain acts constituting criminal acts, which are of

---

[14] Malekian, International Criminal Law, Vol.I, pp.9–10.

course against the rules and principles of the Islamic law.

Although the terminology used in 'Islamic international criminal law' is my own innovation, this type of criminal law has generally existed for a much longer period of time; It has not been previously analyzed within a separate field of law.[15] This is also true in the case of the system of international criminal law. Although the system has long been exercised, it was in the early twentieth century that the system was slowly recognized as an integral part of the public international law. This is because the system of public international law itself consists of many different international laws – including international criminal law.[16] The legal provisions of both systems have therefore previously existed by some degree in their original sources.

It is essential to emphasize that the Islamic concept of international criminal law bases its elements on the well known principle of *nulla poena sine lege or nullum crimes sine lege,* which means that *a conduct cannot be punished as criminal unless some rule of law has already declared conduct of that kind to be criminal and punishable as such.*[17] For this reason the Islamic international criminal law, like the system of international criminal law, essentially builds its framework on the principle of legality and this is particularly important in the recognition of international crimes.[18]

Islamic international criminal law is therefore against the principle of retroactivity which has sometimes been exercised in the system of international criminal law. Accordingly, a crime must first be defined as an action and cannot be criminalized after its commission. For this reason the principle of legality must be regarded as the chief principle of the criminal justice system in Islamic international criminal law. It is for this reason that the *Qur'an* (the main source of the Islamic criminal law) reads that 'We have revealed the Book to you with the truth that you may judge between people according to the complete Code and knowledge of justice which God has given you.'[19] The *Qur'an* therefore makes it clear that the prosecution and punishment of individuals can only be carried out on the grounds of pre−existing criminal law criminalizing the given conduct. This interpretation means that Islamic international criminal law

---

[15] See, for instance, Hamidullah, Muslim Conduct of State; Hamidullah, Muhammad., The Battlefields of the Prophet Muhammad (England, 1953); Khadduri, Majid., Law in the Middle East (1955); Khadduri, Majid., War and Peace in the Law of Islam; Khadduri, Majid., The Islamic Law of Nations: Shaybani's Siyar (Baltimore, 1966); Al−Ghunaimi, Mohammad, Talaat., The Muslim Conception of International Law and Western Approach (Hague, 1968).

[16] Malekian, International Criminal Responsibility of States, pp.47−9.

[17] See chapter one, section 6.

[18] *Id.*

[19] The *Qur'an,* 4:105.

considers the principle of criminalization of a given international conduct as a key element in the international criminal justice system and therefore challenges any type of criminal jurisdiction, the jurisdiction of which is retroactive.[20]

Due to this consideration one can draw the conclusion that the international criminal jurisdiction exercised after the Second World War against perpetrators of international crimes, which based its jurisdiction on retroactive law, would have been recognized as invalid according to Islamic international criminal law. We can however propose that the perpetrators of war crimes during the Second World War could have been punished in accordance with legal principles if the principles of the Islamic international criminal law have been taken into consideration within the framework of the constitution of the International Military Tribunal in Nuremberg. This is because in accordance with Islamic international criminal law, which has a wide range of regulations and principles governing the international humanitarian law of armed conflicts,[21] the perpetrators of international crimes during the Second World War could have easily been punished due to its principle of legality.[22]

The principle of legality in Islamic international criminal law therefore implies respect for two important principles in the criminal justice system of the Islamic criminal law, 'The first is that no obligation exists prior to the enactment of legislation, and the second is that all things are presumed permissible. The application of those rules to the criminal law signifies that no punishment shall be inflicted for conduct which no text has criminalized and that punishment for criminalized conduct is restricted to instances where the act in question has been committed after the legislation takes effect.'[23]

This power of the legalization of the given international conduct in the Islamic international criminal law increases the common value of the law and therefore makes its implementation or enforcement possible. In a broader perspective it decreases the commission of criminal activity at an international level.

---

[20] See chapter one, sub-section 6.2.

[21] See chapter twenty one.

[22] I have however given this example for clarification of the subject matter and not necessarily for the implementation of the Islamic international criminal law on the perpetrators of international crimes in Europe after the Second World War.

[23] al-'Awwa, Muhammad Salim., The Basis of Islamic Penal Legislation, in Bassiouni, M. Cherif (ed.), The Islamic Criminal Justice System (London, Rome, New York, 1982), pp.127–47, p.134.

2.3. A Comparative Definition of Both Systems

Although the system of international criminal law may be defined in a number of ways its definition coincides in many aspects with the definition of Islamic international criminal law. Both systems aim to define preventions, prohibitions, extraditions, prosecutions and punishments. It is the basic principle of both systems to bring the violators of certain specific rules and obligations before an appropriate criminal jurisdiction. Both systems not only aim to protect individuals but also the rights of minorities in relation to international criminal violations. For example, the system of international criminal law strongly prohibits any type of crime against minorities or any type of discrimination against individuals of a group or a nation. Clear examples of these prohibitions in the system of international criminal law can be examined in many instruments of the United Nations concerning racial discrimination, apartheid, genocide and also in a large number of instruments of international human rights.

Islamic international criminal law also has a large number of rules protecting minority groups. These rules of the Islamic international criminal law can especially be found in the main source of the Islamic law i.e. the *Qur'an* and many other sources of this law. For example, the Islamic law prohibits the killing of an individual or individuals who have not engaged in criminal conducts and it strongly prohibits mass killing of groups. Discrimination is not only prohibited, but is also recognized as a serious crime against Islamic human rights. There should thus be no difference between Muslims and non-Muslims in all aspects of social relations. 'The basic principle of the system of international relations in Islam is, in the words of jurists, that 'the Muslims and non-Muslims are equal (sawa').'[24]

Although the Islamic law does not use the legal terminologies of international criminal law such as genocide or apartheid in its sources (since both words are new innovations under the United Nations Organization), its rules and principles obviously prohibit any type of apartheid or genocide. The Islamic law goes even further and not only prohibits apartheid at a national level but also prohibits it at an international level and recognizes it as a serious violation of the law of equality between all nations. This is not however true in the case of international criminal law. This is because in international criminal law apartheid is a practice initiated against a group or nation by an occupying

---

[24] Publications of Centre Culturel Islamique, p.94.

power,[25] or carried out internally by a regime such as in South Africa – officially abolished in 1991.[26] One can say for example that according to *Islamic law* the inequality which may exist in the constitution of an organization concerning the majority of members in favour of a few permanent members can be regarded a type of apartheid against the majority members within the same organization itself. This theory cannot be defined however under the provisions of the Convention on Apartheid in international criminal law. In this respect one can see that the Islamic international criminal law goes further and creates a stronger concept of discrimination and/or apartheid. This is because *according to the Islamic law all men must be equal before the law and before any type of assembly.* It is on this basis that the Islamic law gives very high regard to the equality of representatives of parties to a conflict and accordingly no priority should be given to the legislators in an authentic and equal assembly.

This conclusion means that the obligations of the system of international criminal law governing the crime of genocide and apartheid have been long accepted in Islamic international criminal law and that it has given much stronger character to these categories of international crimes. Having this in mind one must not forget that the Islamic concept of criminal law is much more spiritual in nature, whereas the system of international criminal law is more conventional. This means that the latter is an accumulation of regulations and when these regulations are fulfilled the law is respected, although states may commit criminal acts without being necessarily criminalized in the system of international criminal law. For example the international crimes of genocide and apartheid were not criminalized until the years 1948 and 1973 respectively. This means that both crimes could be committed and were committed during numerous wars including the First and the Second World Wars without any particular punishment. The Islamic system of international criminal law does not however build the concept of international criminal law on conventional obligations between states but on the fact that certain principles are violated, the violation of which constitute crimes under its system. One of the chief differences between these two systems of international criminal law is that one is independent and can be enlarged accordingly, without any need for codification and ratification, while the other is not.

Nearly all the new obligations and rules of the system of international criminal law must always be codified and adopted, in one way or another, and

---

[25] Falk, Richard, A, and Burns, H. Weston., The Relevance of International Law to Palestinian Rights in the West Bank and Gaza: In Legal Defense of the Intifada, 32 Harvard International Law Journal (1991), pp.129-57.

[26] For further analysis see Malekian, International Criminal Law, Vol.I, pp.324-75. White South Africans handed over power to blacks as a result of democratic election in May 1994.

thereafter ratified by different states. Thus, one of the basic weakness of the system is that certain states avoid ratifying certain international criminal conventions and thereby escape their obligations by invoking their non–ratification *e.g.* international Convention on Genocide. The provisions of the Convention have been seriously violated in international conducts of states.[27] Similarly, non–ratification of many other international criminal conventions has also created great difficulties for international criminal law in enforcing its obligations upon the perpetrators of international crimes. In accordance with the Islamic international criminal law, no state can escape its Islamic criminal obligations. All obligations are equally applicable to all states without any need for their ratification.[28]

3. Sources of Both Systems[*]

3.1. Sources of International Criminal Law

3.1.1. Conventions

One of the first legal values of the obligations in the system of international criminal law must be examined from the provisions of a large number of international criminal conventions applicable to a number of international crimes.[29] International criminal conventions have therefore occupied an invaluable place in the system of international criminal law and are considered an important part of the system. International conventional criminal law constitutes the first source of international criminal law. These conventions,

---

[27] For further analysis and references see *Id.*, p.119. For example on the non–ratification of the international Convention on Genocide see Duffett, J., Against the Crime of Silence (New York, London, 1968). Sartre, Jean–Paul., On Genocide (Boston, 1968); Sartre, On Genocide, in Duffett; O'Brien, William V., The Law of War, Command Responsibility and Vietnam, 60 The Georgetown Law Journal (1972), pp.605–64; Lombois, Claude., Droit Pénal International (France, 1971), p.83. Falk, Richard, A., Six Legal Dimensions of the United States Involvement in the Vietnam, in Falk, The Vietnam War and International Law, pp.216–59; Falk, The Vietnam War and International Law (Princeton University Press, 1969), 2 vols; Ferencz, Benjamin B., Compensating Victims of the Crimes of War, 12 Virjinia Journal of International Law (1972), pp.343–56. In particular see the statements of Bertrand Russell and the Russell International War Tribunal held in Stockholm, Sweden, May 2 to 10, 1967 and Roskilde, Denmark from November 20 to December 1 1967. Sartre *id.* The Tribunal was essentially created as a result of different meetings in London in 1966.

[28] See chapter one.

[*] All sources are not necessarily considered here.

[29] Malekian, International Criminal Law, Vol.I, pp.27–8.

agreements, treaties, protocols, declarations, pacts and codes have been signed or ratified from the middle of the nineteenth century up until the present time. Although all states have not participated in the drafting and ratification of all these international criminal conventions, the legal value of these conventions is impossible to reject.

3.1.2. Customs

The second source of the system of international criminal law are the provisions found in customary international criminal law.[30] This source has long been accepted by states in the development of the law without any need for the type of characterization required of obligations in conventional criminal law. Customary international criminal law is thus that part of the system of international criminal law which relys exclusively on the acceptance of certain rules and principles in the practice of states. Clear examples of customary principles are those applicable in time of armed conflicts and these are regarded as an integral part of the law of armed conflict including some of the rules contained in the international humanitarian law of armed conflicts e.g. prohibition of the use of certain weapons – the use of which create unnecessary suffering, wilful destruction and devastation of civilian objects and attack on those who are considered non–combatants.[31]

Another example are the provisions of customary international criminal law applicable to the international crime of piracy.[32] Customary international criminal law may come into existence upon repetition of certain behaviour or may be taken from the provisions of certain conventional international criminal law. For example the provisions of the 1949 Geneva conventions are not only regarded as an integral part of international criminal conventional law but also as an integral part of customary international criminal law.[33] Provisions of many international conventions have in fact been taken from the earlier customary international criminal law and been regulated into international criminal law. Thus, customary international criminal law and conventional international criminal law may repetitiously interchange each others provisions and therefore coincidently develop one another.[34]

---

[30] *Id.*
[31] *Id.*, p.149.
[32] *Id.*, pp.489–92.
[33] *Id.*, pp.139–41.
[34] *Id.*, p.139.

3.1.3. Decisions

The third source of international criminal law are the international jurisdictional decisions and practices which are greatly lacking in the system at present. We cannot however deny that the system has been largely developed through the provisions of the International Military Tribunals in Nuremberg and Tokyo[35] and to some extend from the practice of domestic criminal laws having jurisdiction over international crimes.[36] This source of international criminal law has been particularly effective in the development of laws governing the prosecution and punishment of pirates and war criminals. While the practice of domestic criminal courts, domestic military tribunals and admiral courts have been effective in the development of the system of international criminal law, the effect of these courts must not be exaggerated, due to the limited number of authorities which have been required to practice the provisions of international criminal law.[37] Moreover, although they have been effective in the development of the system of international criminal law, they can never be practically useful to other states in applying them as a source of international criminal law. This is because states rarely accept the application of the domestic practice of other states in their international relations and it is on this basis that the third source of international criminal law is not practical as long as an international criminal court is not established.[38]

It must of course be added that the decisions and directives of the International Court of Justice demonstrates the existence of the tendency of states towards the internationalization and consolidation of provisions of conventional and customary international criminal law. An illustrative example is the genocide convention, the provisions of which have without doubt not only the effect of conventional international criminal law on the contracting parties, but also the effect of customary international criminal law on all states

---

[35] For these international military tribunals see Malekian, International Criminal Responsibility of States, pp.59–67.

[36] Malekian, International Criminal Law, Vol.I., pp.503–6.

[37] The Statute of the International Court of Justice also refers to 'the general principles of law recognized by civilized nations' as a source of international law.

[38] Malekian, Farhad., The Principal Function of an International Criminal Tribunal, Paper submitted to the World Conference on the Establishment of an International Criminal Court to Enforce International Criminal Law and Human Rights, Associated with the United Nations, International Institute of Higher Studies in Criminal Sciences (Siracusa, Italy, November 2–5, 1992), 16 pp.

regardless of their participation in the process of achieving those provisions.[39]

3.1.4. Publicists

The fourth and subsidiary source of international criminal law is the collective opinions of the most distinguished publicists in this field;[40] Views of certain publicists who are well recognized in the system of international criminal law may be considered subsidiary sources in the system. Although the fourth source of the system of international criminal law may be opposed by the opinions of some writers and states, this does not mitigate the value of opinions by publicists who give a balanced and unbiased presentation of the system of international criminal law.[41]

Needless to say that the views of publicists have not the effect of law making power and cannot be regarded as a definite legal interpretation in the system of international criminal law. This is on the basis of their various political, economic, social and cultural involvements. Consequently, the views of publicists do not constitute positive law but may be useful in solving certain legal dilemmas. Moreover, the views of publicists may be greatly helpful in the legislation and promotion of international criminal conventions.

3.2. Sources of Islamic International Criminal Law

The Islamic law has a variety of sources for its definition, interpretation and application. This is a reason for the flexibility of Islamic law and sometimes creates controversy concerning the enforcement of the law between the various doctrines within this law.[42] Some of the sources enumerated in the Islamic law are the *Qur'an*, custom, consensus, *qiyas*, preuves, pre–assumptions, equality, freedom, doctrine and cases. Since there is controversy among Muslims as to the validity of all these sources and no special agreement has been

---

[39] Malekian, The System of International Law, p.19. The International Court of Justice recently formulated an order concerning the genocide of Muslim inhabitants of Bosnia–Herzegovina which has undoubtedly the effect of the third source of international criminal law. See Case Concerning Application of the Convention on the Prevention and Punishment of the Crime of Genocide (8 April, 1993, Order), 25 pp.

[40] See Article 38 of the Statute of the International Court of Justice.

[41] This source is nevertheless very controversial indeed.

[42] Mallat, Chibli., The Renewal of Islamic Law, Muhammad Baqer as–Sadr, Najaf and the Shi'i International (Cambridge, University Press, 1993).

reached to that purpose, we will only study the more acceptable sources of Islamic law which combined from an important framework for the Islamic law and the Islamic concept of international criminal law. A general classification of the Islamic sources are as follows:

i) The *Qur'an*.
ii) The *Sunnah* or the traditions of the Prophet.
iii) The Orthodox practice of the early *Caliphs*.
iv) The practice of the other Muslim rulers not repudiated by the jurisconsults.
v) The opinions of celebrated Muslim jurists:
   a) Consensus of opinion or *Ijma*;
   b) individual opinions *Qiyas*.
vi) The arbitral awards.
vii) The treaties.
viii) The official instructions to commanders, admirals, ambassadors and other state officials.
ix) The internal legislation for conduct regarding foreigners and foreign relations.
x) The customs and usage.
xi) Public interest or *Istislah*.

According to a well known Islamic Persian lawyer the following classification of the sources of the Islamic law are challenged by various Islamic jurisprudence.[43] These are:

a) The *Qur'an*.
b) The *Sunnah*.
c) Wisdom.
d) Consensus or *Ijma*.
e) Individual opinions or *Qiyas*.
f) Preuves.
g) The principle of Justice.
h) The principle of Equality.
i) The principle of Liberation.
j) Doctrine.

[43] Jafary Langaroody, Muhammad Jafar., Islamic Law (in Persian language, Teheran, 1978), p.15. According to Langaroody, the basic sources of Islamic law are the *Qur'an, Sunnah,* analogy and consensus. *Id.,* p.20.

k) Case Law.
l) Custom and usage.
m) Presumptions of fact.

The study of all these sources is obviously impossible here. Only four basic sources of the Islamic law are briefly studied in the following sections. These are a) the *Qur'an* which constitutes the chief source of the Islamic law, b) the Sunnah which means the authentic traditions of the prophet Muhammad, c) *Qiyas* which means an analogy of a case to another case by a jurist and d) *Ijma* denoting the existence of consensus between opinion.

3.2.1. The Qur'an

The *Qur'an*' means to collect, to recite and to unite.[44] The *Qur'an* is the basic source of the Islamic international criminal law. The *Qur'an* not only provides the manner of social life and methods of cooperation between the members of the society, but also the law, rules and regulations which must be respected and applied in relations of individuals, entities and states. The *Qur'an* is known as the law of God, its principles and words are as complete as those which represent the methods of sociology, psychology, family law, commercial law, human rights, criminal law, procedural law, criminology and for our part the basic rules for the system of Islamic international criminal law.

Although certain principles of the *Qur'an* governing the punishment of criminals may be criticized by some writers this does not diminish its legal value, since the principles of *Qur'an* should be read (like many other laws) in conjunction with one another and it must be remembered that the *Qur'an* is a very flexible constitution and can adapt itself to the change of time. This is one of the most important values of the *Qur'an*. The reason for this is that according to the modern international law, any modification and modernization of a treaty almost always requires a new reconsideration and the ratification of the relevant subject. The *Qur'anic* constitution does not however need to be modified since its rules and provisions can always modify themselves to a new situation. This is unique in the system of law in general and in the system of constitutional law in particular. One must not forget that the *Qur'an* may however be interpreted (like many other regulations) in different ways and therefore different conclusions may be reached upon the same issue. This depends on personal judgements and the social status of the person interpreting and for what purposes the political diplomacy of the *Qur'an* is going to be

---

[44] The Glorious Holy Qur'an, Translated by Jullundri, L.A.A.K., (Pakistan, 1962), p.1.

employed.[45]

The *Qur'an* expects cooperation between all individuals, groups, clans and states. Its basic function is to create workable and acceptable principles of international human rights in relations between individuals and states and to promote the principles of equality, justice and brotherhood for all without any form of discrimination in national and international life. The invaluable function of the *Qur'an* in the development of human rights principles cannot therefore be denied from either a jurisdictional or natural law point of view.

3.2.2. Sunnah

The second source of the Islamic law is the *Sunnah* including the *hadith*[46] which means the total sum of the statements, behaviour and authentic social traditions of the Prophet Muhammad.[47] This has been enumerated as one of the reliable sources of Islamic international law.[48] The Qur'an ordains in several passages the importance of this source. It reads, for example, that 'whatsoever the Messenger give you, take it and whatsoever he forbids, abstain from it.'[49] It is also generally stated that the *Sunnah* implies an interpretation and enforcement of the *Qur'an* in accordance with the Prophets traditions.[50] The *Sunnah* must therefore be regarded as an invaluable source in the Islamic law because of the very strong connection between it and the chief source of

---

[45] For political concepts of the *Qur'an* see Maududi, Sayyid Abul A'la., The Islamic Law and Constitution (Islamic Publication Ltd, Lahore, 7th ed. 1980), pp.153–seq.

[46] For further clarification it must be stated that although *Sunnah* and *hadith* constitute the second sources of Islamic international criminal law their legal characterizations must not be confused with one another. *Sunnah* means the manner or mode of life of the Prophet during his lifespan. One of the legal reasons for *Sunnah* constituting a second source in Islamic law is that *Sunnah* both represents and interprets the Qur'an. In other words it is the actual practice of the *Qur'an* during the life of the Prophet. *Sunnah* not only interprets the *Qur'an* but also aids in its practical implementation and enforcement. *Hadith* means the narrations of the Prophet conveyed to man through revelations or hearing. One may say that the second source of Islamic law consists of two interrelated subjects complementing one anothers purposes and more or less representing the same subject matter.

For further study on *hadith* see Azami, M.M., Studies in Hadith Methodology and Literature (Indianapolis, 1977); Azami, M.M., Studies in Early Hadith Literature (Indianapolis, 1978); Bosworth–Smith, R., Mohammed and Mohammedanism (London, 1889); Abul–Fazl, M., Sayings of the Prophet Muhammad (New Delhi, 1980).

[47] For *hadith* see Azami, M.M., Studies in Hadith Methodology and Literature (Indianapolis, 1977); Azami, Studies in Early Hadith Literature.

[48] Hamidullah, Muslim Conduct of State, p.18.

[49] The *Qur'an*, 59:7.

[50] Jafary Langaroody, Islamic Law, p.43.

this law. In other words the Sunnah promotes the progressive development of the *Qur'an*, not only juridically but also from a practical point of view in the system of Islamic law. It is for this reason that the *Sunnah* can be especially referred to in the Islamic international criminal law when certain questions of the law are not clear and need particular clarification in their application. There are for instance numerous examples of the application of the law by the Prophet when an international armed conflict occurred between two or several states. The rules of Islamic international criminal law found in the traditions of the Prophet are nevertheless inferior to the *Qur'an*.[51]

3.2.3. Consensus

The third source of the Islamic law is *Ijma* which means consensus of opinion. This source of Islamic law denotes the high value of collective opinion in agreeing upon a matter and to the democratic jurisdiction of the Islamic system. It must however be emphasized that there are different opinions concerning the key elements of *Ijma* or consensus. According to one class, consensus does not mean the majority opinion but rather a complete agreement between all those who have participated to arrive at a decision. This is the consensus of unanimous agreement.[52] According to another class, consensus is achieved when an overwhelming majority of opinion is reached.[53] According to the third class, in order to achieve consensus neither a unanimous opinion is essential nor agreement concerning the total majority of opinions debated. For this class it is sufficient that a specific group agree upon the existence of certain matter and that the matter is widely known by others and that they do not object or are silent to its existence.[54] Consensus is thereby achieved. This class qualifies the principle of consensus as being highly important, even though for its creation or establishment unanimous consensus has not actually been attained.

Although within the system of Islamic law there are three different overall opinions concerning the process of legally validating the principle of consensus, none of these opinions can reject the existence of consensus as a source of the Islamic law. Obviously the validity of the principle of consensus is not whether or not unanimity has been reached among all Muslim jurists but whether the

---

[51] Hamidullah, Muslim Conduct of State, p.18.

[52] Jafary Langaroody, Islamic Law, p.68.

[53] *Id.*

[54] *Id.*

practice or non practice of certain subject matter has a common value for the community as a whole. This is because if a jurist or several jurists do not agree on the matter of consensus they can simply express their opinions according to the principle of equality of speech and as a consolidated principle of the Islamic law – a later consensus may abrogate the former.[55] This is for two essential reasons. Firstly, an objection to a consensus by analogy to the ethics, jurisprudence and the philosophy of Islamic law is a right of any jurist and secondly, the purpose of abrogating the former consensus through the later consensus is to promote, adapt and develop the concept of Islamic law into the modern need of the community and the practice of various nations in order to achieve peaceful settlement of international disputes. The principle of consensus in the Islamic international criminal law does not therefore necessarily mean unanimity between the opinions of jurists but, according to modern deduction and interpretation, a concurring vote of the majority of participators in a recognized Islamic assembly. Thus, consensus in Islamic international criminal law is an action which creates a sanction against the criminal conduct of certain individuals, groups or states, the criminality of which has already been proven in the international community but has not been specifically identified in the form of a consensual resolution against the given criminal conduct.[56]

The principle of consensus in the Islamic international law and international criminal law can be compared to the high majority of decisions normally achieved in the General Assembly of the United Nations in the form of resolutions relating to certain issues.[57]

---

[55] Hamidullah, Muslim Conduct of State, p.22.

[56] This source of Islamic international criminal law can also be compared with those principles of the system of international criminal law which have come into existence in the process of time and have not been necessarily codified or regulated within especial agreements, but are respected and sometimes considered an integral part of customary international criminal law.

[57] Many of these resolutions deal with questions of international criminal law including crimes against humanity, war crimes, crimes against peace, genocide, apartheid, international humanitarian law of armed conflicts, the invalidity of occupations, intervention, self-determination, drug offenses and terrorism. The historical review of the work of the General Assembly implies that most of these resolutions have been rejected by one or several of the permanent members of the Security Council. This means that unanimity was not reached in the General Assembly. However, this does not preclude the validity and enforcement of the relevant resolutions of the General Assembly. The reason for this is that the type of the consensus achieved in the adoption of resolutions of the General Assembly is not only the result of the voting process but is also highly important in the elimination of criminal activities conducted by certain groups or states. Malekian, Farhad., The Monopolization of International Criminal Law in the United Nations, A Jurisprudential Approach (Uppsala, 1993), pp.76–89.

3.2.4. Juridical Analogy

A juridical analogy, analogical reasoning or Qiyas constitutes the fourth and subsidiary source of Islamic international criminal law. Juridical analogy is essentially based on the opinion of an individual jurist who by analogical reasoning applies the existing decision of a jurisdiction, a rule of Islamic law in the *Qur'an* or the traditions of Mohammad to another case. A certain similarity must always exist between the subjects being compared to one another. A juridical analogy by a jurist is essentially based on his deductions and interpretations which according to him coincide with another matter and can consequently be implemented to solve the given case.

A juridical analogy by a jurist in the Islamic international criminal law may be compared with the fourth source of the system of international law i.e. publicist as the subsidiary means for the determination of the rules of international criminal law. A juridical analogy by a jurist may only be referred to if a given case cannot easily be treated by and in accordance with other sources of the Islamic law. The opinion of a jurist may be found in the collections of judicial decisions called *Fatawa*, in the works of the writers of the Islamic international law, responsa prudentium, proceedings of conferences and the Modern works on the Islamic international law.[58]

According to Professor Langaroody a considerable amount of caution must be exercised in the case of a juridical analogy by a jurist. Accordingly, a juridical analogy cannot be made with any law or decision which has already stated the actual reason for its existence.[59] For example, when a law states that the reason for the invalidity of a contract is a lack of age or the absence of a legal guardian, a juridical analogy in such cases is indeed without grounds.[60] According to his view the law must be 'silent' about the motivation for its existence and this is the essential reason for a juridical analogy being expressed.[61] Moreover, if a jurist cannot discover the reasons for the existence of a law, he/she should not make juridical analogy to the law with suspicion.[62] According to Professor Langaroody some essential principles must be respected when expressing a juridical analogy. *Inter alia* are i) the source of the juridical analogy, ii) the subject for which the law is silent, iii) the law to which analogy must be made, iv) the reason for the juridical analogy, *v)*

---

[58] Hamidullah, Muslim Conduct of State, pp.23–4.

[59] Jafary Langaroody, Islamic Law, p.83.

[60] *Id.*, pp.83–4.

[61] *Id.*, p.84.

[62] *Id.*, p.84.

the reason for which the law is silent and so forth.[63]

Another writer asserts that *Qiyas* is a subsidiary source of law. It is considered as a mode of *Ijtihad*, which means individual judgement in a legal dilemma or question based on the interpretation and the application of the principles of Islamic law. Its function is to discover the law. He further states that *Qiyas* 'authority is disputed, for it involves human thinking and bias. The original case *(asl)* which a jurist makes the basis for his reasoning is sometimes open to question. Hence the dispute.'[64] It follows then that the methods employed for the discovery of the law should be made adaptable in order to apply it to new situations. For this purpose *Qiyas* must revert to its original position in order to be useful and practical. According to the same writer, the methods used in the application of *Qiyas* or analogical reasoning are of two types;[65] One is certain and the other probable. The *Qur'an* and Sunnah are the main sources of the Islamic law and the third source *Ijma* together constitute the certain methods in Qiyas above. As a result the conclusion arising from the above analogical reasoning is reliable.[66] In contrast to this, the probable method is not reliable since it bases its analogical reasoning on resemblance, suitability, rotation, probing and division. The conclusion by this method is consequently uncertain.[67]

There are although certain criticisms against Qiyas constituting the fourth source of the Islamic law, the application of this source for the solving of certain questions of the law promotes and makes the system of Islamic law an adaptable and a flexible law. Consequently in a broader perspective it encourages the solving of international problems with analogical reasoning and the use and application of different methods for promoting pacific settlements of international disputes. The use of this source is particularly important in the system of Islamic international criminal law which does not employ the new legal terminologies of the system of international criminal law in its original form.

[63] *Id.*, pp.85–ff.

[64] Hasan, Ahmad., Analogical Reasoning in Islamic Jurisprudence – A Study of the Juridical Principle of Qiyas (Islamic Research Institute, Islamabad, Pakistan, 1986), p.463.

[65] *Id.*, p.463.

[66] *Id.*, 463.

[67] *Id.*

3.3. A Comparative Examination of Sources of Both Systems

Although the sources of the system of international criminal law are comparatively the creation of humankind and the human will for the promotion of international peace, security and justice, the sources of this system overlap in many respects with the Islamic concept of international criminal law and therefore the possibility that there are *mutatis mutandis* between the both systems is indeed incorrect. Although the Islamic international criminal law is formulated according to divine command, it has certain principles, rules and regulations which are not only not contrary to basic elements in the system of international criminal law but actually promote the system in many respects.

Both systems desire peaceful international relations and the promotion of peaceful settlements in international disputes. Whilst the main source for the system of international criminal law may be said to be conventional international criminal law, the basic provisions of these conventions such as conventions on genocide, apartheid, the Geneva conventions on the law of armed conflicts, the conventions on the protection of natural environment or those of cultural protection display more or less similar values to the Islamic international criminal law. One may even assert that the Islamic system of international criminal law gives special regard to all provisions of international criminal conventions as long as they overlap, follow or adapt themselves to the chief principles of the Islamic law in protecting man and nature from all forms of violations. A similar conclusion can be drawn about other sources in both systems. As a general rule the other sources of Islamic international criminal law are essentially the development and evolution of their basic source i.e. the *Qur'an* and therefore cannot be opposed to its framework.[68] To examine these comparatively common values in the context or purpose of law in general makes interrelations between both systems possible and therefore may solve many international conflicts between states.

4. Subjects of Both Systems

The subjects of international criminal law in general and the subjects of international law in particular have been discussed from various points of view. There has been much controversy as to what does or does not constitute a

---

[68] This is because 'the relevant portions of the Qur'an and the *Sunnah* form permanent positive law of the Muslims in their international dealings; state legislations and treaty obligations establish temporary positive law; and all the rest provide non-positive or case law and suggested law respectively.' Hamidullah, Muslim Conduct of State, p.36.

subject under international law. Many writers have expressed different opinions and the general impression is that states and certain international organizations are respectively considered the main subjects of the system of international law. Although many writers have expressed that individuals are also the subjects of international law, their position is still unsettled. An explanation for this is that individuals in the system of international law do not fulfil the traditional conditions required for their admissibility such as a juridical character – which states and certain international organization own; Moreover, any complaint made by an individual is presented by their state. One cannot however deny the fact that individuals may bring a case before regional juridical bodies such as the European Human Rights Court. This Court unfortunately has an exclusively beneficiary function and not the role of admissions of individuals as main subjects of the law. Even if one accepts that individuals are subjects of international law, their legal positions is surely vastly different to other types of subjects under international law. It may therefore be asserted that individuals are presently considered as beneficiary subjects of international law. A similar conclusion can also be drawn about the system of international criminal law.[69]

Contrary to the above, the Islamic international law gives special consideration to individuals and recognizes them as the basic subject of its law.[70] Moreover, 'the Muslim law of nations was ordinary binding upon individuals rather than territorial groups. For Islamic law, like all ancient law, had a personal rather than a territorial character and was obligatory upon the Muslims, as individuals or as a group, regardless of the territory they resided in. ... from a philosophical viewpoint, ... Islam, as a universal religion, laid emphasis on individual allegiance to a faith which recognized no boundaries for its kingdom: for under a system which claims to be universal territory ceases to be a deciding factor in the intercourse among people.'[71]

The Islamic international law also considers states and organizations its subjects and therefore its provisions can be equally applied to all these subjects

---

[69] See Malekian, International Criminal Law, pp.30–49.

[70] See, for instance, Ghunaimi, The Muslim Conception of International Law and Western Approach, pp.127–8.

[71] Khadduri, War and Peace in the Law of Islam, pp.45–6. Furthermore, 'Piety and obedience to God were the criteria of a good citizen under the Islamic ideology, rather than race, class, or attachment to a certain home or country. Failing to achieve this ideal, the Muslim jurists did not give up the concept of the personality of the law, that is, its binding character on individuals, not on territorial groups.' *Id.*, p.46.

without any type of discrimination.[72] The reason for this is that the Islamic law is constituted by divine command and therefore builds its recognition of subjects on the spiritual personality of an individual and not on the fulfilment of juridical conditions, territorial acquisitions and military installations. The philosophy underlying this reason is that superficial qualifications do not constitute an integral part of an individual. Thus, the Islamic international law provides equality before the law for all.

5. The Concept of Crime in Both Systems

What and what does not constitute an international crime has been variously discussed. It is for this reason that there is not yet an acceptable list of the most consolidated international crimes in the system of international criminal law. One of the most essential reasons for this is that all states have not participated in the conclusion of all international criminal conventions and therefore do not submit themselves to provisions to which they have not given their written consent. This situation has existed for a long time and was especially notable after the Second World War. For this reason there have been various movements within the United Nations to codify international crimes and to bring the most consolidated international crimes under the provisions of one overall code. Earlier attempts by the United Nations in this field began in early 1948 and continued up to 1954. The result was a Draft Code of Offences against the Peace and Security of Mankind submitted to the International Law Commission in 1954. Although the draft Code was not successful, it did become an essential reason for the future development of the system of international criminal law. The 1954 Code was suspended for several reasons, one of which was the very controversial question as to what constitutes aggression. After the Definition of Aggression in 1974, the draft Code was again reconsidered in the United Nations in 1978. Since that time the International Law Commission has worked on the question of what constitutes an international crime under the provisions of the Code of Crimes against the Peace and Security of Mankind and a Draft Code was submitted to the Commission by the special Rapporteur in 1991. The Code may be improved and adopted in the near future.

---

[72] According to one writer the subjects of Islamic international law are *i)* every independent state which has some type of relations with foreign states, *ii)* part sovereign states *iii)* rebels who have acquired a power and a territory having independent international legal personality, *iv)* pirates and highwaymen, *v)* resident aliens in Islamic territory, *vi)* citizens of Muslim states who reside in foreign countries, *vii)* apostates, *viii)* internationally protected persons who are subjects of a Muslim state. Hamidullah, Muslim Conduct of State, p.11.

5.1. The List of Crimes

It may be useful to enumerate the international crimes which are recognized in the system of international criminal law (I.C.L.), the Code of Crimes against the Peace and Security of Mankind (the Code) and the Islamic international criminal law (Islamic I.C.L.).[73] P means prohibited, Cp means conditionally prohibited, and S means the law is silent.

List of the International Crimes in the Code	I.C.L.	Islamic I.C.L.
1. Aggression	P	P	P
2. War Crimes	P	P	P
3. Intervention	P	P	P
4. Colonial domination and other forms of Alien Domination	P	P	P
5. The Unlawful Use of Weapons	P	P	P
6. Mercenaries	P	P	P
7. Slavery	P	P	P
8. Crimes Against Humanity	P	P	P
9. Genocide	P	P	P
10. Racial Discrimination / Apartheid	P	P	P
11. Torture	P	P	P
12. The Crime of Unlawful Medical Human Experimentation	S+P	P	S+P

[73] Crimes under Islamic law may be divided into the following categories; Firstly, those which constitute crimes against a person such as murder, fornication, adultery or bodily harm. Secondly, crimes against property such as theft and highway robbery. Thirdly, crimes against honour such as calumny against chastity, the consumption, sale, purchase, importation or exportation of alcohol and narcotics or involvement in prostitution.

13. Piracy	S	P	P
14. Hijacking	S	P	S+P
15. Taking of Hostages	P	P+CP	P+CP
16. Crimes Against Internationally Protected Persons	P	P	P
17. Terrorism	P	P	P
18. Drug Offences	P	P	P
19. Crimes Against Cultural Property	P	P	P
20. Crimes Against the Natural Environment	P	P	P
21. Unlawful Acts Against Certain Establishments on the Sea and Maritime Navigations	S	P	S
22. Mail Offences	S	P	S
23. Falsification and Counterfeiting Currency	S	P	P
24. Obscene Publications Offence	S	P+CP+S	P
25. Prohibitions on Alcohol	S	S	P

5.2. Differences

The above list of crimes demonstrates that there are indeed few differences between the two systems. Needless to say the Code of Crimes against the Peace and Security of Mankind is the integral part of the system of international criminal law and is in the process of adoption in the United Nations Organization. What is really important here is that the differences between the two concepts are more political than juridical and to this it must also be added that the legal or political implementation of both systems relys on the interpretation of their provisions and therefore their implementation may, in certain circumstances, vary from one another.

In certain situations the list of crimes which are enumerated in accordance with Islamic international criminal law may be extend to other crimes which are not recognized in the system of international criminal law, or to those crimes which have been recognized in the early twenty century as national or international crimes but whose recognition has later been abolished. A clear example of this is the prohibition of importation of alcohol into certain countries. For instance, at the beginning of this century it was prohibited to import alcohol into the United States and there were severe regulations and penalties against those who committed that crime. This crime, which does not constitute a crime now, is still a recognized crime in accordance with Islamic international criminal law and is presently practised by certain Islamic states such as Iran. This type of non–criminalization and criminalization of certain acts can also be examined in other areas of these two systems.

6. Punishment

6.1. Lack of Methods in International Criminal Law

One of the chief purposes of the system of international criminal law is to bring the perpetrators of international crimes before an appropriate jurisdiction and to apply an appropriate punishment for the commission of activities constituting international crimes. Although this is one of the chief purposes of the system of international criminal law, strictly speaking the system has scarcely identified all its methods, levels and degrees of punishment. This is one of the more serious problems in the implementation of the system of international criminal law and the system is indeed incomplete for this reason. The reason for this is that the system owns a large number of international criminal conventions for the recognition of criminality but no direct punishment method is to be found in the actual system. All that can be said is that the system of international criminal law largely depends on the provisions of national criminal courts, which are not equivalent to one another and their implementation methods and provisions greatly vary.[74] One of the essential reasons for the non–existence

---

[74] Take for example the death penalty, Swedish criminal legislation long ago abolished its enforcement, while in the United States the death penalty is one of the methods of punishment for criminals.

of a decisive method, degree and level of punishment is that there is not yet an international criminal court which can bring all criminals before an appropriate international criminal jurisdiction for their prosecution and punishment. The lack of such as important body for the enforcement of the system of international criminal law indirectly encourages its violation and makes the commission of certain international crimes more probable.

The most recent example is the war between different ethnic groups in Yugoslavia in which numerous international crimes have been committed. Parties to the conflict were invited to accept a cease fire on numerous occasions with no effective result and the war initiated the genocide of Muslim inhabitants of Herzegovina.[75] It is on this ground that the United Nations has been active in bringing the perpetrators of international crimes from the war before a temporary international criminal jurisdiction for prosecution and punishment.[76]

This lack of method, degree and level of punishment in the system of international criminal law was also considered in preparing the Charter of the International Military Tribunal in Nuremberg. The enforcement of the system of international criminal law on the perpetrators of international crimes during the Second World War had two major difficulties. The first difficulty was that the United States, the United Kingdom, the Soviet Union and France were faced with the non-existence of an international criminal court to enforce the provisions of the system of international criminal law. The second difficulty was that there was no method, degree and level for the punishment of the Major War Criminals due to the lack of an international criminal court. Both difficulties were passed over by the implementation of retroactive law and the military strength of the strong political powers. Consequently, difficulties were not fundamentally examined and resolved. Both difficulties are still two of the

---

[75] See Case Concerning Application of the Convention on the Prevention and Punishment of the Crime of Genocide (8 April, 1993, Order), 25 pp. See also Malekian, The Principal Function of an International Criminal Tribunal, Paper submitted to the World Conference on the Establishment of an International Criminal Court to Enforce International Criminal Law and Human Rights, Associated with the United Nations, 16 pp. Malekian, Farhad., An Inquiry into the Severe Violations of International Criminal Law in Bosnia-Herzegovina, (A letter to the Members of the Security Council of the United Nations and the General Secretary of the Organization, 27/May/1993), 12 pp.; Malekian, Farhad., A letter to the Members of the Security Council of the United Nations and the General Secretary of the Organization, July 7, 1993, 5 pp.; Malekian, The Monopolization of International Criminal Law in the United Nations, pp. 109, 110, 111 and 201.

[76] In February 1993, the Security Council of the United Nations decided 'that an international criminal tribunal shall be established for the prosecution of persons responsible for serious violations of international humanitarian law committed in the territory of the former Yugoslavia since 1991.'

most important reasons for the non-enforcement of the provisions of the system of international criminal law at an international level.

6.2. Flexibility of Punishment in Islamic International Criminal Law

The Islamic concept of criminal law is a very complete system from a juridical point of view and provides methods, degrees and levels of punishment. In other words, in Islamic international criminal law jurisdiction and punishment constitute an integral part of the law and therefore there is no need for the adoption of certain regulations and rules for the enforcement of its provisions. Although there are a number of punishments enumerated in the main source of Islamic law (the *Qur'an*) against the perpetrators of crimes and although some of these methods may strongly be criticized when compared with the provisions of the modern system of international criminal law, the Islamic concept of criminal law is very *flexible* and the methods, degrees and the levels of punishment can *adapt* themselves to the needs of the modern time.

In fact the basic philosophy of Islam is to adapt itself to the circumstances of the time and to be capable of enforcement. Thus, although the basic jurisdiction in the Islamic international criminal law is fixed by its original source, this does not prevent the adaptation of the law to its other sources and even to the modern system of international criminal law. This is proven by the practice of many Islamic states which do not necessarily inflict the old system of punishment on their criminals. One cannot however deny that some of the provisions of the old system of punishment may still be enforced by a few states. This type of implementation obviously does not present the whole system of Islamic law. A similar analogy is also true in the case of the Islamic international criminal law. It must however be emphasized that the method, degree and level of punishment in the Islamic international criminal law may not be the same as in the system of international criminal law. In contrast, the methods, degrees and levels of punishment in the system of international criminal law may easily come under the Islamic international criminal law because of their modern characterizations and be adapted into the Islamic law as long as they fulfil its purposes and functions.

The Islamic criminal law recognizes three different classifications of punishments. These are fixed penalties, retribution, and discretionary punishment as decided by an Islamic judge. Fixed penalties are generally applicable to seven categories of crimes. These are adultery, false accusation of unlawful intercourse, highway robbery, theft, rebellion against the Islamic authorities, drinking alcohol, and apostasy. Some of the punishments in Islamic criminal law are very severe and therefore their direct enforcement without modifications and re–considerations are surely contrary to the methods of punishment in most criminal systems of the world. They ought to be modified – if the system of Islamic criminal law is assumed to be effective.

6.3. Comparative Conclusions

Comparing the above conclusions it is obvious that both systems have a system of punishment and jurisdiction, with the difference that the system of international criminal law relys on the jurisdiction and punishment which may be provided by different national criminal jurisdictions whereas Islamic international criminal law relys on its own provisions. This means that the latter is juridically much more comprehensive than the other and is also self–executive. The purpose of both systems is to bring the perpetrators of international crimes before jurisdiction for prosecution and punishment. Their purposes are not contrary to one another but rather compliment one anothers aims and functions. Their methods of punishment may be read in conjunction with one another if, and only if, certain adaptations and modifications are made to the old methods of punishment in the Islamic international criminal law. It must however be emphasized that the method of punishment in Islamic international criminal law has a *flexible* character and can adapt itself to the theory of punishment in the modern criminal justice system. The old system of punishment may even be asserted as an abolished institution.

Chapter Three

Aggression

1. Aggression in International Criminal Law

States have frequently waged war in their international relations. The concept of just or unjust, lawful or unlawful, legitimate or illegitimate war has long been considered in the writings of numerous international writers. There have been profound arguments as to what does or does not constitute a just or unjust war. Just and unjust wars have various advocates.[1] These arguments have been particularly discussed in the writings of classical international writers from Europe on the Law of Nations like Francisco Victoria (1480-1546),[2] Balthazar Ayala (1548-1584),[3] Hugo Grotius (1563-1608),[4] Samuel Pufendorf (1632-1694),[5] Cornelius van Bynkershoek (1673-1743),[6] Christian Wolff (1679-1754),[7] and others. These arguments were however the evolution and the development of the idea of the classical philosophers such as Heraclitus, Plato, Aristotle, Cicero,[8] and Augustine.[9]

Two of the most significant developments in the concept of just and unjust

---

[1] William, Ballis., The Legal Position of War: Changes in its Practice and Theory From Plato to Vattel (Hague, 1937), pp.131-4.

[2] De Victoria, Francisco., De Indis et Ivre Belli Relectiones, The Classics of International Law, edited by Scott, James Brown., (1917).

[3] Ayala Balthazar., De Jure et Officiis Bellicis et Disciplinac Militari Libri, Vol.II, The Classics of International Law edited by Scott, James Brown., (1919).

[4] Grotius, Hugo., *De Juri Belli ac Pacis Libri Tres*: Classics of International Law, Vol.II, Translated by Kelsey, Francis W., (1925).

[5] Pufendorf, Samuel., De Jure Naturae et Gentium Libri octo. The Classics of International Law., Edited by Scott, James Brown., Vol.II (1934).

[6] van Bynkershoek, Cornelius., Quaestionum Juris Publici Libri duo, The Classics of International Law., edited by Scott James Brown., Vol.II (1930).

[7] Wolff, Christian., Jus Gentium Methodo Scientifica Pertractatum, The Classics of International Law, edited by Scott, James Brown., Vol.II. (1934).

[8] Ballis, The Legal Position of War, p.31. Cicero's opinions on the question of war were in contrast to those of Plato and Aristotle. Cicero emphasized the "juridical status of war". *Id.*

[9] *Id.*, pp.30-1.

war came as a result of the First World War and the employment of the terminology 'aggressive war' in the context of certain treaties between states. The First World War resulted in the formation of the Commission on the Responsibility of Authors of the War, the Peace Treaty of Versailles in 1919[10] and the Enforcement of Penalties.[11] The 1919 Peace Conference referred to 'war of aggression.'[12] The 1919 Covenant of the League of Nations is another important instrument condemning aggressive war in the international relations between states.[13] Articles 10 and 16 of the Covenant had an important function in the whole framework of the League of Nations. The League aimed at the promotion of peace through the peaceful settlement of disputes and the prohibition of war.

Three other important instruments dealing with aggressive war and aiming at its prevention were the Protocol for the Pacific Settlement of International Disputes, 1924,[14] the Treaty of Mutual Assistance, 1925,[15] and the General Treaty for Renunciation of War as an Instrument of National Policy (which is known as Kellogg–Briand Pact or Pact of Paris), 1928.[16] All the above mentioned and many other instruments were however violated during the Second World War. The International Military Tribunal was not successful either in the settlement of the definition of 'aggressive war', even for reasons which were the basis of its establishment.

The problem of defining 'aggression' was again raised in the drafting of the Charter of the United Nations and became the most controversial dilemma after the ratification of the Charter. Articles 2 (4), 39, and 51 of the Charter deal with this controversial international crime. Article 2 (4) of the Charter without any reference to the term 'aggression' emphasizes that "All Members shall refrain in their international relations from the threat or use of force against the territorial integrity or political independence of any state, or in any

---

[10] The Treaty of Versailles was singed on 28 June 1919 and entered into force between the Contracting Parties on 10 January 1920.

[11] Malekian, International Criminal Responsibility of States, p.55; Malekian, International Criminal Law, Vol.I, p.57.

[12] Malekian, International Criminal Responsibility of States, p.103; Malekian, International Criminal Law, p.57. See also Brownlie, International Law and the Use of Force by States (Oxford, 1963), p.52.

[13] The Covenant of the League was signed at Versailles in 1919 and entered into force on 10 January 1920.

[14] The Protocol was signed at Geneva, on 2 October 1924.

[15] It was signed at Locarno, on 16 October 1925 and entered into force on 14 September 1926. 54 L.N.T.S., p.289.

[16] It was signed at Paris, on 27 August 1928 and entered into force on 24 July 1929. 94 L.N.T.S., p.57.

other manner inconsistent with the purposes of the United Nations." Article 39 refers to the term 'aggression' by stating that 'The Security Council should determine the existence of any threat to the peace, breach of the peace, or act of aggression and shall make recommendations, or decide what measures shall be taken in accordance with Articles 41 and 42 to maintain or restore international peace and security." To conclude, Article 51 concerns the matter of aggression and self-defence.[17]

The unclear terms and provisions used in the context of the above articles are the reason why it took the United Nations, because of various political controversies, almost thirty years to define the term 'aggressive war'. It finally ended in a resolution entitled the Definition of Aggression. Article 1 of the Definition reads that 'Aggression is the use of armed force by a State against the sovereignty, territorial integrity or political independence of another State, or in any other manner inconsistent with the Charter of the United Nations, as set out in this Definition.' This definition is completed with the words of Article 2. It reads that 'The first use of armed force by a State in contravention of the Charter shall constitute *prima facie* evidence of an act of aggression although the Security Council may, in conformity with the Charter, conclude that a determination that an act of aggression has been committed would not be justified in the light of other relevant circumstances, including the fact that the acts concerned or their consequences are not of sufficient gravity.' A careful reading of the above provisions in conjunction with the provisions of Articles 3 and 4 indicates that the definition of aggression can still be subjected to juridical and particularly controversial political arguments without any effective conclusions. These articles read:

Article 3. Any of the following acts, regardless of a declaration of war, shall, subject to and in accordance with the provisions of article 2, qualify as an act of aggression:

(a) The invasion or attack by the armed forces of a State of the territory of another State, or any military occupation, however temporary, resulting from such invasion or attack, or any annexation by the use of force of the territory of another State or part thereof;

(b) Bombardment by the armed forces of a State against the territory of another State or the use of any weapons by a State against the territory of another State;

(c) The blockade of the ports or coasts of a State by the armed forces of another State;

---

[17] For the article see chapter nineteen.

(d) An attack by the armed forces of a State on the land, sea or air forces, or marine and air fleets of another State;

(e) The use of armed forces of one State which are within the territory of another State with the agreement of the receiving State, in contravention of the conditions provided for in the agreement or any extension of their presence in such territory beyond the termination of the agreement;

(f) The action of a State in allowing its territory, which it has placed at the disposal of another State, to be used by that other State for perpetrating an act of aggression against a third State;

(g) The sending by or on behalf of a State armed bands, groups, irregulars or mercenaries, which carry out acts of armed force against another State of such gravity as to amount to the acts listed above, or its substantial involvement therein.

Article 4. The Acts enumerated above are not exhaustive and the Security Council may determine that other acts constitute aggression under the provisions of the Charter.

The concept and definition of aggression has also been entered into one of the Articles of the Draft Code of Crimes against the Peace and Security of mankind.[18] The definition of aggression in the Draft is similar to the definition in the resolution on aggression adopted by the General Assembly of the United Nations in 1974. Both the resolution and draft recognize aggression as constituting an international crime, the perpetrators of which should be prosecuted and punished. The draft must however be completed and receive the certain necessary support from states. The adoption or acceptance of the draft because of the present situation in the world is very doubtful indeed.

2. Aggression in Islamic International Criminal Law

2.1. Definition

Under Islamic international criminal law aggression may be defined as an action or inaction which directly or indirectly jeopardizes the jurisdictional independence and security of another state by means of ideological conflicts

---

[18] Report of the International Law Commission on the work of its forty–first session, 2 May – 21 July 1989, General Assembly official records: forty–fourth session supplement No. 10 (A/44/10), pp.173–9.

and/or armed invasions.[19] A war which is conducted in one way or another for the purpose of glory or economic gains is certainly considered an aggressive war. Islamic international criminal law permits war in certain situations for the path of divine law or the protection of the rights of man from unjustified acts of aggression and therefore a war which does not contain these aims or is combined with the purposes of luxury is considered unlawful. A war which is conducted for the purpose of occupation, colonialization, seizure of territories or to reduce a territory to the status of trusteeship is also considered an aggressive war and is thus prohibited under Islamic international criminal law.[20]

The scope of aggression in Islamic international criminal law is rather broader than that found in the system of international criminal law. This is because the former recognizes at least two types of aggression. These are ideological and armed aggressions. Whilst in the system of international criminal law aggression is limited by the 1974 resolution to armed force – if the Security Council does not recognize other acts as constituting aggression.[21]

2.2. Prohibitions

Aggressive war is considered a prohibited act under the concept of Islamic international criminal law. Islamic law contrary to interpretations by Western writers not only does not permit war but also restricts the waging of war in certain inevitable situations in relations between states. This is because Islamic law basically promotes peaceful relations between all mankind and this theory should not be modified by the causes of war. Aggression is evil and against the moral and legal philosophy of divine law. For this reason, the *Qur'an* vividly clarifies its basic attitudes towards aggression and states that 'God does not love the aggressors.'[22] This basic philosophy has also been developed in the context of other verses of the *Qur'an* and it is a consolidated principle of Islamic international criminal law that war should not be waged as long as other

---

[19] It must be stated that the term 'aggression' was first employed in Islamic international criminal law. Thirteen centuries later the term was introduced into the Western system of international criminal law, at the beginning of the twentieth century.

[20] The *Qur'an*, 2:190–93.

[21] Although it is true that the concept of ideological aggression was introduced into the system of international criminal law by the Communist regime of the former Soviet Union, this concept of aggression was not successful in the international legal realm and therefore eventually lost relevance.

[22] The *Qur'an*, 2:190.

elementary channels for the peaceful settlement of international disputes have not been exhausted.[23] This means that under Islamic international criminal law states are prohibited from conducting war against those states which offer peace and are brave enough to face the real elements of conflicts by means other than war. The *Qur'an* commands the conflicting parties to refrain from armed conflict by stating, 'say not unto one who offereth you peace.'[24] This statement can be examined within other verses of the *Qur'an* and especially the basic philosophy of Islam *i.e.* peace is strongly advocated in the relevant verses. The *Qur'an* clarifies, 'And Allah summoneth to the abode of peace.'[25]

2.3. Peaceful Settlement of Disputes

Peace is imperative in jurisprudence of *Shari'ah or Islamic law*.[26] Disputes must be solved by peaceful means and parties to a conflict are obliged to exhaust all possible means for a peaceful settlement. These include negotiation, arbitration, mediation and conciliation. The law of arbitration has especially developed under Islamic jurisdiction and the *Qur'an* provides a number of provisions regarding the scope and the validity of arbitration. One of the verses of the *Qur'an* runs that 'Allah doth command you to render back your trusts to those to whom they are due; And when ye judge between man and man, that ye judge with justice: Verily how excellent is the teaching which he giveth you!

---

[23] According to one writer, 'Islamic States today have widely accepted the general prohibition of 'threat or use of force' in international relations, as embodied in Art. 2 (4) of the UN Charter. The question whether it curtails the scope and application of Jihad may be considered as follows: *(a)* as the obligation to wage Jihad, in the form of an armed struggle, underlies the Koranic injunction 'not to begin hostilities' and the ethical admonishment 'Allah loveth not aggressors'. (Q 2:190), the prohibition of resorting to the use of force in contemporary international law does not represent an antithesis to the Islamic obligation of Jihad; *(b)* since Jihad, in the form of an armed struggle, is a collective obligation, and its invocation lies within the authority, judgement, and discretion of the head of State or responsible State institutions, the Membership of contemporary Islamic States in the UN system and their undertaking to resort to force only in accordance with international law has limited the right of invoking Jihad to cases of self–defence.' Moinuddin, Hasan., The Charter of the Islamic Conference and Legal Framework of Economic Co–Operation among its Member States: A study of the Charter, the General Agreement for Economic, Technical and commercial Co–operation and the Agreement for Promotion, Protection and Guarantee of Investements among Member States of the OIC (Oxford, 1987), pp.31–2.

[24] The *Qur'an*, 4:94.

[25] The *Qur'an*, 10:25.

[26] For some considerations on the terminology of Shari'ah see Watt, Montgomery W., Islam and the Integration of Society (London, 1961) pp.199–209.

For Allah is He who heareth and seeth all things.'[27] One of the strongest reasons for the development of this *Qur'anic* verse was the practice of Muhammad – the Prophet of Islam – whose arbitration for the peaceful settlement of disputes reached the highest level of justice in the Islamic world.[28] Since the second source of Islam i.e. *Sunnah* constitutes the traditions, mode of life and the statements of the Prophet, the peaceful settlement of international disputes for the prevention of war, including aggressive war, must be regarded as the most reliable method for the prevention of hostilities between conflicting parties. *Ijma* – the third source of Islamic law – also confirms the important validity of arbitration for the peaceful settlement of disputes.[29]

In order to stop bloodshed and aggressive activities between conflicting parties, peaceful settlements of disputes and especially by nomination of arbitrators are recognized as one of the important methods of solving political disputes under Islamic international criminal law. Ali Ben Abi Taleb, the first of the twelve recognized Imams in Islamic religion (*shi'a*),[30] in order to prevent bloodshed accepted the arbitration institution as an effective method of stopping aggressive activities by a conflicting party. This was when Muawiyat Ben Abu–Sufyan refused to recognize the right of Ali Ben Abi Taleb to attain leadership (Caliphat) in the Islamic world.[31] This case indicates the importance of settling disputes through peaceful channels.

2.4. Inevitable Situations

Islamic international criminal law permits resorting to war only in certain inevitable situations and therefore recognizes it as a defensive action or defensive war. Otherwise, a war may be recognised as an aggressive war and constitute a violation of its certain regulations governing lawful war. A war which is conducted for the following reasons may be recognized as lawful:

---

[27] The *Qur'an*, 5:8.

[28] El–Ahdab, Abdul Hamid., Arbitration with the Arab Countries (Denver, Boston, 1990), pp.14–7.

[29] *Id*, p.15.

[30] The first fourth Rashidin Caliphs were Abu Bakr, Umar, Uthman and Ali.

[31] El–Ahdab, pp.16–7.

2.4.1. Defensive War

A war which is conducted for the purpose of self-protection or self-defence cannot be recognized as an aggressive war as long as the principle of proportionality is respected during the war.[32] Thus, according to Islamic international criminal law it is the recognized right of a state to fight for the purpose of self-defence or self-protection. This right is regarded as an integral right in the independent sovereignty of states. Consequently *jihad* (under this section) means a defensive war and not as an aggressive war. This means that the terminology of *jihad* may be qualified as terms of self-defence against those who have initiated an armed attack.[33] Moreover, this implies that any interpretation of *jihad* meaning an aggressive war is without grounds. *Jihad* aims to prevent unlawful acts. Accordingly, 'The *jihad* ... is a measure of reprisal in self-defence or self-help.'[34] Self-defence is also a fact in the system of international criminal law. Although the terminology '*jihad*' is not used in the system, it does permit defensive war for the purpose of self-defence. The Charter of the United Nations also permits '*jihad*' for the purpose of self-defence, with the reservation that it does not directly employs the terminology '*jihad*' used in Islamic international criminal law but the term 'self-defence' instead.[35]

2.4.2. Assisting Victims

When a war is conducted in order to repel acts of aggression against a nation which is the victim of an aggressive war, such conduct does not constitute an act of aggression.[36] According to Islamic international criminal law when a

---

[32] See also chapter nineteen, section 5.

[33] According to one writer, 'the basic assumptions derived from the Koranic obligation to wage Jihad in the from of armed struggle qualify it to be considered as the *bellum justum* of Islam because it is to be waged for a just cause as a consequence of some wrong or injury inflicted upon the Muslims; it includes the inherent right of self-defence; and it must be conducted in accordance with upright intentions and not for material gains or the sake of glory and power. On the other hand, the duty to wage Jihad, that is, a perpetual struggle against all that is evil and against disbelief distinct from armed struggle, remains. ... The right to invoke and wage Jihad in the form of an armed struggle by modern Islamic States has undergone fundamental changes in the light of contemporary international law which prohibits the threat or use of force in international relations.' Moinuddin, Hasan., The Charter of the Islamic Conference and Legal Framework of Economic Co-Operation among its Member States, p.28.

[34] Al-Ghunaimi, p.177.

[35] Article 51 of the Charter of the United Nations.

[36] Al-Ghunaimi, p.209.

state has been the target of an aggressive war other states both Muslim and Non–Muslim have an international legal right to give assistance to that state. This assistance is given to the victim state in order to restore peace and justice as commanded by divine law. This principle of Islamic international criminal law has been precisely advocated in the system of international criminal law but under the direction of the Security Council of the United Nations. Article 43 of the Charter reads that 'All Members of the United Nations, in order to contribute to the maintenance of international peace and security, undertake to make available to the Security Council, on its call and in accordance with a special agreement or agreements, armed forces, assistance, and facilities, including rights of passage, necessary for the purpose of maintaining international peace and security.'[37]

Islamic international criminal law, because of its theological foundation was mostly implemented in Islamic states in ancient times. It must however be asserted that assistance may also be given to other societies, nations or states by Muslim states for the purpose of defeating an aggressive armed force. In other words a broader interpretation of this principle of the right to struggle against aggressors under Islamic law is that Islamic international criminal law recognizes the legal right of any state to give assistance to any other state which is the victim of an *absolute* act of aggression. As a consequence it is the illegal or unlawful notion of an act which identifies it as aggressive and religious factors are not necessarily important. This means that Islamic international criminal law protects all nations from acts of aggression regardless of their religion. This theory is based on the two principles of equality between humans and brotherhood; Constituting two of the prominent reasons for the development of Islamic law in general.

2.4.3. Protection of Fundamental Rights

According to Islamic international criminal law a war which is conducted for the purpose of protecting certain fundamental rights recognized under the Islamic system cannot be considered an aggressive war. This is for example, 'to allow the followers of revealed religions to practise their faith freely.'[38] In other words Islamic international criminal law protects human rights and where these rights are systematically violated by the authorities of a notorious state, other

---

[37] For further consideration of see, generally, Malekian, The Monopolization of International Criminal Law in the United Nations.

[38] Al–Ghunaimi, p.209.

states may resort to armed force in order to protect individuals who are the victims of infringements of human rights. This is called humanitarian intervention under the system of international criminal law and is the subject of controversial discussion.[39] Nevertheless, the United Nations has systematically resorted to armed force by means of peace–keeping operations, where according to it there has been systematic violations of the principles of international law. This is with the reservation that economic and political interests in the Security Council have normally taken priority over other factors.[40]

2.4.4. Fulfilment of Serious Obligations

Islamic international criminal law may also permit war if its purpose is to force a state to fulfil its certain *necessary* obligations in treaty provisions with an Islamic state and which have not been accomplished according to the terms of the treaty. According to Islamic international criminal law the principle of *pacta sunt servanda* must be fully respected by the parties to a treaty.[41] In other words, parties are to abide by their obligations. These are such obligations as respecting the rights of certain Muslim minorities who are under the jurisdiction of non–Muslim state(s), to redress wrongs and to pay different types of taxation agreed upon by the terms of a treaty. Similar provisions can be found under the system of international criminal law, which may permit certain states to wage war against a state which has not fulfilled its serious international obligations towards the international legal community as a whole. For instance, Article 2 (5) of the Charter of the United Nations reads that 'All members shall give the United Nations every assistance in any action it takes in accordance with the present Charter, and shall refrain from giving assistance to any state again which the United Nations is taking preventive or enforcement action.' This sub–paragraph should be read in conjunction with chapter VII of the Charter governing action with respect to threats to the peace, breaches of the peace, and acts of aggression.

---

[39] Falk, Richard., Human Rights and State Sovereignty (New York, London, 1981).

[40] The United Nations does not act for example against the Serbians who are committing genocide against Muslims in the present Yugoslavian war. It does not act either against the Chinese government which is guilty of restricting the legitimate rights of Tibetans. The Kurdish genocide by the Turkish government does not provide sufficient grounds for the United Nations to give humanitarian support to the victims in that case either.

[41] See chapter one, sub–section 6.1.

2.5. Jihad

2.5.1. Definition

In Islamic international criminal law the term '*jihad*' is basically a combination of both the legal and literal definitions of the word. This gives the term a special characterization and should be discussed in conjunction with the relevant provisions found in the verses of the *Qur'an*. Importantly, the definition of 'war' in Islamic international criminal law has been poorly analyzed in relation to the definitions of the term '*Jihad*' by most European writers; Their definitions are not authentic and thereby misleading. For example, one of the most well known Professors of public international law from Oxford University defines *jihad* as 'holy war'. This means 'a war against the unfaithful.'[42] However such a serious misinterpretation is understandable when one realizes that such western sources refer to jurists who have wrongly interpreted the term *jihad*.[43] There is actually another word in the *Qur'an* which may be translated as meaning war. This is the word *qital* and essentially means fighting.[44]

Jihad is basically constructed from the word *jahada* which means struggle, strive, attempt, endeavour or effort. Thus, *Jihad* does not necessarily mean war but a continuous struggle for the purpose of the establishment, re-establishment, building, rebuilding and promotion of various social institutions or relations including the jurisdiction of the divine.

Jihad in Islamic international criminal law also means to mobilize oneself against that which creates inequality between nations. This does not necessarily mean that a nation is at war with another nation(s).[45] *Jihad* may also refer to the legitimate right of a state to conduct war which is exclusively for the purpose of *self-defence* or has the character of a *defensive war* when certain

---

[42] Brownlie, Ian., International Law and the Use of Force by States (Oxford, 1963), p.6.

[43] According to one writer, 'There is no doubt that the institution of Jihad exists in Islamic theological and legal doctrine, and there is equally no doubt about its mention in the Koran and the hadith of the Holly Prophet. However, the precise scope and concrete application of the doctrine has, in our opinion, been a matter of great controversy and, perhaps, even misinterpretation. From the foregoing discussion of the basic Koranic provision on warfare it has become clear that *the Koran does not sanction a state of permanent warfare against the non-Muslim world*.' Emphasis added. Moinuddin, The Charter of the Islamic Conference and Legal Framework of Economic Co-Operation among its Member States, p.26.

[44] In Arabic '*harb*' also means war.

[45] Khadduri, The Islamic Law of Nations: Shaybani's Siyar, p.15. See also further section 2.5.2., p.58.

necessary conditions are fully respected.[46] Therefore the term 'war' in the system of Islamic international criminal law may be variously defined.[47] This is also true for the system of international criminal law. It is important to emphasize that *jihad* does not mean holy war against other nations or non-Muslims.[48] This is because waging war is prohibited as a whole under Islamic international criminal law and war should only be conducted when it is for the purpose of self-defence, otherwise it constitutes an aggressive or offensive war. *Jihad* is a defensive war.[49]

Of course, we do not deny that the *Qur'an* in certain verses refers to the waging of war against those who are violators but these verses should not be interpreted in isolation from other relevant verses and especially from relevant *historical* events.[50] Such verses supported those Muslims whose covenants were repeatedly violated by '(i) the pagan Arabs and (ii) the Jews.'[51] The scope of applicability of those verses should not therefore be interpreted as constituting continuous war. Moreover, historically 'the Muslims became more accustomed to a state of dormant jihad rather than to a state of open

---

[46] See chapter nineteen, sub-section 3.

[47] In one sense, the term 'Jihad in the technology of law is used for expending ability and power in fighting in the path of God by means of life, property, tongue... .' Hamidullah, Muslim Conduct of State, p.150.

[48] According to one writer, 'Let us to conclude this brief exposé with some words on a question which is most misunderstood in non-Muslim circles. It refers to the notion commonly held of the holy war. The entire life of a Muslim, be it concerning spiritual affairs or temporal ones, is a discipline regulated by the Divine law. If a Muslim celebrates even his service of prayer without conviction (for ostentation, for instance), it is not a spiritual act of devotion, but a crime against God, a worship of the self punishable in the Hereafter. On the contrary, if a Muslim takes his meals, for the purpose of having necessary force to perform his obligations regarding God, even if he cohabits with his wife, as an act of obedience to the Divine law, which orders him that, these acts of need and pleasure constitute saintly acts, acts of devotion, meriting all the divine rewards promised for charity... Such being the concept of life, a just struggle cannot be anything except a holy act. All war is forbidden in Islam, if it is not waged for a just cause, ordained by the Divine law. The life of the Prophet shows only three kinds of wars: defensive, punitive and preventive. ... To establish liberty of conscience in the world was the aim and object of the struggle of the Prophet Muhammad, and who may have a greater authority in Islam than he? This is the 'holy war' of the Muslims, the one which is undertaken not for the purpose of exploitation, but in a spirit of sacrifice, its sole object being to make the World of God prevail. All else is illegal. *There is absolutely no question of waging war for compelling people to embrace Islam; that would be an unholy war.*' Emphasis added. Publications of Centre Culturel Islamique., Introduction to Islam (Park Lane, Secunderabad, 1376 H/ 1957 A.C.), p.144.

[49] See also chapter nineteen.

[50] For this misinterpretation see Nawaz, M.K., The Doctrine of 'Jihad' in Islamic Legal Theory and Practice, 8 The Indian Year Book of International Affairs (1959), pp.32-ff, pp.47-8.

[51] Al-Ghunaimi, p.179.

hostility.'[52] It must however be stated that Islamic legal principles are eternal and should prevail permanently but this does not exclude authentic interpretations of them.

Islamic religion is a religion of peace and it is against its principle of 'immunity' to embrace Islam through force. Verses containing phrases such as 'war', *'qital'*, 'fight', 'attack' and 'disbelievers' should certainly be interpreted within their historical context, where Muslims were endangered by the aggressive threats or criminal activities of other groups. Some of these verses were especially revealed during times of crisis for Muslims. Verses containing these phrases are not therefore general orders under the Islamic system of law but are particular orders given to certain Muslims in given historical contexts to defend themselves (under the command of God) from aggressive or hostile conduct by those who were against the Islamic religion and especially at the time of its revelation and consequent development.[53] It is not therefore

---

[52] Khadduri, The Islamic Law of Nations: Shaybani's Siyar, p.17.

[53] The above verses were revealed for instance because of conflicts or disagreements with Muslims or because a given party had a strong tendency to violate their treaty obligations. Thus, they are applicable to the conditions under which Muslims suffered from the unlawful acts of other groups and thus they have no aim to embrace those who were impartial and not aggressive against Muslims. They run that:

'1. A Declaration of immunity from God and His Apostle to those of the polytheists with whom you made an agreement of mutual alliance (because they acted treacherously against the agreement.)

2. So you walk about through the land freely for four sacred months, and know that you cannot weaken God and surely God will bring disgrace to the unbelievers.

3. And as an announcement from God and His Apostle to the people on the day of the Great Pilgrimage the God and His Apostle are free from liability to keep the agreement of alliance with the polytheists; but if you polytheists repent and take the right way, it will be better for you, and if you turn back to act treacherously against God and His Apostle, then know that you cannot weaken God; and proclaim grievous chastisement to those who acted treacherously.

4. Except those of the polytheists with whom you made an agreement, so they have not failed in anything in their agreement because they did not go against you in the least, and they did not back any one against you, so fulfil their agreement to the end of their term, surely God loves the righteous.

5. So when the Sacred months shall have passed away, slay the polytheist warmongers wherever you find them, and seize them as captives and besiege them and lie in wait for them in every ambush; but if they repent and take the right way and offer prayers and pay the poor–rate then leave their way clear and release them, surely God is Great Forgiving, Most Merciful.

6. And if anyone of the polytheists seeks asylum, grant him asylum, till he has heard the message of God, then escort him to his place of security; this is because they are a people without knowledge.

7. How can there be an agreement between the polytheists and God and His Apostle, except with those you have made a treaty at the Sacred Mosque? Therefore as long as they adhered to their agreement with you, you should also adhere to your agreement with them, surely God loves the righteous.

8. How can an agreement be made with them, when they overcome you, they do not pay regard in your case, to the ties of kinship nor of covenant? They please you with their mouths, but their

surprising to see that the *Qur'an* contains verses against offensive activities and war. By the same token this is also true in the case of Christianity which was prevented and restricted by the Emperors of Romans at the time of its revelation.

2.5.2. *Jihad* as a Means of Defeating Aggressors

In order to understand the meaning of the relevant verses of the *Qur'an* relating to the word *jihad* they must not only be considered in conjunction with one another but must also be examined in relation to their revelations. These verses were revealed in order to defeat an aggressor or to resort to the right of self-defence.[54] This means that one should not interpret them in isolation to

---

hearts are averse from you; and most of them are transgressors.

9. They took a mean and impure price as a recompense for reversing and making severe and impractical the Commandments of God, so in this way they hindered people from His Way; indeed most evil are those deeds what they do.

10. They do not pay regard to ties of kinship nor of covenant in the case of a believer, and these are they who have transgressed the limits.

11. Yet if they repent and take the right way and offer prayer and pay the poor rate, then they are your brethren-in-faith; and We relate Our Commandments in detail for those people who have knowledge and can understand.

12. And if they violate their oaths of peace, after their agreement and revile your religion, then you too fight against these leaders of unbelief; surely they are violators of their oaths, therefore your oaths are not for them; in this way they may desist from doing mischief.

13. Will you not fight against a people who violated their oaths, and aimed to expel the Apostle, and they attacked you first; do you fear them? So God is most deserving that you should fear Him, if you are believers.

14. Fight against them and God will chastise them by your hands, and bring disgrace on them and assist you against them and relieve the hearts of a believing people.

15. And remove the rage of their hearts, and God turns mercifully to whom He wills, and God is Knowing, Wise.' The *Qur'an*, 9:1-15.

[54] Islamic external relations had essentially, from the time of the revelation of Islamic religion, a defensive and not offensive function. The efforts of the Prophet Muhammad, beginning from the City-State of Medina, were mostly to unite the Arab nations and this was the sole purpose of the Islamic religion at that time. For this reason, since pagan Arabs and some others such as Jews were waging war against the Prophet and his followers, the external policy of some of the verses of the *Qur'an* were used against those who were aggressors and conducted offensive war against Islamic development. The words used in these verses do not imply the waging of war against other nations for any other reason. For this reason one must state that 'the precedents taken from the Muslim diplomatic history of that period cannot serve as an adequate basis for the future conduct of the Islamic state towards non-Muslim states. Several injunctions dealing with this topic are confined to the Arabs and incumbent only on them as such. The legal and political theory of Islam gives a special regard to the Arabs and considers their unification in a politico-religious community of primordial importance as this unity would be the kernel of the propagation of the Faith. ... Presumably, even the acts which some may qualify as acts of aggression against the pagan Arabs do not constitute models for the future policy of the Islamic

their legal and historical contexts. Here, we examine several verses which have important functions in Islamic international criminal law. These are verses 190 to 193 which may be interpreted as an integral part of the very broad status of the term *jihad*. The historical event concerned was the conclusion of the treaty of *Hudaybiyah* when Muslims were troubled by religious doubt concerning several important matters. The reason for this was that Muslims were conducting a pilgrimage and were not sure whether the Meccans would permit them to practice their rituals and the question arose as to whether it was right to fight against the Meccans if they resorted to force within a sanctuary and during the sacred months.[55] For this reason the 193 verse was revealed. The verse therefore runs, 'And fight against them until there is no more persecution or tumult.'[56] This verse stipulates the right of self-defence for the victim and also creates sufficient right for victims to defeat their enemy or aggressor. This verse must also be analyzed in connection with aforementioned verses in the *Qur'an*.[57]

Jihad greatly encourages the right of self-defence but not war. According to one of the verses of the *Qur'an* relating to the right of self-defence and defeating aggressors, '*Fight in the way of God against those who fight against you, but begin no hostilities; surely God does not love the aggressors.*'[58] The words of this verse are indeed clear when analyzed in their historical context. The verse also states, 'fight in the way of God' and means that one should struggle for the promotion of human rights in general and human dignity, respect and freedom of religion in particular. The second phrase completes the right to fight with the stipulation that this is only to occur 'against those who fight against you, but begin no hostilities' This means that a fight can only be

---

state towards the unbelievers outside Arabia. However, neither towards the pagan Arabs nor towards the unbelievers the Islamic state, during the life time of Muhammad, was aggressive.' Ghunaimi, p.181. All activities of Muslims during the life span of the Prophet Muhammad must also be analyzed in relation to the oppressive activities of others against his life when he had to seek refuge constantly and at the same time promote Islam. Consequently, 'the Prophet's war like policy was confined to defensive measures. He never envisaged a war of aggression.' *Id.*, p.183. This means that the events during the life span of the Prophet could in no way advocate 'the theory of aggressive *jihad* as maintained by Muslim classical writers.' *Id.*, p.183. One of the main reasons for this misinterpretation by certain Islamic and Western writers is that the terminology and phrases in the *Qur'an* and *hadith* have been badly translated by these writers and another reason is that the Western writers, some with and some without prejudice, have given different interpretations to Islamic law. See, for instance, Bo Johnson, Islamisk rätt: Studier i den islamiska rätts- och samhällsordningen (Stockholm, 1975), pp.32-*seq.*

[55] Al-Ghunaimi, p.166.

[56] The *Qur'an*, 2:193.

[57] See the above sections.

[58] The *Qur'an*, 2:190.

carried out in self–defence. In other words this phrase emphasizes the right to resort to self–defence and also the principle of proportionality. Hostility must not be carried out against those who are not aggressors. The third phrase denotes this important fact. It states that 'surely God does not love the aggressors.' This also implies that an aggressor is condemned under divine law.

The above provisions are also strengthened by the provisions of the next verse of the *Qur'an* which reads, 'And slay them whenever you find them, and turn them out from where they have turned you out; persecution and tumult are worse than slaughter; but fight them not at the Inviolable Place of Worship unless they first attack you in it, but if they do fight you, then slay them, such is the reward of the infidels (who oppress the innocent).'[59] 'But if they cease, God is Oft–forgiving, Most Merciful.'[60] This verse permits and prevents a number of activities during actual fighting. These are the following seven points:

Firstly, when one is being attacked one is legally permitted to attack for the purpose of self–defence.

Secondly, the principle of proportionality must be respected at all times.

Thirdly, 'persecution is worse than slaughter.' This phrase implies the importance of freedom of religion and lays blame with those who persecute others for religious reasons; in the case Muslims who may have been persecuted by non–Muslims or Meccans in early historical times. This means that interference in the matter of religion is prohibited by Muslim law and no one should be forced to accept other religions or to be persecuted by others on the grounds of their religion, whether upon Muslim or non–Muslim territory.

Fourthly, a fight must be carried out in certain recognized places or war should not be conducted where it is prohibited. This very important and significant principle is stated by the words, 'but fight them not at the Inviolable Place of Worship unless they first attack you in it.' A broader and proper modern interpretation of this principle is that one should not attack civilians, civilian installations, hospitals, agricultural fields, schools, churches, mosques or any other places which are not traditionally and conventionally recognized as places of war. All civilian needs must be recognized as inviolable and places of worship must be provided for by both conflicting parties. Attacks should only be carried out against military installations and military activities. The above principle must be recognized as one of the most important principles of Islamic international criminal law and has been regulated into the provisions of 1949 Geneva Conventions and 1977 Protocols governing the protection of civilians

---

[59] The *Qur'an*, 2:191.
[60] The *Qur'an*, 2:192.

and civilians installations.

Fifthly, it is a recognized right of those who are attacked in an inviolable place of worship to attack enemies for the purpose of self-defence. This principle is limited by the next principle in order to implement the status of proportionality in time of conflict.

Sixthly, one who has been attacked should cease to attack if the enemy desist from such an attack. This is one of the most significant developments in the humanitarian law of armed conflicts under the Islamic system of international criminal law and is not even found in the modern system of international criminal law.[61]

Seventhly, the one who has been attacked should give amnesty to those who have ceased to attack. This is the principle of forgiveness or the principle of mercy and is strongly advocated by Islamic international criminal law.[62]

The above seven principles constitute an integral part of the framework of the term '*jihad*' and its broad motivations against violators or enemies. These principles also clarify various misunderstandings of the term '*jihad*' in Western juridical writings and politics.[63]

The third and sixth principles are strengthened by the provisions of the next verse of the *Qur'an*. This verse reads, 'And fight against them until there is no more persecution or tumult, but everywhere Justice of God prevail. Domain and Jurisdiction is only for God Almighty; but if they cease, then there is no hostility except against the oppressors.'[64] It must be emphasized that the phrases and provisions of this verse must be read in conjunction with one another and it should not be deduced that all men must be forced to embrace the principles of the Islamic religion.[65] This is because Islamic law or religion means obedience to the law by and through individual access, in which the awareness of the conscience of an individual is the most determining factor in being recognized as a Muslim under divine law. In other words Islam cannot be injected and one should achieve Islam by external and internal individual peace – by what is known as the principle of the universality of divine law.

---

[61] See Malekian, Farhad., Condemning the Use of Force in the Gulf Crisis (Uppsala, 1992).

[62] Hamidullah, The Battlefields of the Prophet Muhammad, p.35. That is why Muhammad is also called the 'Prophet of Mercy'. See also the *Qur'an* on a general amnesty, 2:58.

[63] See, for instance, Bo Johnson, Islamisk rätt: Studier i den islamiska rätts- och samhällsordningen, pp.32–41.

[64] The *Qur'an*, 2:193.

[65] Islamic law respects a person who respects their faith and this is regardless of religious belief.

2.6. Acts Constituting Aggression

The Islamic system of international criminal law qualifies any of the following acts as an act of aggression and therefore constituting a crime within the system. It must however be emphasized that the expression 'a Muslim state' in the following sections does not make any distinction between i) a state which is exclusively ruled by Islamic law and authorities, ii) a state, the majority of the population of which are Muslims and iii) a state, the constitution of which broadly contains Islamic provisions. Any of the following acts constitutes as an act of aggression:

− − A serious violation of a treaties obligations, violations of which endanger the national or international security of a Muslim state.

− − Any armed attack by a state against the territorial jurisdiction of a Muslim state.

− − Invasion, occupation, colonialization or any other act by a state which isolates a part of the territorial jurisdiction of a Muslim state.

− − Ideological attacks by a state against a Muslim state which may seriously destabilize its political jurisdiction.

− − A deliberate and designed attack upon the Muslim or non−Muslim citizens of a Muslim state who are in the territory of another state by the authority of the host state.

− − A deliberate and designed attack by a third state upon the nationals of a Muslim state who are inhabitants under the territorial jurisdiction of another state.

− − Attacks on the refugee camps in the territory of one state by the armed forces of another state.[66]

---

[66] Especially attacks by other groups or idolatrous tribes against Muhammad the Prophet of Islam, who sought refuged in one place or another, were recognized as acts of aggression.

Chapter Four

War Crimes

1. War Crimes in International Criminal Law

The system of international criminal law has developed the concept of war crimes on many occasions. War crimes were essentially categorized in the constitution of the International Military Tribunal for the Prosecution and punishment of the Major War Criminals. They were the only international crimes in the procedures of the Nuremberg Tribunal which were not juridically speaking retroactive and had some origin in the customary and conventional international criminal law. The development of this type of international crime in the positive international criminal law may be divided into five constructive periods, which are particularly important in the recognition and legal characterization of certain acts as constituting war crimes.[1] We do not deny that this development has not been effective in preventing and prohibiting the commission of certain acts during armed conflicts. It will nevertheless have an important function and effect in the establishment and consolidation of an appropriate international criminal court which can exercise jurisdiction over the perpetrators of war crimes.[2]

1.1. The First Development

The first development toward this end was under the 1907 Convention IV, Respecting the Laws and Customs of War on Land. According to this Convention any attack or bombardment for whatever purpose on dwellings, villages, towns or any building which is undefended is prohibited. The

---

[1] It must be emphasized here that violations of other international criminal conventions may also be recognized as constituting war crimes but because of their broad application we have mentioned them in other relevant sections.

[2] A clear example is the establishment of the United Nations Committee (1992) in order to investigate the creation of a temporary international criminal tribunal over the perpetrators of war crimes in Yugoslavia.

Convention also prohibited the commission of other acts in war time.[3] These imposed certain responsibilities on the conflicting parties concerning the prohibition of attacks on the life of non-combatants and the property of municipalities, damages to the institutions of religions, charity and education, works of art and historic monuments.[4] The 1907 'Convention integrated natural law and customary law into international conventional law and it was a step towards the creation of international humanitarian law.'[5]

1.2. The Second Development

The second development on the recognition of war crimes occurred after the First World War in the Preliminary Conference of Paris in 1919. This Peace Conference established a Commission to investigate which acts constituted violations of the rules of war and were therefore war crimes. The Commission enumerated thirty two acts as constituting war crimes, many aspects of which overlap with the concept of war crimes in Islamic international criminal law.[6] In order that one can examine the similarities between the war crimes in these two legal systems we are obliged to list them here.[7] It must however be emphasized that the below list is more representative of customary international criminal law than conventional law. The reason being that international conventional criminal law governing the law of armed conflicts had not yet been developed at that time. These are:

(1) Murders and massacres; systematic terrorism.
(2) Putting hostages to death.
(3) Torture of civilians.
(4) Deliberate starvation of civilians.
(5) Rape.
(6) Abduction of girls and women for the purpose of enforced prostitution.
(7) Deportation of civilians.
(8) Internment of civilians under inhuman conditions.
(9) Forced labour of civilians in connection with the military operations of

---

[3] Article 25.

[4] Articles 46, 50 and 56.

[5] Malekian, International Criminal Law, Vol.I, p.105.

[6] See *infera*.

[7] The United Nations War Crimes Commission., History of the United Nations War Crimes Commission and the Development of the Laws of War (London, 1948), pp.34–5. See also Malekian, International Criminal Law, Vol.I, pp.106–7.

the enemy.

(10) Usurpation of sovereignty during military occupation.

(11) Compulsory enlistment of soldiers among the inhabitants of occupied territory.

(12) Attempts to denationalize the inhabitants of occupied territory.

(13) Pillage.

(14) Confiscation of property.

(15) Exaction of illegitimate or of exorbitant contributions and requisitions.

(16) Debasement of currency, and issue of spurious currency.

(17) Imposition of collective penalties.

(18) Wanton devastation and destruction of property.

(19) Deliberate bombardment of undefended places.

(20) Wanton destruction of religious, charitable, educational and historic buildings and monuments.

(21) Destruction of merchant ships and passenger vessels without warning and without provision for the safety of passengers and crew.

(22) Destruction of fishing boats and relief ships.

(23) Deliberate bombardment of hospitals.

(24) Attack on and destruction of hospital ships.

(25) Breach of other rules relating to the Red Cross.

(26) Use of deleterious and asphyxiating gases.

(27) Use of explosive or expanding bullets, and other inhuman appliances.

(28) Directions to give no quarter.

(29) Ill-treatment of wounded and prisoners of war.

(30) Employment of prisoners of war on unauthorised works.

(31) Misuse of flags of truce.

(32) Poisoning of wells.

(33) Indiscriminate mass arrests (added by the United Nations War Crimes Commission).[8]

1.3. The Third Development

The third development in the system of international criminal law regarding war crimes was under the Charter of the International Military Tribunal for the Prosecution and Punishment of Major War Criminals. The Charter originally defined the concept of war crimes and was also the first international organ established by the victorious states which officially used the terminology of 'war

---

[8] For no. 33 see The United Nations War Crimes Commission, *id.*, p.478.

crimes'.[9] This historical definition became an important reason for the development of the concept of war crimes in the system of international criminal law under the Charter of the United Nations and in particular the 1949 Geneva Conventions and its 1977 Protocols.[10] The Charter of the International Military Tribunal in Nuremberg reads that war crimes are 'violations of the laws or customs of war. Such violations shall include, but not be limited to, murder, ill–treatment or deportation to slave labour or for any other purpose of civilian population or in occupied territory, murder or ill–treatment of prisoners of war or persons on the seas, killing of hostages, plunder of public or private property, wanton destruction of cities, towns or villages, or devastation not justified by military necessity.'[11] The above definition obviously secures its legal applicability by defining its scope under both positive and customary law – both sources may however reach similar conclusions.[12] The article describes whether war crimes are violations of the laws of war and/or the customary rules of armed conflicts. The enumeration of what acts constitute war crimes is only for illustrative purposes and is therefore not conclusive. This means that many other acts may also be recognized as constituting war crimes and gives rise to the concept of the criminality of perpetrators.

1.4. The Fourth Development

The provisions in the 1949 Geneva Conventions are the fourth development in the recognition of war crimes under the system of international criminal law. These Conventions have not only an important function in the recognition of this category of international crime but also have an important role in the legal framework of international humanitarian law of armed conflicts. These conventions are the 1) Geneva Convention for the Amelioration of the Condition of the Wounded and Sick in Armed Forces in the Field, 12 August 1949, 2) Geneva Convention for the Amelioration of the Condition of Wounded, Sick and Shipwrecked Members of Armed Forces at Sea, 12 August 1949, 3) Geneva Convention Relative to the Treatment of Prisoners of War, 12 August 1949, and 4) Geneva Convention Relative to the Protection of

---

[9] See Malekian, International Criminal Responsibility of States, pp.62–6.

[10] Malekian, International Criminal Law, Vol.I, p.122.

[11] Article 6 (b).

[12] Malekian, International Criminal Law, Vol.I, p.112.

Civilian Persons in Time of War, 12 August 1949.[13]

These conventions lay down a number of provisions, the violation of which can constitute war crimes. These crimes include murder, extermination, violence to life, mutilation, torture, humiliating, cruel and degrading treatment, taking of hostages, prevention of aid to the sick and wounded, attacks against medical services and attacks against hospital ships, reprisals against the wounded, the sick and personnel, unlawful act or omission by the Detaining Power causing death or seriously endangering the health of a prisoner of war, scientific experimentation and any act which is contrary to the normal procedure in hospitals and executions without previous judgment pronounced by a regularly constituted court.[14]

These four Geneva Conventions have particularly specified that the commission of certain acts in an armed conflict constitute grave breaches. This is a new innovation in the law of armed conflicts. Earlier relevant conventions have not been identified as such. Importantly, the grave breaches in the Geneva Conventions are more or less similar to those breaches which Islamic international criminal law prohibits during armed conflicts, such as wilful killing and destruction not justified by military necessity.[15]

The content of one of the Geneva Conventions exclusively relates to the protection of civilian populations from unlawful armed activities. This subject is developed under the Geneva Convention Relative to the Protection of Civilian Persons in Time of War, 12 August 1949.[16] According to this Convention a number of acts constitute greave breaches under its provisions;[17] Among these are wilful killing, wilful causing of great suffering or serious injury to body or health, torture, degrading and inhuman treatment, including biological experiments, compelling a protected person to serve in the forces of a hostile power, unlawful deportation or transfer or unlawful confinement of a protected person, wilful deprivation of the rights of a protected person to a fair and regular trial, the taking of hostages and the extensive destruction and appropriation of property not justified by military necessity and carried out unlawfully and wantonly.

---

[13] *Id.*, pp.122–41.

[14] *Id.*

[15] See *infra*.

[16] The Convention was signed in Geneva on 12 August 1949 and came into force on 21 October 1950. 75 United Nations Treaties Series, p.287.

[17] Article 147 along with Articles 50, 51 and 130 is common to the first three of the four Conventions of 1949.

1.5. The Fifth Development

The fifth development of the law of armed conflicts and the recognition of certain activities as constituting war crimes can be examined in the Geneva Protocol I Additional to the Geneva Conventions of 12 August 1949, and Relating to the Protection of Victims of International Armed Conflicts, 12 December 1977 and the Geneva Protocol II Additional to the Geneva Conventions of 12 August 1949, and Relating to the Protection of Victims of Non-International Armed Conflicts, 12 December 1977. These Protocols contain some of the rules of armed conflicts not regulated into earlier conventions. They also have a complementary character regarding subjects which were not clarified by earlier conventions.

Protocol I especially emphasizes that the term 'armed conflict' includes those conflicts in which peoples are fighting for the purpose of liberation and freedom from colonial domination and alien occupation and against racial regimes in the exercise of their right of self-determination; as provided in the Charter of the United Nations and the Declaration on Principles of International Law concerning Friendly Relations and Co-operation among States in accordance with the Charter of the United Nations.[18]

Some of the important provisions of the Protocol contribute to the treatment of the sick and shipwrecked in a humanitarian way. The Protocol has especially prohibited *(a)* medical or scientific experiments, *(b)* the removal of tissue organs for transplantation and *(c)* physical mutilations. The Protocol emphasizes that medical units shall be respected and prohibits attacks of reprisal against medical personnel, religious personnel and medical units.[19] Other important provisions concern the protection of civilians, civilian populations and civilian property from inhuman attacks, including indiscriminate attacks such as attack by bombardment, reprisal and an attack which may be expected to cause incidental loss of civilian life, injury to civilians, damage to civilian objects or a combination of these activities. The protocol also prohibits attacks on un-defended or demilitarized zones, dams, dykes and nuclear electrical generating stations. Certain persons in special situations should be treated with priority; Such as rape victims, women, pregnant women, mothers having dependant infants and children, who are arrested, detained or interned for reasons relating to the armed conflict.[20]

---

[18] Resolution 2625 (XXV) of October 24, 1970 of the General Assembly of the United Nations.

[19] Article 20.

[20] See Articles 76 and 77.

Wilful violations of some of the above provisions may be considered as grave breaches, such as attacking civilian populations, installations potentially harmful to civilian objects if damaged or destroyed, non–defended localities and demilitarized zones, transference by an occupying power of parts of its own population into the territory it occupies, or the deportation or transference of the population of the occupied territory, unjustifiable delay in the repatriation of prisoners and racial discrimination or *apartheid* practices.[21]

The Geneva Protocol II Additional to the Geneva Conventions of 12 August 1949, and Relating to the Protection of Victims of Non–International Armed Conflicts of 1977 has a similar characteristic to Protocol I.[22] Protocol II however, specifically relates to any 'non–international armed conflict' which may occur due to internal reasons: 'The scope of Protocol II in comparison with Protocol I is very restricted.' Protocol II contains three important humanitarian principles. The first relates to the fundamental guarantees protecting those who do not take a direct part in armed activities.[23] The second concerns those persons whose liberty has been restricted.[24] The conflicting parties must respect certain rules regarding persons such as the wounded and sick, who shall be protected and receive medical care, they shall be allowed to practise their religion, women shall be held separate from men, except in the case of family unity and places of internment and detention shall not be located close to the combat zone. The third humanitarian principle relates to the respect of generally recognized principles for penal prosecutions such as the principle of innocence until proven guilty, the right to defence, conviction on the basis of individual responsibility and the application of the law in force and not retroactive law.[25] The Protocol also protects, by various means, medical units and prohibits attacks on civilian populations and their objects by one means or another – such as agricultural areas for the production of foodstuffs.

[21] See Article 85 of Protocol I.

[22] The Protocol was opened for signature in Berne, on 12 December 1977 and came into force on 7 December 1978.U.N. Doc. A/32/144 Annex II; International Committee of the Red Cross, *Protocols Additional to the Geneva Conventions of 12 August 1949, Geneva*, Geneva, 1977, pp.89–101; 16 ILM (1977), p.1442.

[23] See Article 4.

[24] See Article 5.

[25] See Article 6.

2. War Crimes in Islamic International Criminal Law

2.1. Codification

Islamic international criminal law was the first system of criminal law to codify rules for the conduct of international and non-international war. Islam provides for the precise rules during a state of war.[26] The Islamic international criminal law prohibits war between Muslims, Muslims and non-Muslims. The reason for this is that the Islamic international criminal law basically prohibits war and recognizes that conflicts between nations must be solved through negotiations, mediation, sending of diplomats, arbitrations and other peaceful means of settlement.[27] The second reason is that Islamic law considers itself a universal law applicable to all social relations between humans including war, which is morally evil and creates unnecessary suffering.

Islamic international criminal law has therefore placed much emphasis upon the solving of international conflicts through consultation and negotiation between chief members of both conflicting parties.[28] This is in fact a tradition of the Prophet Mohammed who prohibited war as long as peaceful agreements could be concluded between the conflicting parties. Yet, even if no agreement could be reached, unlimited war was still not permitted; certain principles such as declaration of war, invitation to cease fire in order to help to the wounded

---

[26] The *Qur'an*, constituting the main source of the Islamic law, has devoted a number of verses concerning the law of war. The relevant provisions of the Islamic international criminal law must however be analyzed and examined with regard to other systems of law principally based on and developed from the rules of war; For example the system of 'law of nations' was created and developed from the rules of war. One can scarcely reject the fact that the rules of war were the main reasons for the creation and development of the international humanitarian law of armed conflicts. The League of Nations as well as the United Nations were both established because of the events of the two World Wars. A great majority of international criminal conventions have been regulated and ratified as a result of numerous international wars. Although we obviously do not support a state of war as an essential reason in the development of the system of international law, it is also true that most modifications, alterations, abolitions, prohibitions, criminalizations, modernizations and humanizing legal systems have been effectively promoted by the consequences of various wars.

[27] This philosophy and rule can be seen in Article 2(3) of the United Nations, which reads that 'All Members shall settle their international disputes by peaceful means in such a manner that international peace and security, and justice are not endangered.' The provisions of Article 53(1) concerning the Pacific Settlement of Disputes completes the context of the above sub-paragraph. It reads that 'The parties to any dispute, the continuance of which is likely to endanger the maintenance of international peace and security, shall, first of all, seek a solution by negotiation, enquiry, mediation, conciliation, arbitration, judicial settlement, resort to regional agencies or arrangements, or other peaceful means of their own choice.'

[28] Khadduri, War and Peace in the Law of Islam, pp.98-101.

fighters and a definite human morality governed warfare.[29] Consequently, in the final stage, if a conflict of armed forces occurred the principles of morality and legality had to be respected by the conflicting parties.[30]

In general Islamic international criminal law, contrary to the system of international criminal law, forbids reprisals and struggles for the maintenance of the principle of proportionality in all time. The *Qur'an* (the main source of the Islamic law) states that 'All prohibited things are under the Law of Retaliation; if then any one acts aggressively against you, inflict injury on him according to the injury he has inflicted on you, and fear God, and know that God is with those who refrain from doing evil deeds and are righteous ones.'[31] Thus, Islamic international criminal law has recognized (as does the system of international criminal law) the nature of self-defence and also fundamentally bases the concept of self-defence on the proportionality principle.[32] A defensive war can take two forms. Firstly, when the enemy has invaded a Muslim territory. Secondly, although the enemy has not invaded any territory its activities are in contradiction to prevailing conduct.[33] The relevant version of *Qur'an* concerning self-defence emphasizes that 'Fight in the path of God against those who fight against you, but do not transgress. Lo! God does not love transgressors.'[34] This version of the Islamic international criminal law denotes without doubt respect for the principle of proportionality in all situations. It also denotes the fact that in all military situations the law of war must be respected. A serious violation of the law of armed conflicts may therefore be recognized as a war crime under Islamic international criminal law.[35]

---

[29] Allahdin, Abdullah., Extracts from the Holy Quran and Sayings of the Holy Prophet Mohammad, 7th ed. (India, 1933), p.193.

[30] See sub-section below.

[31] The *Qur'an*, 2:194.

[32] See chapter nineteen, section 2.

[33] Hamidullah, Muslim Conduct of State, p.154. According to one writer there may be other reasons for waging war. These are *i)* a violation of an agreement by a party, *ii)* considering certain religious duties not obligatory such as taxation, *iii)* hypocrisy and *iv)* apostasy. *Id.*, p.156. Another writer asserts that Islamic international criminal law in the early days of its development recognized five different periods regarding the status of war against non-Muslims. These were: '(i) a period of trust, forgiveness and withdrawal, (ii) a second period summoning them to Islam, (iii) a third period of fighting in self-defence, (iv) a fourth period of aggressive fighting at certain times, (v) a fifth period, of aggressive fighting in general or absolute terms.' Al-Ghunaimi, The Muslim Conception of International Law and Western Approach, p.74.

[34] The *Qur'an*, 2:190.

[35] The system of Islamic international criminal law may legitimize giving assistance in certain circumstances to a nation which seeks humanitarian help. The *Qur'an* 8:72. See also chapter twenty one.

2.2. Acts Constituting War Crimes

Islamic international criminal law has a wide range of rules applicable to an armed conflict.[36] These rules must not be violated and must be taken as the most serious and effective rules for the implementation of the Islamic international humanitarian law of armed conflict. The following acts are strictly prohibited in time of an armed conflict and considered war crimes in accordance with the Islamic international criminal law.[37] The following classification of war crimes may therefore be listed:

A.
1) Massacre.
2) Killing and destruction which are not necessary.
3) Killing of non-combatants.
4) Killing of those who accompany combatants but are considered non-combatants and do not assist the actual fighting in any way.
5) Killing hostages.
6) Killing hostages for retaliation.
7) Killing envoys.
8) Killing envoys for the purpose of retaliation.
9) Continuing to kill after vanquishing the enemy.

B.
1) Violations of acts which are prohibited according to the existing treaties.
2) The employment of poisonous weapons.
3) To force prisoners to fight against their own armed forces.
4) Killing those who are impartial concerning the result of the war.
5) Killing of refugees (Mustamin)
6) Killing all those who are traders, merchants, business men and under any other position who does not actually fight.
7) Inflicting death by burning a prisoner.
8) Amputation of the parts of body.

---

[36] See chapter nineteen.

[37] For some of these prohibitions see, generally, Hamidullah, Muslim Conduct of State, pp.204–13; Hamidullah, The Battlefields of the Prophet Muhammad, p.17; Al-Ghunaimi, The Muslim Conception of International Law and Western Approach, pp.148–50; Khadduri, War and Peace in the Law of Islam, pp.103–4; Allahdin, Extracts from the Holy Quran and Sayings of the Holy Prophet Mohammad, p.193; Khadduri, The Islamic Law of Nations: Shaybani's Siyar, pp.76, 87. See also Arabi, Abdel Rahman, L'Islam et la guerre à l'Epoque du Prophète Mahomet (Ambilly, 1954); Fyzee, A.A.A., Outlines of Muhammadan Law (London, 1955).

9) Mutilation of dead bodies.

C.
1) Killing women.
2) Killing mothers who have dependent infants.
3) Killing those who are incapable of fighting such as those who are handicapped, blind, insane, lunatic, delirious, old men and women.
4) Killing minors who have not take part in the actual fighting.
5) Rape.
6) Adultery and fornication with families.
7) All types of sexual abuse.
8) Killing parents not for the purpose of self-defence.
9) Killing monks, priests and hermits.
10) Killing a national of the enemy state who is already resident under the jurisdiction of another.
11) Killing neutrals, including physicians and journalist who do not take part in the actual fighting.
12) Mistreatment of prisoners of war by one means or another.
13) Torture.
14) Excess and wickedness.
15) Degrading treatment of sick and wounded and prisoners of war.
16) Humiliation of men.
17) Treachery and perfidy.

D.
1) Killing civilian populations.
2) Destruction of civilian establishments.
3) Any type of wanton destruction.
4) Forcing civilians to fight.

E.
1) Killing peasants.
2) Destruction of properties unnecessarily.
3) Destruction and devastation of agriculture.
4) Destruction and devastation of forests (crimes against the natural environment).
5) Mutilation of beasts.
6) Slaughtering beasts which are not necessary for food.
7) Burning an animal.

Chapter Five

Poisonous Weapons

One of the more important criminalizations under Islamic international criminal law is the prohibition of the use of poisonous weapons in warfare.[1] Accordingly, 'Le poison est donc considéré comme moyen de guerre illicite.'[2] This principle is one of the most important principles in the humanitarian law of armed conflicts and has not yet been properly consolidated in the system of international criminal law.

There has long been controversy concerning the prohibition and criminalization for such weapons in the system of international criminal law and despite the fact that the 1925 Protocol concerning the use of poisonous gases prohibits the use of poisonous weapons, the Protocol has repeatedly been violated in international relations. Two of the most notorious cases are the employment of atomic bombs on Hiroshima and Nagasaki in 1944 and the use of poisonous weapons in the Vietnam War up to 1969.[3]

Although a new convention between the super powers orders the destruction of various nuclear weapons, the provisions of this agreement apparently do not bind all states and the nuclear weapon capabilities of a considerable number of states are still untouched. Islamic international criminal law gives significant priority to the prohibition of the use of poisonous weapons and it is here that the real humanitarian value of the law is deeply admirable.

The prohibition of poisonous weapons under Islamic international criminal law has been for two essential reasons. Firstly, the Islamic law of armed conflicts commands that armed attacks must always be waged in a humane

---

[1] Muhammad al-Amir, Kitab al-Iklil Sharh Muktasar Khalil (Cairo, A.H. 1224), p. 160; Hilli, Tabsirat al-Muta`allimin (Damascus, A.H. 1342), p.103. Quoted in Khadduri, War and Peace in the Law of Islam, p.104. See also Weeramantry C.G., Islamic Jurisprudence: An International Perspective (1988), p.138; Singh, Nagendra, India and International Law, Vol.I (New Delhi, 1973), p.216.

[2] Rechid, L'Islam et le Droit des Gens, p.481.

[3] For further analysis and references see Duffett, J., Against the Crime of Silence (New York, London, 1968); see also Falk, Richard A.(ed.), The Vietnam War and International Law (Princeton, 1969), 2 vols.

manner – denoting the bravery of the soldiers in the actual fight.[4] Secondly, armed attacks which are based on poisonous weapons are against the moral aspects of human dignity and are consequently against divine law.[5]

[4] Rechid, L'Islam et le Droit des Gens, p.481.

[5] It is appropriately stated by Professor Weeramantry that 'In the context of nuclear weapons, chemical warfare and defoliation of the countryside which are concerns of importance to contemporary international law, the Islamic tradition is of vital significance as contributing an important strand with which to strengthen current norms of humanitarian law.' Weeramantry, Islamic Jurisprudence, p.138.

Chapter Six

Crimes Against Humanity

1. Criminalization in International Criminal Law

The term 'crimes against humanity' was first formulated in the Charter of the International Military Tribunal in Nuremberg for the prosecution and punishment of Major War Criminals.[1] Crimes against humanity were defined as 'murder, extermination, enslavement, deportation, and other inhumane acts committed against any civilian population, before or during the war; or persecutions on political, racial, or religious grounds in execution of or in connection with any crime within the jurisdiction of the Tribunal, whether or not in violation of the domestic law of the country where perpetrated.'[2] This definition has been rapidly developed and enlarged in the system of international criminal law by the establishment of the United Nations Organization and the formulation of a number of international criminal conventions applicable to crimes against humanity. Some of the most recognized instruments which have been ratified by a great number of states include, the Convention on Prevention and Punishment of the Crime of Genocide, 1948, the International Convention on the Suppression and Punishment of the Crime of Apartheid, 1973, Geneva Convention for the Amelioration of the Condition of the Wounded and Sick in Armed Forces in the Field, 12 August 1949, Geneva Convention for the Amelioration of the Condition of Wounded, Sick and Shipwrecked Members of Armed Forces at Sea, 12 August 1949, Geneva Convention Relative to the Treatment of Prisoners of War, 12 August 1949, Geneva Convention Relative to the Protection of Civilian Persons in Time of War, 12 August 1949, the Geneva Protocol I Additional to the Geneva Conventions of 12 August 1949, and Relating to the Protection of Victims of

---

[1] Malekian, International Criminal Law, Vol.I, p.267.

[2] Article 6 (c) of the Charter of the International Military Tribunal annexed to the London Agreement of 8 August 1945.

International Armed Conflicts, 12 December 1977 and the Geneva Protocol II Additional to the Geneva Conventions of 12 August 1949, and Relating to the Protection of Victims of Non–International Armed Conflicts, 12 December 1977 and a number of conventions relating to the crime of slavery.[3] All these conventions have formulated provisions recognizing the commission of certain acts in both war and peace as constituting crimes against humanity. This concept is regardless of the race, colour, national or ethnic origin of an individual or group.

2. Criminalization in Islamic International Criminal Law

In Islamic international criminal law it is not necessarily the acceptance of certain regulations and the legislation of certain rules within the domestic and the international criminal systems which identifies which acts do and which acts do not constitute a crime. It is the effect and basic elements of the natural or moral law which prohibits and criminalizes given international criminal conduct.

One must not forget that an individual under Islamic law is recognized as an integral part of the human community and from a more far reaching aspect, an integral part of a universal human life. This means that injury to a person or discrimination between two persons is considered a crime against the entire international human society.

It must therefore be emphasized that the provisions regulated within the content of conventions applicable to crimes against humanity in international criminal law are *not*, regarding Islamic international criminal law, innovative and consequently do not contradict the provisions of Islamic law or the provisions of Islamic international criminal law. For example, the Nuremberg Tribunal recognized murder and extermination of civilians as constituting crimes against humanity. Islamic international criminal law has long ago prohibited the murder and mass killing of civilians and identified such crimes as against the fundamental principles of divine law; In other words a crime against humanity. The same is true in the case of deporting those who do not take part in actual fighting, even though they have other religions, political and ethnical origins.[4] Islamic international criminal law, like the system of international criminal law, criminalizes the extermination and murder of individuals. The practice of deporting individuals (for whatever reason) constitutes crimes against humanity

---

[3] For further analysis and discussions see, generally, Malekian, International Criminal Law, Vols. I and II.

[4] See chapter four on War Crimes.

once the practice has occurred. Islamic international criminal law essentially prohibits the persecution of individuals on religious, racial and political grounds.

Accordingly all these acts may constitute crimes regardless of whether or not an individual, group or government which has committed such crimes was aware of their criminalization under Islamic international criminal law. This is because (according to the Islamic theory) it is not the awareness and information about the criminalization of an act which prevents the commission of related criminal conduct, it is rather the nature and the ill characterization of an act which provides the necessary information as to whether or not it constitutes a criminal conduct in accordance with the principles of legality. Ignorance and/or negligence concerning the law or the order of the law does not prevent the prosecution and punishment of a person who has committed crimes against humanity. *The system of Islamic international criminal law has in other words a very high degree of moral force, while this is fundamentally lacking in the system of international criminal law. The former not only bases its legal sanctions on the principle of legality but also on the natural and moral wrong of criminal conduct, while the latter on the recognition of the system by each individual state.*[5] This means that the criminalization of the given conduct in the system of international criminal law depends on each individual states decision. In contrast the law or obligations are already fixed under the Islamic international criminal law.

The criminalization of a given conduct in Islamic international criminal law therefore has a legal characterization which cannot be ignored and deleted by way of interpretation, this can only be accomplished through the humiliation and monopolization of legal and moral power. Thus, when one speaks of the criminalization of apartheid and discrimination under Islamic international criminal law, one does not need to decide whether the state in which such activities are carried out is Muslim or non-Muslim. This is because in Islamic law it is the spirit of human beings which is identified with dignity and not necessarily the system of law.[6] It must of course be emphasized that *the principle of legality* has long been revealed in the system of Islamic international criminal law.[7] This system is therefore relevant when one deals with the types of crimes against humanity committed during the Second World War.

---

[5] For the principle of legality in Islamic international criminal law see chapter one sub-section 6.2.

[6] See, generally, chapter one.

[7] Moreover, subjects in Islamic law are not authorized to codify the law.

Chapter Seven

Slavery

1. Slavery in International Criminal Law

1.1. Abolition

Slavery is one of the oldest institutions practiced by almost all nations. The practice had been legally permitted by the European system of international law and there had not therefore been any effective movement against the institution of slavery up until the end of nineteenth and beginning of the twentieth centuries. To sell and to buy human beings was considered an important branch of national and international trade.[1] It was basically upon the institution of slavery that the economy of some European countries and the United States in particular developed.[2] It must not however be ignored either that the criticisms made against this institution were also effectively started by the countries which had made broad income from this cheap labour. The desire to abolish or maintain the institution of slavery in the United States was one of the most essential reasons for the American Civil War.[3] This and many other movements in European societies against the institution e.g. the long struggle for the creation of the right of visit and search of vessels, became an essential reason for the formulation of the first agreements concerning the abolition of slavery.[4]

According to a new tradition which began in the life of navigation concerning the slow evolution of the right of visit, trade in humans was assimilated to the crime of piracy, which meant the prosecution and punishment of those who carried slaves came under universal criminal jurisdiction. This assimilation was not however very useful as a whole. States which supported this practice could still engage in the trade by their vessels crossing territorial or international

---

[1] Malekian, International Criminal Law, Vol.I, pp.209–11.

[2] *Id.*, p.212.

[3] *Id.*, p.213.

[4] *Id.*, p.214.

water ways. The legal problems concerning this issue were that firstly, under national systems the institution was not abolished and secondly, they could still trade without being suspected of carrying slaves. Thirdly, states which legitimated the institution did not capture the vessels of states involved in the trade. Fourthly, the institution of slavery was not prohibited by a positive international criminal law and could therefore easily be supported by domestic legislations.[5] Many bilateral and multilateral agreements were ratified by states between the period 1890–1938.[6] Nevertheless, none of these instruments were effective for the international abolition and criminalization of the institution of slavery.

1.2. Criminalization

Slavery was not internationally characterized as an international crime, even with the establishment of the League of Nations in which many states officially condemned the institution of slavery. The struggle for the abolition of the institution of slavery by states finally resulted in the adoption of the 1926 Convention on slavery. This Convention has been reconsidered and amended through the establishment of the United Nations in a Protocol of 1953. The new amendment of the 1926 Convention was not satisfactory and did not apply to all forms of slavery – including the abolition of all types of slavery.[7] As a result a Supplementary Convention on the Abolition of Slavery, the Slave Trade and Institutions and Practices Similar to Slavery was adopted in the United Nations Conference in Geneva in 1956. The new Convention is the extension of the scope of the 1926 Convention on Slavery and both the Convention and the Supplementary are assumed to cover all forms of slavery at an international level.[8]

The definition of the institution of slavery has been extended in the above instruments due to the needs of the time. According to the 1926 Convention slavery is the status or condition of a person over whom any or all of the powers attaching to the right of ownership are exercised. The Convention has put more weight on the abolition of slave trade and this is on the grounds that the slave trade has been most instrumental in the development and extension

---

[5] *Id.*, p.217.

[6] *Id.*, p.221.

[7] *Id.*, pp.220–3.

[8] *Id.*, p.223. The instruments on slavery have also been accompanied by other instruments for the suppression of white slavery. See *id.*

of the institution of slavery. The Convention therefore divides the slave trade into four types of categories. These are i) all acts involved in the capture, acquisition or disposal of a person with intent to reduce him to slavery, ii) all acts involved in the acquisition of a slave with a view to selling or exchanging him, iii) all acts of disposal by sale or exchange of a slave acquired with a view to being sold or exchanged and, iv) every act of trade or transport in slaves.[9] The Convention also emphasizes the abolition of compulsory or forced labour and requires all state parties to take all effective measures which may seem necessary for the prevention of compulsory or forced labour extending into conditions analogous to slavery.[10] Although the Convention has prohibited slavery and slave trade, it does not consider the territories placed under the sovereignty, jurisdiction, protection, suzerainty or tutelage of a contracting party as a strong reason for cases of slavery. In fact the international juridical position of these territories could be compared to the slavery of one country to another. This is on the grounds that such protector states had almost total control over all the economic resources of the relevant states. However, the system of international criminal law of that time was not prepared, as it is today, to recognize that the institution of slavery can exist even though the elements of slavery stated in the 1926 Convention do not exist. Secondly, states were and are very cautious regarding the scope and method of applicability of the system of international criminal law, especially where the system limits their activities within their territorial jurisdictions. These and many other reasons undermined the legal position of the 1926 Convention and caused its amendment by the 1953 Protocol and finally by the 1956 Supplementary Convention on the Abolition of Slavery, the Slave Trade and Institutions and Practices Similar to Slavery. The Convention has developed and extended the concept of the definition of slavery and its institutions.[11] All these agreements and many

[9] Article 1.

[10] Article 5.

[11] The most relevant articles of the 1956 Supplementary Convention are as follows:

Article 1: Each of the States Parties to this Convention shall take all practicable and necessary legislative and other measures to bring about progressively and as soon as possible the complete abolition or abandonment of the following institutions and practices, where they still exist and whether or not they are covered by the definition of slavery contained in Article I of the Slavery Convention signed at Geneva on 25 September, 1926:

(a) debt bondage, that is to say, the status or condition arising from a pledge by a debtor of his personal services or of those of a person under his control as security for a debt, if the value of those services as reasonably assessed is not applied towards the liquidation of the debt or the length and nature of those services are not respectively limited and defined;

(b) serfdom, that is to say, the condition or status of a tenant who is by law, custom or agreement bound to live and labour on land belonging to another person and to render some determinate service to such other person, whether for reward or not, and is not free

others on white slavery constitute the main instruments applicable to the international crime of slavery under the system of international criminal law. The application of these instruments has not however been fully successful due to the creation of other types of slavery under various national systems.[12]

to change his status;

(c)   any institution or practice whereby:

  (i)   women, without the right to refuse, is promised or given in marriage on payment of a consideration in money or in kind to her parents, guardian, family or any other person or group; or

  (ii)   the husband of a women, his family, or his clan, has the right to transfer her to another person for value received or otherwise; or

  (iii) a women on the death of her husband is liable to be inherited by another person;

(d)   any institution or practice whereby a child or young person under the age of eighteen years is delivered be either or both of his natural parents or by his guardian to another person, whether for reward or not, with a view to the exploitation of the child or young person or of his labour.

Article 3: I. The act of conveying or attempting to convey slaves from one country to another by whatever means of transport, or of being accessory thereto, shall be a criminal offence under the laws of the States Parties to this Convention and persons convicted thereof shall be liable to very severe penalties.

2. (a) The States Parties shall take all effective measures to prevent ships and aircraft authorized to fly their flags from conveying slaves and to punish persons guilty of such acts or of using national flags for that purpose.

(b) The States Parties shall take all effective measures to ensure that their ports, airfields and coasts are not used for the conveyance of slaves.

3. The State Parties to this Convention shall exchange information in order to ensure the practical co-ordination of the measures taken by them in combating the slave trade and shall inform each other of every case of the slave trade, and of every attempt to commit this criminal offence, which comes to their notice.

Article 7: For the purpose of the present Convention:

(a)   'slavery' means as defined in the Slavery Convention of 1926, the status or condition of a person over whom any or all of the powers attaching to the right of ownership are exercised, and 'slave' means a person in such condition or status;

(b)   'a person of servile status' means a person in the condition or status resulting from any of the institutions or practices mentioned in Article I of this Convention;

(c)   'slave trade' means and includes all acts involved in the capture, acquisition or disposal of a person with intent to reduce him to slavery; all acts involved in the acquisition of a slave with a view to selling or exchanging him; all acts of disposal by sale or exchange of a person acquired with a view to being sold or exchanged; and, in general, every act of trade or transport in slaves by whatever means of conveyance.

[12] See, generally, Awad, Mohamed., Report on Slavery (United Nations, New York, 1966); Sellin, J. Thorsten., Slavery and the Penal System (New York, Oxford, Amsterdam, 1976).

2. Slavery in Islamic International Criminal Law

2.1. Manumission

According to the legal, social, economic and political philosophy of Islamic international criminal law mankind is equal in all social phenomena. Islamic jurisdiction therefore prohibits any type of action degrading a person to the statute of slavery.[13] Therefore, slavery is 'unlawful' under Islamic law.[14] We cannot deny however that during war the taking slaves was, in certain circumstances, permitted in order to *prevent bloodshed*.[15] This is because the Islamic law of armed conflict basically consists of the law of battle and the humanitarian law of armed conflict. This regulation is neutralized by the command that priority is not given to Muslims as all are equal before the divine law.[16] Moreover, 'La législation islamique déclare action 'laide' la vente de l'homme libre, parce que le mot 'vente' signifie échange de biens (choses), tandis que l'homme libre n'est pas un bien. L'homme esclave n'est pas non plus un bien. L'homme réduit à l'esclavage subit une punition temporaire pour s'être opposé par les armes au triomphe et à l'extension de la vraie religion. La durée de son esclavage est une épreuve qu'il traverse. Il dépend absolument de lui d'abréger la durée de cette épreuve par sa conduite. Une fois affranchi, il ne diffère en rien des autres membres de la société, quelle que soit sa couleur. Il a le droit de prétendre à tout ce que l'homme peut obtenir sur terre par son

---

[13] 'In the time when Islamic government was not founded in Arabia, the believers had to release the slaves of the disbelievers by giving ransom to them, but when Islamic government was founded then no one could keep slaves under their possession against Islamic Law. When Islamic government was founded then the Arabian Muslims abolished slavery from many parts of the world. They released many slave subjects from the possession of the great tyrant kings. So in the Holy Qur'an God commands to the believers that they should release every kind of slaves in the way of God.' Jullundri, Ali, Ahmad Khan., Translation of the Glorious Holy Qur'an (Lahore, 1962), p.60.

[14] *Id.*, p.iii.

[15] Rechid, L'Islam et le Droit des Gens, p.474.

[16] According to one writer, 'It is noteworthy that the divine injunctions deal only with the means of emancipation, non provided slavery as an imperative system. This is due to the fact that Islam tries to solve the problem of slavery on a pragmatic basis. When Islam emerged, slavery was a world wide recognized institution deeply rooted in all societies to the length that any abrupt banishment of the system would result in shaking the very fundations of society. For this, Islam's policy in putting an end to slavery is rather practical. Islam restricted the causes of slavery and widened the possibilities of freeing the slaves. Such device is capable, in the course of time, of abolishing the system of slavery without affecting the social values or entiling economic crisis.' Al-Ghunaimi, The Muslim Conception of International Law and Western Approach, p.191. See also *id*, p.190.

mérite et son travail.'[17]

Therefore, releasing slaves became even a custom and *tradition* of the Prophet Muhammad who basically condemned the killing of individuals and insisted that Muslims must, as much as possible, not conduct war and must come to peaceful solutions with their enemies. He was therefore against hostile conduct and according to him, war was against the principles of family unity. He emphasized the release of those captured during war and without taking any reward for such action.[18] For example, after one of the most recognized Islamic Wars i.e. Badr, the Prophet ordered the release of all those who were captured during the war and did not degrade them to the statute of slavery.[19]

2.2. Abolition

Islamic international criminal law prevents acts of slavery in any form and it is a well recognized rule in the *Qur'an* that in certain situations punishment of a person who has committed a crime can be mitigated, discontinued or even neglected if he releases a slave(s). Islamic international criminal law has from its very beginning encouraged the abolition of the institution of slavery by one means or another. A number of verses in the *Qur'an* deal with this radical matter concerning slavery and the common value of man in freedom, justice, equality and brotherhood. For example the *Qur'an* states that:

And it is not lawful for a believer to kill a believer except by mistake, and whoever kills a believer by mistake, he should free a believing slave, and blood–money should be paid to his (victim's) family, but first they should verify themselves that they are really the next of the kin of slain person, and if the slain be from a tribe who is your foe and slain is a believer, then a believing slave should be freed only, and, if he is from a tribe between whom and you there is a treaty, the blood–money should be paid to his (slain's) next of kin and a believing save should be freed, ...[20]

The existence of the institution of slavery in the Islamic jurisdiction must also be examined in the light of the time in which the Islamic law was revealed to the Arab nations as the divine law and must be analyzed and compared with the

[17] Rechid, L'Islam et le Droit des Gens, p.476.

[18] See *infra*.

[19] See also below sections.

[20] The *Qur'an*, 4: 92. See also 2:177.

jurisprudence of various nations of the world towards slavery such as the Greeks, Romans[21] and even the practices and tendencies of the various churches.[22]

It is also worth noting that the use of slaves was not prohibited in early religious practice. For instance in 595, 'Pope Gregory the Great sent a priest, Candidus, to Britain to buy pagan slave boys *(pueros Anglos)*, seventeen to eighteen years old, to work on monastic estates.'[23] Christians in Europe considered slaves as 'the domestic enemy'. Therefore, they treated slaves as a legally unrecognized class of people who did not enjoy the protection of domestic laws. Female slaves were often preferred to male slaves. This was probably because females were easier to control.[24,25]

Islamic law permitted the institution of slavery on the one hand while simultaneously promoted its abolition in social relations on the other.[26] This is exactly the policy of the provision which is enacted under the system of international criminal law concerning the first agreements made on the

[21] According to Professor Weeramantry 'slavery as practised in Greece, Rome or modern America was a condition of rightlessness which had no parallel in Islamic law. ... The master's authority was not unlimited or free of the control of the state as it was under the Greeks, the Romans or indeed in America. Further, the slave had equal rights before the criminal law and any body who committed his murder suffered capital punishment.' Weeramantry, Islamic Jurisprudence: An International Perspective, pp.138–9.

[22] As mentioned in the previous section, it was from the middle of nineteenth up to the beginning of twentieth centuries that the abolition of slavery was encouraged by the European law of Nations.

[23] Evans, Deniel., Slave Coast of Europe, 6 Slavery & Abolition / A Journal of Comparative Studies (1985), p.43.

[24] *Id.*, p.47.

[25] Malekian, International Criminal Law, Vol.I, p.210. According to a comparative study 'Nous n'avons rencontré dans les livres ce'lestes antérieurs au Koran, et tels qu'ils nous sont connus, aucune parole rappelant le genre humain à sa liberté primitive. Au contraire, dans le Lévitique (XXV, 44–45), nous lisons ce qui suit: 'Ton esclave mâle ou femelle, c'est des nations, tes voisins, que tu l'acquerras, ainsi que parmi les fils des passagers et des colons, qui habitent avec toi; c'est d'eux et de leurs familles, résidant parmi vous et ayant enfanté en votre pays, que vous tirerez vos esclaves, et ils seront votre propriété. Ce sera un héritage dont profiteront vos fils après vous et qu'ils posséderont perpétuellement.' L'Evangile n'a pu amener la suppression de l'esclavage; les moines, les prélats, les papes eux–mêmes, avaient des esclaves en foule. Les plus grands Etats chrétiens, proclamant la liberté de la personne humaine, se donnant la mission de propager la civilisation, ont eux–mêmes pratiqué l'esclavage pendant de longs siècles. La Grande–Bretagne, les Etats–Unis, l'Espagne, etc., ne l'ont aboli qu'au XIX siècle. En trois siècles, l'Afrique 'sortit' trente millions d'esclaves.' Rechid, L'Islam et le Droit des Gens, p.477.

[26] See section below.

abolition of slavery.[27] Moreover, one must always remember that slave trade and slavery existed well before Islamic law and that the latter has not only not promoted the institution of slavery but is also, strictly speaking, against its practice. For example, when a slave women has breastfed the baby of a Muslim women who cannot herself provide milk, she must be given freedom immediately and should be regarded as if she had never been a slave.[28] Islamic international criminal law, in order to abolish the institution of slavery, provides certain priorities under certain circumstances for a Muslim slave to be given amnesty. Thus, one could give mercy or quarter which meant the act of giving life to a defeated enemy.[29]

2.3. Protection

In order to gradually abolish slavery Islamic jurisprudence recognized certain rights for slaves and by this methodology proselytized non–Muslims. It recognizes equality between a slave and his master with regards to food, clothing and a place of dwelling. Simultaneously, it must be emphasized that 'Islam does not allow compulsion to convert even slaves to Islam.'[30] The *Qur'an* (the main source of Islamic international criminal law) has not only exhorted the liberation of slaves but has also emphasized that Muslim states should allot part of their budgets for the manumission of slaves. This meant that income from taxation was to be paid to the masters of the slaves in order to release slaves from that condition. In other words Islamic law has long struggled against the institution of slavery and insisted that the institution is a common problem and cannot be solved in isolation from other social phenomena. An old interpretation of this rule of the *Qur'an* governing the liberation of slaves by manumission from state income was that a master should not refuse a suggestion by a slave who wishes to work and return his value.[31] For the purpose of a quick abolition of slavery the Prophet decreed that Arabs could not be enslaved.[32] According to one view:

Islamic classical institution of slavery is distinguished by two main

---

[27] Malekian, International Criminal Law, Vol.I, pp.217–30.

[28] Rechid, L'Islam et le Droit des Gens, p.476.

[29] See chapter twenty, section 4.

[30] Hamidullah, Muslim Conduct of State, pp.210–11.

[31] *Id*, pp.210.

[32] *Id.*, pp.210.

characteristics, i.e. (I) the human treatment of the slave with the view to raise his morale. A slave should be treated on the same footing with his master as regards food, clothing and dwelling and, (II) the wide possibility given to the slave to be emancipated. Both the Qur'an and the tradition exhort pious Muslims, against considerable worldly and heavenly rewards, to free their slaves. The slave has also, under certain conditions, the chance of claiming his own freedom. ... slavery in traditional Islam was virtually meant to be an adequate medium of proselytizing non–Muslims rather than denigrating some individuals. Yet history records some deplorable incidents which occurred in spite of the legal precepts that Islam has advanced with a view to minimize slavery. Slavery however, persisted in some Muslim societies until recently when it was legally abolished in those countries.[33]

Although one cannot deny the fact that the Muslim Arabs (like many other generic groups) have taken slaves during wars with non–Muslims, this was exercised by all nations and was an old customary rule. One must not forget that one of the core reasons for this practice in Islamic law was that Islamic law was principally against the killing of individuals in any way and since prisoners of war under the old traditions could be killed,[34] Islam privileged the institution as long as it could be effective in stopping bloodshed.[35] One essential historical difference between the concept of slavery in the system of international criminal law and Islamic international criminal law is that according to the former the taking of slaves was lawful at all times whereas according to the latter the taking of slaves was only permitted in connection

---

[33] Al–Ghunaimi, The Muslim Conception of International Law and Western Approach, pp.149–50.

[34] For instance, after the battle of Badr, 'The prisoners were ... treated in an exemplary manner in spite of the fact that the Muslims had least to favour them. The Prophet distributed them among his solidery for safe custody, and enjoined them expressly to treat them well. The command did not remain unheeded: those of the prisoners who had no clothes were provided with dress. ... Some of the Muslims fed them with their bread and contented themselves with mere dates in view of the good treatment enjoined. Tabariy, History, p.1337.' Hamidullah, The Battlefields of the Prophet Muhammad, p.17.

[35] Id., p.17. Therefore, 'according to the Holy Quran to make men or captives, slaves is not lawful for the believers. Everywhere in the Holy Qur'an God commands the believers that they should release even the slaves of the disbelievers by giving ransom to their masters, then how those believers could keep their own slaves under their possession, so they at once freed their slaves in the way of God without taking ransom. God also commands about the prisoners of war that they also should be freed under obligation after the end of the war when the enemy lays down its arms.' Jullundri, The Glorious Holy Quran, p.60.

with and in the course of a war.[36]

The institution of slavery was not only not promoted by Islamic international criminal law but also had a strong tendency towards its abolition. It was also admissible that if a Muslim or non-Muslim who fought for a Muslim army was taken prisoner by the enemy for the purpose of slavery, they should be recognized as a freeman again when released from the jurisdiction of the enemy state.[37] The Islamic law also provided a similar rule for prisoners taken by Muslim armies but whom actually succeeded in coming under another jurisdiction and even though they were 'slaves' were thereby recognized as freemen.[38] Islamic international criminal law had several different regulations concerning enslavement resulting from armed conflicts. As we have stated elsewhere, the virtue of the Islamic law (including Islamic international criminal law) is that these laws can adapt themselves to various historical changes. Alterations can be made to Islamic international criminal law by specific and relevant interpretations of its certain principles, approaches and applications, while the basic philosophies and aims of this law remain unchanged. The early practices of Islamic international criminal law regarding the treatment of slaves in order to gradually abolish slavery can be seen in the light of its core principle concerning the equality of all man before the law and especially the promotion of the principle of brotherhood for all irrespective of race, colour, language, religion, ethnic origin, social position or political view.

2.4. Criminalization

The principles of Islamic international criminal law regarding the institution of slavery have the character of the methods used in the treatment of criminal behaviour in the science of criminology. In fact one can assert that Islamic international criminal law is principally characterized as criminological law. This is a law which has not only the rules and regulations governing the prohibition, prevention, prosecution and punishment of criminals, but also has the methods by which criminals and criminal behaviour can be cured and rehabilitated. It is

---

[36] It must therefore be emphasized that 'The object of permitting slavery in (pre-practice of) Islam is not the exploitation of an unfortunate follow-being. Far from that, its aim is first to provide shelter to the prisoners of war who have lost everything, and for some reason or other are not repatriated; and secondly to educate them and give them the opportunity of acquiring culture in Islamic surroundings, under the government of God. Slaves are obtained only in legitimate war, waged by a government. Private razes, kidnapping or even sale of infants by their parents have no legal sanction whatsoever.' Publications of Centre Culturel Islamique, p.63.

[37] See also chapter twenty one.

[38] Hamidullah, Muslim Conduct of State, p.243.

in the light of these different types of values that the criminalization of slavery, slave trade and institutions similar to slavery come under a consolidated principle in Islamic international criminal law. For confirmation of this one can simply refer to the constitutions of all states which have in one way or another been effected by the principles of the Islamic law and have ratified all relevant international conventions on the prohibition of slavery. A principal virtue of Islamic international criminal law is the modernization of its principles through adaptation and interpretations. The abolition and criminalization of all types of slavery is a fact and reality in Islamic international criminal law today which cannot be denied by any juridical, theological or philosophical argument.

Chapter Eight

Genocide

1. Genocide in International Criminal Law

Genocide constitutes a consolidated international crime in the system of international criminal law.[1] The 1948 Convention on the Prevention and the Punishment of the Crime of Genocide was essentially formulated to condemn the mass killings of groups during the Second World War. Although legislation against the crime of genocide is rather new, the crime has been repeatedly committed in the relations between states for many centuries. According to the Convention, in order for a crime to be identified as genocide several principles must exist. These are the intent to destroy, in whole or in part, a national, ethnical, racial or religious group. The following acts constitutes genocide: *(a)* Killing members of the group; *(b)* Causing serious bodily or mental harm to members of the group; *(c)* Deliberately inflicting on the group conditions of life calculated to bring about its physical destruction in whole or in part; *(d)*

---

[1] For the crime of genocide, see Genocide as a Crime Under International Law, 41 A.J.I.L. (1947), pp.145–51; Stuyt, A.M., Genocide, 23 Nederlands Juristenblad (1948), No.9 pp.125–51 and No.10 pp.157–163; Kunz, Josef. L., The United Nations Convention on Genocide, 43 A.J.I.L. (1949), pp.738–46; Kuhn, Arthur. K., The Genocide Convention and State Rights, 43 A.J.I.L. (1949), pp.498– 501; Finch, George, A., The Genocide Convention, 43 A.J.I.L. (1949), pp.732–8; Perlman, Philip. B., The Genocide Convention, XXX Nebraska Law Review (1950, no.1), pp.1–10; Drost, Peter., The Crime of State: Genocide, Vol.II (London, 1959); Sartre, Jean–Paul., On Genocide (Boston, 1968); Blischenko, Igor, P., Modern International Law and Genocide, Nos. 16–7 Etudes Internationales de Psycho–sociologie Criminelle (1969); Lombois, Claude., Droit Pénal International (France, 1971), pp.64–6; Reisman, W.M., Responses to Crimes of Discrimination and Genocide: An Appraisal of the Convention on Elimination of Racial Discrimination, I the Denver Journal of International Law and Policy (1971), pp.29–64; Bedau, Hugo Adam., Genocide in Vietnam, 53 Boston University Law Review (1973); Bryant, Comment, *Part I: Substantive Scope of the Convention*, 16 Harvard International Law Journal (1975); Richard (ed.)., Genocide in Paraguay (Temple University Press, Philadelphia, 1976); Edwards, Contribution of the Genocide Convention to the Development of International Law, 8 Ohio Northern University Law Review (1981), pp.300–ff; von Glahn, Gerhard., Law Among Nations (New York, 1981), pp.306–10; Kuper, Leo., Genocide: Its Political Use in the Twentieth Century (New Haven and London, Yale University Press, 1981), pp.21–2; Malekian, International Criminal Responsibility of States, pp.87–92; Bassiouni, M. Cherif., Introduction to Genocide, in 1 Bassiouni (1986), pp.281–86; Malekian, International Criminal Law, Vol.I, pp.287–323.

Imposing measures intended to prevent births within the group; *(e)* Forcibly transferring children of the group to another group.

One of the serious criticisms against the crime of genocide in the system of international criminal law is that the legal application of the concept of this crime is very difficult and in most cases may be purely hypothetical. This is because the convention does not clarify the definition of 'intent' or 'intent to destroy' and many other terms such as 'in part', 'deliberately inflicting' and so forth.[2] All these terms are conditional and can therefore be interpreted differently. One difficulty is that one cannot assert when the 'intent to destroy' has begun. It is very doubtful whether the killing of just one member of a group is sufficient to constitute genocide. This is because the legal language of the Convention speaks of the crime of genocide 'in whole' and 'in part'. The definition of the term 'in whole' may be much more relevant than the definition of the term 'in part'. Since the term 'in part' can apply to any number of people and the legislator, by the term 'in part', did not only mean the killing of, deliberately inflicting on, imposing measures to, and forcible transferring of just one member of a group. These are some of the greater difficulties found in the application of the relevant provisions of the convention of genocide. There have been many instances denoting the commission of the crime of genocide, nevertheless no government has admitted having committed the crime of genocide. There is also another problem with the genocide convention, in most cases the perpetrators of the crime of genocide are those who decide about the enforcement of the provisions of the Convention. Although we cannot deny that some governments like the Iraqi and Turkish governments have been identified as having committed the international crime of genocide, this has never been implemented as a reason to stop the commission of acts of genocide.

2. Genocide in Islamic International Criminal Law

2.1. Prohibitions

Islamic international criminal law, like the system of international criminal law, prohibits the mass killing of individuals or groups for whatever purposes. This includes any form of plan and practice which is essentially designed to destroy a group and nation in any way and /or by whatever means. Mass killing constitutes a serious crime against humanity and a punishable crime under Islamic international criminal law. Although Islamic international criminal law

---

[2] For further examination see Malekian, International Criminal Law, Vol.I, pp.295–9.

does not necessarily speak of the type of genocide formulated in the genocide Convention, it does prohibit the killing of members of groups, regardless of whether or not the act has been committed in whole, in part or only against a single member of a given group. It is the intention of killing, causing serious bodily harm, destroying or imposing forceable measures upon the members of any group which constitutes a crime. This is regardless of whether or not the criminal act has been committed against several or a single member of a group. In Islamic international criminal law it is the motive of ill-action which gives rise to the concept of crime and not the existence or non-existence of various elements enumerated in the genocide Convention. As a general principle of Islamic criminal law bloodshed is basically prohibited by divine law and a person who has committed crime cannot obtain mercy under the Islamic sovereignty of law, at least as long as certain specific punishments have not been inflicted upon them. Still, mercy and amnesty largely depend on the character of a crime and whether or not the crime is a forgivable one.

2.2. Classification

Islamic international criminal law is against any type of mass killing and/or destruction and recognizes such acts as being against the whole theory of the Islamic legislation in the *Qur'an*. The legal reasoning in Islamic international criminal law rests on the effect of such crime on the community of nations. Although many nations may exist statistically, they are still considered an integral part of one nation by Islamic law. The crime of mass killing or genocide can easily be classified under one of the categories of crimes recognized as *Quesas* in Islamic international criminal law. *Quesas* (constituting the second category of crimes) do not necessarily have a fixed definition or penalty and they have basically evolved through various social needs including judicial process, analogy reasoning, political consideration and even the adaptation of modern philosophies of crime and criminology.

This category of crime in Islamic criminal law criminalizes among other things, murder and intentional crimes against a person. Since in the genocide Convention intention to commit genocide constitutes one of the important elements for the recognition of the crime of genocide, the crime therefore simply falls under *Quesas* or the second category of crimes in the Islamic criminal justice system. The reason why the crime of genocide can be classified under this category is that this category guarantees both concepts of genocide. These two concepts are: Murder which results in the death of the victim of the crime of genocide and; The intention to kill but the action has not resulted in the death of the victim.

2.3. Criminalization in Human Rights

Other reasons why mass killing is prohibited under Islamic criminal law are its principles of human rights under which murder, killing and intentional injury for whatever reason are prohibited and recognized as prosecutable and punishable crimes. The value of Islamic international human rights and its rules and principles against the crime of mass killing or genocide can be especially examined under the rules of warfare.[3] Although we have examined this in other sections, Islamic international criminal law prohibits any type of collective killing of groups who are not combatant and this is irrespective of whether or not the victims of the crime belong to other groups which have or have not the same nationality as one of the conflicting parties. It is upon this principle that Islamic international criminal law takes chronological priority to the system of international criminal law in the case of criminalizing genocide as an international crime. This means that the International Military Tribunal in Nuremberg could have recognized the killing of Jewish nationals as constituting the crime of genocide, if and only if they had taken into consideration the long establishment of the Islamic international criminal law against the perpetrators of war crimes and crimes against humanity including the international crime of genocide. Although our purpose is only to present the facts and principles of Islamic international criminal law in the elimination of serious international crimes and although we have only assumed here to draw comparative conclusions, no serious objections could have been made against the Tribunal if it had simply referred to the existence of a large number of customary international criminal principles which had already been codified within the international laws of other nations in the international community. This would mean that many criminals would not have escaped prosecution and punishment for reasons of retroactivity and the jurisdiction of the Tribunal would less have been criticized in the public history of international criminal law, as it often is today.

---

[3] See chapters four and twenty two.

Chapter Nine

Discrimination / Apartheid

1. Apartheid in International Criminal Law

The system of international criminal law has widely recognized that discrimination between various races and groups constitutes an international crime. The strongest form of discrimination is called apartheid, which is the main reason for the recognition of discrimination as an international crime.[1] Apartheid is different types of segregation and discrimination committed against any group of individuals. The system of apartheid has a broad chapter of its own in international criminal law and there are several international criminal conventions and a large number of resolutions and other instruments applicable to this international crime. The basic convention applicable to this category of international crime is the International Convention on the Suppression and Punishment of the Crime of Apartheid, 1973. The crime of apartheid was originally practiced by the South African government against the majority of its own population. It was legally abolished in 1991, although the root of discrimination still continues.

According to international criminal law, in order for a crime to be recognized as apartheid it must be committed against a group of individuals. The system of international criminal law does not however provide a particular definition for 'a group of individuals' and it is therefore very difficult to establish the criteria as to what constitutes a group in order for an act to be recognized as a crime under the provisions of the apartheid conventions.[2]

---

[1] It must be emphasized here that both the terms 'genocide' and 'apartheid' were structured and defined after the establishment of the United Nations and did not earlier exist in the terminology of the system of international criminal law. However, the term 'genocide' was coined between the two World Wars by the Jurist Raphael Lemkin. Sartre, Jean, Paul., On Genocide in Duffett, J., Against the Crime of Silence (New York, London, 1968), p.612.

[2] Rubin, L., Apartheid in Practice (1971); Graefrath, Bernhard., Convention Against the Crime of Apartheid, Vol. XI German Foreign Policy (1972), pp.395−402; Tomko, J., Apartheid−medzinarodny zlocin proti l'undstvu, (Summary in English), 58 Pravny Obzor (1975), pp.289−304; Feimpong, J.K & S Azadon Tiewel., Can Apartheid Successfully Defy the International Legal System? 5 The Black Law Journal (1977), pp.287−311; Feimpong, J.K & S Azadon Tiewel., Can

According to the 1973 Convention apartheid is a crime against humanity and this inhuman act is the consequence of the policies and practices of racial segregation and discrimination. According to the Convention apartheid may be committed by individuals, organizations or institutions. The Convention has particularly stated that the crime of apartheid constitutes 'a serious threat to international peace and security.'[3] It therefore recognizes all such individuals and entities as criminals. The term 'apartheid' has been more specifically defined by the Convention.[4]

Apartheid Successfully Defy the International Legal System? 5 The Black Law Journal (1977), pp.287–311; Seltzer, Garry., The Rule of the South Africa Criminal Code in Implementing Apartheid, 8 Georgia Journal of International and Comparative Law (1978), pp.176–94; Gracia-Amador, F. V., The Crime of Apartheid: Responsibility and Reparations, Review of Contemporary Law (1981), pp.31–8; International Conference on Sanction Against South Africa, UNESCO House, Paris, 20–27 May 1981, Vol.I Main Documents, United Nations Center Against Apartheid (New York, 1981); Paris Declaration, International Conference on Sanctions Against South Africa (And Special Declaration on Namibia), 27 May 1981, Published by the United Nations Center Against Apartheid; Clark, Roger. S., The Crime of Apartheid, in Bassiouni, M Cherif., International Criminal Law, Vol.I (1986), pp.299–323; Reddy, Enuga S., Apartheid: The United Nations and the International Community (New Delhi, 1986); Reddy, Enuga S., India and the Struggle Against Apartheid, 26 I.J. I.L. (1986), pp.551–67; Ji, Ge., Apartheid – An Outstanding Issue in World Politics, 30 Beijiling Review: A Chinese Weekly of News and Views (1987), pp.14–7; Malekian, International Criminal Law, Vol.I, *op.cit.*, pp.324–75.

[3] Article 1.

[4] Article II of the Convention defines the crime of apartheid. It reads that:

For the purpose of the present Convention, the term 'the crime of *apartheid*', which shall include similar policies and practices and racial segregation and discrimination as practiced in southern Africa, shall apply to the following inhuman acts committed for the purpose of establishing and maintaining domination by one racial group of persons over any other racial group of persons and systematically oppressing them:

(a) Denial to a member or members of a racial group or groups of the right to life and liberty of person:

    (i) By murder of members of a racial group or groups;

    (ii) By the infliction upon the members of a racial group or groups of serious bodily or mental harm by the infringement of their freedom or dignity, or by subjecting them to torture or to cruel, inhuman or degrading treatment or punishment;

    (iii) By arbitrary arrest and illegal imprisonment of the members of a racial group or groups;

(b) Deliberate imposition on a racial group or groups of living conditions calculated to cause its or their physical destruction in whole or in part;

(c) Any legislative measures and other measures calculated to prevent a racial group or groups from participation in the political, social economic and cultural life of the country and the deliberate creation of conditions preventing the full development of such a group or groups, in particular by denying to members of a racial group or groups basic human rights and freedoms, including the right to work, the right to form recognized trade unions, the right to education, the right to leave and to return to their country, the right to a nationality, the right to freedom of movement and residence, the right to freedom of opinion and expression, and the right to freedom of peaceful assembly and association;

(d) Any measures including legislative measures, designed to divide the population along racial lines by the creation of separate reserves and ghettos for the members of a racial group or

2. Apartheid in Islamic International Criminal Law

Obviously Islamic international criminal law neither employs the term apartheid in its constitution nor the definition provided in the apartheid convention. It however recognizes a very serious form of discrimination, the scope of which is principally much broader than the definition of the crime of apartheid in the system of international criminal law. Islamic law has, since the time of its creation, internationalized the human society and has therefore recognized that individuals are the main elements in any social structure. It is on this basis that any criminal act against an individual constitutes a crime against the whole society and therefore a prosecutable and punishable crime. The same theory of the Islamic criminal justice system has been entered into the Islamic international criminal law, characterizing any criminal activities against an individual by individuals, groups and governments as constituting a crime against humanity. The main reason for this is that an individual in the Islamic international criminal law constitutes by themselves a form of society. This philosophy is precisely where the concept of the Islamic international criminal law contradicts the legal philosophy of the system of international criminal law. In the latter, apartheid and discrimination are practiced against a group irrespective of how the number of individuals integrated in a group are defined. Islamic international criminal law does not base the concept of discrimination on the existence of a group against which discrimination and apartheid are practiced. The Islamic criminal law has a wide range of rules applicable to the crime of discrimination and consequently recognizes it as a serious crime against humanity, regardless of whether or not a criminal act was committed against a group or a single individual. The logic behind this philosophy from Islamic international criminal law is that in order to determine whether or not an act of discrimination or apartheid has been committed, one must refer to the purpose and aim of the criminal act and against whom it was committed and not to the number of individuals or the group of individuals against whom the criminal activities were carried out.

Islamic international criminal law prohibits, prevents and criminalizes any type of discrimination between race, colour, language, belief or nationality. This is

---

groups, the prohibition of mixed marriages among members of various racial groups, the expropriation of landed property belonging to a racial group or groups or to members thereof;

(e) Exploitation of the labour of the members of a racial group or groups, in particular by submitting them to forced labour;

(f) Persecution of organizations and persons, by depriving them of fundamental rights and freedoms, because they oppose *apartheid.*

because (according to the Islamic law) all men are equal before its jurisdiction and has therefore given an international characterization to the principles of brotherhood, equality, liberation and an authentic criminal justice system. Under Islamic international criminal law discrimination constitutes an international crime against the fundamental rights of mankind. This includes even discrimination against other groups of people who have different religion, colour, race, sex, language, culture or political statutes. It is upon this basic consideration that other groups can also live side by side with Muslim groups in brotherhood, equality and justice. As a result of this basic aspect of Islamic law any type of apartheid or discrimination between men is essentially a prohibited crime and constitutes a crime against the social principles of equality. The legal and moral philosophy of this principle arises from one of the Verses of the *Qur'an* reading that 'Surely we have accorded dignity to the sons of Adam.' This verse implies that all men have fundamentally come from one generation and therefore human spiritual dignity is the same all over the universe of God.

The Islamic international criminal justice system recognizes the inherent right of all members of the community of nations to enjoy an equal standard of life, not only without any due consideration to race, colour, national or ethnic origin but also from the practical aspects of equality, including an equal economic and living standard for all men. It is the manifestation of this type of consideration and re-consideration of the social structure that creates equality in Islamic law. It therefore rejects and criminalizes all types of social and institutional priority between humans.

Chapter Ten

Torture

1. Torture in International Criminal Law

1.1. Non-Criminalization

Torture constitutes one of the most serious international crimes in the system of international criminal law.[1] This is however an innovation in the system, otherwise torture has been legally inflicted under most domestic legislations as an integral part of political, juridical and criminal procedures. This can especially be examined in the historical backgrounds of criminal jurisdictions where it was impossible for jurists to access evidence denoting the criminality of the accused. For this reason they inflicted torture in order to obtain confessions or information regarding the commission of certain criminal activities. Some states however did not officially permit the infliction of torture but in practice their criminal jurisdictions were profoundly combined with the institution of torture and torture constituted an effective instrument in order to obtain confession. For instance under the English system torture was considered an integral part of criminal procedures where there was no proof of criminality or it was insufficient to prove guilt. The English system especially employed torture when there was a crime against the monarch or when it was considered that a political crime against English sovereignty had been committed.[2]

The institution of torture was also employed in order to obtain confessions for the commission of certain acts by those who were considered political criminals or those whose activities were against the security of the State. Torture was also carried out on slaves who had, according to their owners, committed certain acts which were against their status.[3] Torture of political prisoners and slaves might also have other aims such as humiliating the accused or frustrating other

---

[1] Malekian, International Criminal Law, Vol.I, pp.376-463.

[2] Id, p.397.

[3] Id., pp.387-9.

related persons.[4] In all cases, torture could also be inflicted as an effective punishment of the accused or actual criminals. For this reason there was often no difference between those who were accused and those who were criminals. This was because torture was inflicted upon both those accused and actual criminals, even though the former could be found innocent. An accused could even be killed under torture because of the strong physical and psychological effects – even when no proof of guilt was found.[5]

1.2. Criminalization

The beginning of twentieth century brought into consideration some of the most important legal principles regarding the institution of torture and it was considered that the infliction of torture was inhuman and should be abolished under criminal legislations. The criminalization of torture was not however effective until the establishment of the United Nations. Still, the early works of the Organization only had hortatory effect in the prohibition of torture, although some resolutions were adopted for such a purpose. The most important instruments in international criminalization of torture are as followings:

i) The 1949 Geneva Conventions which in Articles 3 and 99 prohibits the use of torture;

ii) The Universal Declaration of Human Rights (1948), Article 5;

iii) The United Nations Standard Minimum Rules for the Treatment of Prisoners (ECOSOC Resolution (1955, 1957), Article 31;

iv) The International Covenant on Civil and Political Rights (1966), Article 7;

v) The Declaration on the Protection of All Persons from being Subjected to Torture and Other Cruel, Inhuman or Degrading Treatment or Punishment (1975), Article 3;

vi) The United Nations Code Conduct for Law Enforcement Officials (1979), Article 5;

vii) The United Nations Principles of Medical Ethics (1982), Principle 2;

viii) The Convention against Torture and Other Cruel, Inhuman or Degrading Treatment or Punishment (1984).

ix) The 1989 Convention on the Right of Child.

---

[4] *Id.* pp.393–5.

[5] *Id.*, pp.389–90.

There are also some regional instruments applicable to this international crime which have been codified and developed due to specific requirements at a given time. These instruments do have a regional perspective but are nevertheless considered of prominent importance in the prohibition of the institution of torture under the criminal jurisdiction of many states. These regional instruments are namely:

A) The prohibition of the use of torture in Article 3 of the European Conventions on Human Rights (1950);
B) The American Convention on Human Rights (1969), Article 5 (2);
C) Draft Convention Defining Torture as an International Crime (Inter-American), 1980;
D) The African Charter on Human Rights (1981), Article 5;
E) Draft European Convention on the Protection of Detainees From Torture and From Cruel, Inhuman or Degrading Treatment or Punishment (Inter-European) 1983;
F) The European Convention for the Prevention of Torture and Inhuman or Degrading Treatment or Punishment 1987.

The most significant instrument under the system of international criminal law applicable to the crime of torture is the international Convention against Torture and Other Cruel, Inhuman or Degrading Treatment or Punishment (10 December 1984).[6] Because of the high humanitarian purposes of the Convention and the existence of a number of other international instruments applicable to this international crime, as well as the broad prohibition of torture under the legislations of most states, the provisions of the convention must be regarded as having approached the effect of customary international criminal law. This means that no state should deny the international legal effect of the convention concerning the criminalization and prohibition of the crime of torture. In my view the 1984 Convention has the effect of international *jus cogens*.

According to the Convention, torture is defined as 'any act by which severe pain or suffering, whether physical or mental, is intentionally inflicted on a person for such purposes as obtaining from him or a third person information or a confession, punishing him for an act he or a third person has committed or is suspected of having committed, or intimidating or coercing him or a third

---

[6] Adopted and opened for signature, ratification and accession by General Assembly resolution 39/46 of 10 December 1984. Report: A/39/708 and Corr.2. Enter into force: 26 June 1987, in accordance with article 27(1).

person, or for any reason based on discrimination of any kind, when such pain or suffering is inflicted by or at the instigation of or with the consent or acquiescence of a public official or other person acting in an official capacity. It does not include pain or suffering arising only from, inherent in or incidental to lawful sanctions.'[7] This definition of torture is without prejudice to any other instrument on the prohibition and criminalization of torture which may apply provisions with wider perspectives.[8] For instance, the convention prevents states from the commission of other acts under their criminal jurisdictions such as cruel, inhuman or degrading treatment or punishment which do not amount to torture.[9]

Several other important matters concerning prohibition, criminalization, prosecution, punishment, extradition and other administrative matters are also stated in the convention. Accordingly, states are under conventional obligations to take effective legislative, administrative, juridical or other measures to prevent acts of torture and no circumstances should be reason for employing torture. This means that torture is prohibited during all times including war and no plea of superior order is acceptable for the justification of torture.[10] States are also prevented from expelling or extraditing a person when there is a risk of imposing torture on the accused.[11]

According to the Convention a state(s) is also obliged to 'ensure that all acts of torture are offences under its criminal law. The same shall apply to an attempt to commit torture and to an act by any person which constitutes complicity or participation in torture.' States should punish those who have committed torture in any way.[12] This even includes those who have come under their jurisdiction but for whom extradition is impossible for one reason or another.[13]

The 1984 Convention also recognizes the duty of states to assist one another regarding criminal proceedings in cases of the crime of torture in conformity with treaty obligations which may exist between them.[14] They should ensure that prohibition governing the crime of torture is fully respected in the training of law enforcement personnel, civil or military personnel, medical personnel,

---

[7] Article 1 (1).
[8] Article 1 (2).
[9] Article 16.
[10] Article 2.
[11] Article 3.
[12] Article 4.
[13] Articles 5, 6, 7 and 8.
[14] Article 9.

public officials and other persons who may be involved in the interrogation, custody or treatment of any individual subjected to any form of arrest, detention or imprisonment.[15]

They should also guarantee redress for a person who is subjected to torture and a statement which is obtained as a result of torture shall not be invoked as evidence in any proceedings against the accused. The convention also encourages states in creating and participating in a Committee against Torture which can have the function of an impartial administration in the prevention of torture under the jurisdiction of states.[16]

The 1984 Convention has recognized the prevention, prosecution and punishment of the crime of torture. Although torture has also been criminalized within other international instruments applicable to this international crime, torture has been inflicted under the criminal and political jurisdictions of states and many governments have denied that they have committed the international crime of torture. This crime has been especially committed by states which prevent all forms of political movements under their jurisdictions and thus the infliction of torture on political prisoners is one of the most prevalent forms of this international crime.[17]

---

[15] Article 10.

[16] Articles 14, 15 and 17–24.

[17] 'The events of the twentieth century prove that torture has frequently been employed by governments in order to impose their ideology upon the national population or upon foreign nationals particularly in the time of war. The prohibitions governing the institution of torture have not therefore been effective in eradicating the use of torture at national and international levels. The use of torture has especially been sanctioned as a weapon against dissident political movements. Reports prepared by international organizations confirm the fact that the victims of torture are very often individuals who have refused to conform to the ideology of the state. In other words torture is used as a means of maintaining political control. Torture is also used to maintain economic control without which political control is impossible.' Malekian, International Criminal Law, Vol.I, p.440. According to two writers, 'Thus, it may be concluded that no political system in any part of the globe is necessarily immune from the practice of torture, because overall circumstances may change, and adoption of torture is based on perceived expedience.' M. Cherif Bassiouni and Daniel Derby., The Crime of Torture in Bassiouni, 1 International Criminal Law, pp.363–97, p.370. The same writers also conclude that 'It is appropriate to mention here, however, that at least one reliable organization (Amnesty International) has recently compiled a world survey of torture that reports incidents and patterns of torture on every continent and in states of all cultural, political and religious characters.'*Id.* See *also* Amnesty International: Report on Torture (1975); Torture in the Eighties, An Amnesty International Report (1984). Amnesty International lists 67 states in which torture was employed. The employment of torture and other inhuman acts under national authorities is also reported by the General Assembly of the United Nations and other international bodies. For example see The opinion of the European Court of Human Rights in 1978. Council of Europe, European Commission on Human Rights, Applications N 5310/71, Ireland against the United Kingdom of Great Britain and Northern Ireland, Report of the Commission adopted on 25 January 1976 (Published version– Rule 29 § 3 of the Rules of Court of the European Court of Human Rights, Strasbourg). See also Annexes

2. Torture in Islamic International Criminal Law

2.1. Definition

Islamic international criminal law prohibits any harm or injury to individuals. For this reason information which is extracted under the infliction of torture is invalid. Torture is thus not permitted under Islamic international criminal law. The prohibition of torture under Islamic law rests on the fact that information which is extracted by the use of torture is not reliable, since the mind of the victim cannot function appropriately and information which has been given is the result of suffering and pain under torture and not a normal reflection of the mind of the victim.

Torture in Islamic international criminal law may therefore be defined as the enforcement of unlawful and immoral measures by force which are not acceptable in Islamic theory and are against the spiritual dignity of the victim as they are imposed by physical or psychological force; This is regardless of whether or not the actual and relevant acts of torture cause any forms of physical or psychological suffering. The reason for this is that Islamic law does not base the recognition of torture on the physical or psychological tolerance of the victim but on the theory that the spiritual dignity of man must be respected at all times regardless of the physical and psychological strength of the victim. Contrary to this definition, in the system of international criminal law for an act to constitute torture it must create physical suffering and although other cruel, inhuman or degrading treatments are prohibited they do

I and II to the Report of the Commission adopted on 25 January 1976, *id.* Council of Europe, European Court of Human Rights, Case of Ireland against the United Kingdom: Judgment (Strasbourg, 18 January 1987); Torture in the Eighties, An Amnesty International Report (1984), pp.14-5, and 50-61. See *also* Torture and inhuman treatment of children in detention in South Africa and Namibia, Resolution 43/134, 8 December 1988, U.N. Press Release, Department of Public Information, Press Release G.A/7814, 19 January 1989, Resolutions and Decisions Adopted by the General Assembly During the First Part of Its forty-third Session from 20 September to 22 December 1988, pp.404-5; Torture and inhuman treatment of children in detention in South Africa and Namibia, Resolution 44/143, 15 December 1989, Adopted without a vote, Report: A/44/827, U.N. Press Release, Department of Public Information, Press Release G.A/7977, 22 January 1990, Resolutions and Decisions Adopted by the General Assembly During the First Part of Its forty-fourth Session from 19 September to 29 December 1989, pp.438-9. A further prohibition of the use of torture is emphasized in the 1989 Convention on the Rights of the Child annexed to Resolution 44/25. Adopted without a vote, Report: A/44/736 and Corr.1, U.N. Press Release, Department of Public Information, Press Release G.A/7977, 22 January 1990, Resolutions and Decisions Adopted by the General Assembly During the First Part of Its forty-fourth Session from 19 September to 29 December 1989. See also pp.143-4, *infra.*

not constitute torture. This means that the system has a restricted definition of the term torture and its scope of applicability may be limited in certain specific situations.[18]

2.2. Administration of Justice

Islamic law places a significant weight on respecting the dignity of man and on appropriate methods of social relations between individuals and the administrative conduct of an Islamic state. This is because in Islamic law, rules must be carried out with full respect regarding each individual subject and as a fundamental principle of Islamic law a person must not be forced to accept certain information or duties. This principle is the extension of the principle of freedom and equality of all persons before Islamic law and relys on the fact that the Islamic religion is not a religion of force and no person should therefore be forced to embrace Islam. The development of this principle is the development of the principle of freedom of thought, information, equality, brotherhood and more significantly the administration of civil and criminal jurisdiction in the favour of all individuals.

It is an acceptable principle in the Islamic criminal justice system that method of proof profoundly relys on an oath taken from the accused on the *Qur'an* and this method is also applied to both the victim and witness.[19] This principle is obviously carried out on those who are Muslims and the principle loses its juridical effect in the case of a non–Muslim.[20] Thus, those who implement

---

[18] Malekian, International Criminal Law, Vol.I, pp.431–4.

[19] See also Bassiouni, Sources of Islamic Law, and the Protection of Human Rights in the Islamic Criminal Justice System, in Bassiouni, The Islamic Criminal Justice System, pp.3–53, at 23.

[20] 'Foreigners residing in the Islamic territory are subject to Muslim jurisdiction, but not to Muslim law, because Islam tolerates on its territory a multiplicity of laws, with autonomous judiciary for each community. A stranger would belong therefore to the jurisdiction of his own confessional tribunal. If he is a Christian, Jew or something else, and if the other party to the litigation is also of the same confession – no matter whether this other party is a subject of the Muslim State or a stranger – the case is decided by the confessional court according to its own laws. Generally no distinction is made between civil and criminal cases with respect to this jurisdiction. ... However, it is always *lawful for* non–Muslim to renounce this privilege and go before the Islamic tribunal, provided both parties to the suit agree. In such an eventuality, Islamic law is applied.' Moreover, 'the concern for legality has forced the Muslim jurists to admit that if a crime is committed, even against a Muslim, who is the subject of the Muslim State, by a foreigner in a foreign country, and this foreigner later comes peacefully to the Muslim territory, he would not be tried by the Islamic tribunals, which are not competent to hear a case that had taken place outside the territory of their jurisdiction.' Publications of Centre Culturel Islamique, pp.95–6.

Islamic principles of criminal justice should accept the oath taken from the accused, victim or witness on the grounds that every person is competent unless the contrary is proven. The logic behind this process is that the Islamic criminal justice system is itself essentially based on the principles of the *Qur'an* and it should not therefore reject the statements of an accused taken by an oath relying on the *Qur'an*. The whole procedure is also based on the principle of good faith to the sovereignty of *the Qur'an*. Obviously an improper oath is against the Islamic criminal justice system and is punished with severe penalties. It should not however be interpreted that torture can be inflicted on the accused or a guilty person as a form of witness interview.[21]

2.3. Prohibitions

Islamic criminal law or Islamic international criminal law prohibits torture for any purpose and by sudden means. This includes torture during various criminal procedures such as arrest, arbitrary arrest, pre-trial detention, detention and when an accused is found guilty. Under Islamic criminal law the criminally accused is certainly innocent until proven guilty by an impartial and fair criminal court basing its judgement on the established law and the evidence denoting possible criminality. Under no circumstances should a criminally accused be subjected to torture and humiliation in any way. This is also true in the case of prisoners of war who have already stopped fighting. According to one writer, 'Dans la lutte armée entre nations, le but qu'on se propose consistant à – pour mieux dire, devant être de – briser la résistance de l'ennemi, le soldat, qui en est l'instrument principal, une fois rendu inoffensif par la captivité, volontaire ou forcée, ne doit pas être mis à mort, ni subir de tortures.'[22]

One of the articles of the Universal Islamic Declaration of Human Rights[23] points to this important and significant prohibition of torture under the Islamic criminal justice system. The scope of the article also broadly covers all those who are taken by authorities for other reasons than criminal accountability such as political prisoners and prisoners of war. Accordingly,

---

[21] Although torture has been prohibited by Islamic criminal law, it is frequently employed for various purposes by most Islamic states.

[22] Rechid, Ahmed., L'Islam et le Droit des Gens, 2 Recueil des Cours, Académie de Droit International (1937), pp.371–506, p.470.

[23] See chapter twenty two.

Right to Protection Against Torture

No person shall be subject to torture in mind or body, or degraded, or threatened with injury either to himself or to anyone related to or held dear by him, or forcibly made to confess to the commission of a crime, or forced to consent to an act which is injurious to his interests.[24]

The provisions of the above article rely heavily on the Islamic criminal justice system based on the sources of Islamic law, in particular the *Qur'an* and their effect on the creation and development of Islamic cultural heritage including the maintenance of brotherhood, neighbourhood, friendship and universal respect for the dignity of a person in all forms of social conduct. Infliction of torture is thus prohibited by Islamic criminal law and Islamic international criminal law.

2.4. Practice

The constitutional legislations of Islamic states also denotes the prohibition of torture and respect for the dignity of man in social conduct with all types of administrative justices. With Islamic state, as we have mentioned elsewhere, we mean a State which is ruled in accordance with Islamic law and practice and also has a culture broadly based on the Islamic religion.

One cannot deny however the fact that Islamic criminal law in general and the legislations of Islamic states in particular are violated by the practices of many states exercising the Islamic legal system.[25] Torture is inflicted on the criminally accused and in particular political prisoners. This has been carried out irrespective of the motives of the politically accused and also regardless of the principles of Islamic international criminal law and the system of international criminal law in general. The infliction of torture on political prisoners has been carried out for several reasons such as extracting information, confession, punishment, prevention of certain acts and more often for the purpose of stabilizing and guaranteeing the authority of those who have political control in an Islamic State. This is not however surprising when one examines the commission of the same international crime and the violation of the principles of the system of international criminal law under the supervisions of other states.[26]

---

[24] Principle VII.

[25] Arkoun, Mohammad., The Death Penalty and Torture in Islamic Thought in Bockle, F. and Pohier, J. (ed.)., The Death Penalty and Torture (New York, 1979), pp.75–82.

[26] See footnote 17.

Chapter Eleven

Crimes Against Internationally Protected Persons

1. Criminalization in International Criminal Law

The system of international criminal law has for sometime been codified by the rules and provisions of positive international criminal law, recognizing certain activities against internationally protected persons as constituting international crimes.[1] This conventional criminal recognition is rather new, however the crime has long been recognized alongside the customary rules of international criminal law. The most important provisions which have been regulated concerning internationally protected persons can be found in the 1961 Vienna Convention on Diplomatic Relations. This Convention has especially emphasized that the provisions of the Convention are drafted to ensure the efficient performance of diplomatic missions representing member states. According to the Convention diplomatic protection applies to the heads of official missions, which means ambassadors, ministers and *chargé d'affairs.*[2] Thus the Convention has, as a whole, guaranteed certain immunities for diplomatic missions in order that they can appropriately perform their international diplomatic functions.[3]

As a result of many attacks on internationally protected persons and in particular diplomatic missions, the Convention on the Prevention and Punishment of Crimes against Internationally Protected Persons including Diplomatic Agents was signed in 1973 and came into force in 1977. The Convention constitutes one of the most significant conventions in the system of international criminal law regulated under the auspices of the United Nations on the prevention and punishment of international crimes. The most relevant

---

[1] Crimes against internationally protected persons and crimes of taking hostages are basically similar. For a careful analysis, discussion and references see Malekian, International Criminal Law, Vol.II, pp.28 et seq.

[2] See the Preamble of the Convention.

[3] For an intensive discussion and references see Malekian, p.35.

provisions of the Convention concern the criminalization of certain acts against protected persons as constituting international crimes. Accordingly, protected persons are; i) a head of state, including any member of a collegial body performing the functions of a head of state, a head of government or a minister for foreign affairs, whenever any such person is in a foreign state, as well as members of his family who accompany him; ii) any representative or official of a state or any official or other agent of an international organization of an intergovernmental character including their family. The 1973 Convention criminalizes the following acts whenever they are committed against any internationally protected person(s). These are:

1. The intentional commission of:

   (a) A murder, kidnapping or other attack upon the person or liberty of an internationally protected person;

   (b) A violent attack upon the official premises, the private accommodation or the means of transport of an internationally protected person likely to endanger his person or liberty;

   (c) A threat to commit any such attack;

   (d) An attempt to commit any such attack; and

   (e) An act constituting participation as an accomplice in any such attack shall be made by each State Party a crime under its internal law.

2. Each State Party shall make these crimes punishable by appropriate penalties which take into account their grave nature.

3. Paragraph 1 and 2 of this article in no way derogate from the obligations of States Parties under international law to take all appropriate measures to prevent other attacks on the person, freedom or dignity of an internationally protected person.[4]

In the next section we will see that the provisions of the 1973 Convention on the criminalization of certain acts as constituting international crimes in the system of international criminal law have long been recognized in Islamic international criminal law. Thus, although the words and the significance of the Convention may be considered rather a new clarification of the relevant crimes, such crimes could have been regulated long ago if the European system of

---

[4] Article 2. It must be emphasized that the criminalization of certain acts in the Convention 'could not in any way prejudice the exercise of the legitimate right to self–determination and independence, in accordance with the purposes and the principles of the Charter of the United Nations and the Declaration on Principles of International Law concerning Friendly Relations and Co–operation among States in accordance with the Charter of the United Nations, by peoples struggling against colonialism, alien domination, foreign occupation, racial discrimination and *apartheid*.' See the Preamble to the Convention.

international criminal law was not conservative and had the vision to analyze and assimilate the legal systems of other civilizations in the world without any type of prejudice to those system.

2. Criminalization in Islamic International Criminal Law

2.1. Immunity

A protected person in traditional Islamic international criminal law may be defined as a person who has been delegated certain duties and rights from an authorized person(s) to deliver documents, consult or negotiate certain important matters such as political, military, economic, religious, cultural and social issues which are of prominent importance for the international relations of both parties. A protected person is normally called a messenger and his dignity and duties must be fully respected by any other party.[5] Thus, one important legal characterization of an internationally protected person (or agent) is the inviolability of his position relative to a receiving party.

In the practice of the Prophet it was a recognized fact that the position of those who came to negotiate or deliver messages was inviolable.[6] 'Mahomet a consacré cette inviolabilité. Jamais les ambassadeurs envoyés auprès de Mahomet ou de ses successeurs n'ont été molestés.'[7] In certain situations when a protected person had seriously insulted the Prophet, the Prophet did not violate the protected persons immunity and respected his position during the mission.[8] The Prophet was also especially kind with the envoys of foreign countries and it was his especially recognized habit to give them gifts and other presents. He always recommended to his companions that they should also act with envoys after him in the same manner.[9]

---

[5] Called a diplomat or an internationally protected person today.

[6] Watt,W. Montgomery., Muhammad at Medina (Oxford, 1956), p.58.

[7] Rechid, L'Islam et le Droit des Gens, p.421.

[8] *Id.*, p.422.

[9] Bassiouni, M. Cherif., Protection of Diplomats under Islamic Law, 74 American Journal of International Law (1980), pp.609--33, at 612 and 613.

2.2 The Scope of Protection

Although Islamic international criminal law does not speak of the immunity of the personnel in international organizations such as the United Nations, obviously protection and immunity is also applicable to such personnel during the period under which they carry out their official duties. This is because under the provisions of Islamic law, protection, immunity and privileges are granted to all those whose function is, by one means or another, the negotiation of certain topics, to consult on certain matters, to initiate certain rights and duties and any other matter for which a person has been instructed by a recognized intergovernmental entity to discuss under the temporary jurisdiction of another party.[10] This even includes envoys on journeys which have not been accessed or do not have the characterization of the prevailing definition of the term 'international personality' as defined under the system of international law. This is because under the Islamic concept of law 'international personality' is not provided for by the recognition of other states or organizations, rather the concept of recognition is *self–structured* by the divine law, since each individual by himself is a unit and in a more far – reaching aspect an integral part of one universal unit. Thus protections, immunities and privileges can also be granted to envoys of populations or groups who do not necessarily fulfil the conditions of recognition in the system of international law.[11]

2.3. Criminalization

The Islamic system of international criminal law has a considerable number of traditions and provisions recognizing certain acts against protected persons as constituting crimes and are therefore against the fundamental principles of

---

[10] Publications of Centre Culturel Islamique, p.95.

[11] A serious problem concerning the type of protection provided under the system of international criminal law is that the provisions of the 1973 Convention on the Prevention and Punishment of Crimes against Internationally Protected Persons including Diplomatic Agents do not protect the envoys of the groups or populations whose international personality(s) have been limited by an alien power. Although we do not deny that the 1973 Convention protects the struggle of people for self–determination and according to its preamble its provisions do not restrict such struggles, its provisions because of the conditions for obtaining international personality under the system of international law for states and entities do not recognize acts against the envoys of groups as criminal. However, this is not so within Islamic international criminal law.

Islam.[12] This is because the framework of the Islamic law provides *aman* i.e. immunity to all those who have an internationally protected position.[13] This developed for several reasons, *inter alia* the international relations between states could not develop without the necessary respect for those who come to give messages from other countries. Secondly, Islam exercises special respect for those who are invited and they therefore enjoy certain immunity under the jurisdiction of the host country. It is upon these basic juridical and theological principles that Islamic international criminal law provides special respect for diplomats, the violation of which may constitute crimes against protected persons.[14] The following passage is illustrative of this important matter. Accordingly:

Envoys, along with those who are in their company, enjoy full personal immunity: they must never be killed, nor be in any way molested or maltreated. Even if the envoy, or any of his company, is a criminal of the state to which he is sent, he may not be treated otherwise than as an envoy. The envoys of the impostor Musailimah provide good law to whom the Prophet had said: Had you not been envoy, I would have ordered you to be beheaded.

Envoys are accorded full freedom of prayer and religious rites. The Prophet allowed the delegation of the Christians of Najran to celebrate their service in the very Mosque of the Prophet. Muslim historians mention as a curiosity that these Christians turned their faces towards the East and prayed.

Envoys may only in extraordinary cases be detained or imprisoned. So, the Prophet detained the plenipotentiaries of Mecca until the Muslim ambassador detained in Mecca returned safe to Hudaibiya where the Prophet was camping.

The property of the envoys is exempt from import duties in Muslim territory if reciprocated. ... if the foreign states exempt Muslim envoys from customs duties and other taxes, the envoys of such states will enjoy the same privileges in Muslim territory.[15]

It is indeed clear that approximately fourteen centuries earlier certain persons where recognized within Islamic international criminal law as internationally protected persons.[16] This protection not only extends to heads of states,

---

[12] See also chapter twelve.

[13] Bassiouni, Protection of Diplomats under Islamic Law, pp.613–4.

[14] Malekian, International Criminal Law, Vol.II, p.33.

[15] Hamidullah, Muslim Conduct of State, pp.139–40.

[16] See, generally, Bassiouni, Protection of Diplomats under Islamic Law, pp.609–33.

ambassadors and their families but also to those who for one reason or another had accompanied the protected persons. This could include all those who carried out administrative duties and their family members. All these persons came under special immunity and violations of their privileges were criminalized under Islamic international criminal law.

In Islamic international criminal law to attempt, have complicity in, threaten and/or participate in violating the privileges of protected persons may constitute a crime against an internationally protected person(s). Obviously if a violation has occurred, reparation and restoration must be made where possible to the state of the protected persons. This includes damages to the property of the protected persons and also their companies.

Chapter Twelve

Taking of Hostages

1. International Criminal Law

In the old system of international law the taking of hostages during or after a war was a legitimate right of the conflicting parties.[1] The purpose of taking of hostages was mainly to force the other party or parties to fulfil their obligations. Taking of hostages was especially practised after the conclusion of a war. The practice was abolished during the nineteenth century. This did not however mean that states did not resort to the taking of hostages in order to impose their military, political or economic interests on other states.[2]

Despite the fact that there is an international convention criminalizing the taking of hostages, the practice has been continued not only through individuals and organizations actions but also under the order of states; Up until some years ago the former U.S.S.R. and the United States took hostages against one another, who were only released after certain political agreements were made. The International Convention Against the Taking of Hostage was adopted in 1979. The Convention prohibits the taking of hostages and recognizes it as an international crime.[3]

---

[1] Crimes of taking hostages and crimes against internationally protected persons are basically similar.

[2] For detail analysis of this international crime see Malekian, International Criminal Law, Vol.II. pp.1-27.

[3] The International Convention Against Hostage Taking reads that:

Article 1: 1. Any person who seizes or detains and threatens to kill, to injure or to continue to detain another person (hereinafter referred to as the "hostage") in order to compel a third party, namely, a State, an international intergovernmental organization, a natural or judicial person, or a group of persons, to do or abstain from doing any act as an explicit or implicit condition for the release of the hostage commit the offence of taking of hostages "hostage-taking" within the meaning of this Convention.

2. Any person who:

(a) Attempts to commit an act of hostage-taking, or

(b) Participates as an accomplice of anyone who commits or attempts to commit an act of hostage-taking

likewise commits an offence for the purpose of this Convention.

2. Islamic International Criminal Law

Under the traditional system of Islamic international criminal law, like the system of international law, hostages might be taken if the taking of hostages is stated in an agreement for the purpose of implementing its provisions. Parties to an agreement may have also stated that they could kill hostages if such provisions were disregarded by another party. Although the provisions of such agreements were repeatedly violated by other parties against Muslims, the latter did not resort to killing hostages. Moreover, 'Bonne foi pour perfidie vaut mieux que perfidie pour perfidie.'[4] According to the Prophet, "Restitue le dépôt à qui s'est fié à toi et ne trahis point qui te trahit."[5]

Killing hostages was recognized as against the principal philosophy of Islamic law and the formulation of such a provision in a treaty was therefore due to the maltreatment and threatening of Muslims by other parties. Moreover, the imposition of such a provision for the killing of hostages was invalid according to Islamic international criminal law. The beginning of hostilities between the parties to an agreement was a strong reason for Muslims to immediately and safely return all hostages to their homeland in order to fully respect family unity. For confirmation of this, 'Les hostilités ouvertes, on met les otages en liberté mais s'ils sont des hommes faits, il est obligatoire de les faire parvenir jusqu'à leurs lieux de sûreté; si ce sont des femmes ou des enfants, il est d'obligation de les ramener jusque dans leurs familles.'[6]

According to a very significant principle of Islamic international criminal law, even though Muslim hostages could have been killed and were killed by unbelievers or non-Muslims, Muslims should not kill hostages because of the very important principle of inviolability – applicable to their dignity and juridical position under Islamic law. Thus, killing hostages was not recognized by Islamic international criminal law and was therefore illegitimate.[7]

Article 2: Each State Party shall make the offences set forth in article 1 punishable by appropriate penalties which take into account the grave nature of those offences.

Article 3: 1. The State Party in the territory of which the hostage is held by the offender shall take all measures it considers appropriate to ease the situation of the hostage, in particular, to secure his release and, after his release, to facilitate, when relevant, his departure.

2. If any object which the offender has obtained as a result of the taking of hostages comes into the custody of a state Party, that State Party shall return it as soon as possible to the hostage or the third party referred to in article 1, as the case may be, or to the appropriate authorities thereof.

[4] Rechid, L'Islam et le Droit des Gens, p.433.

[5] *Id.*

[6] *Id.*

[7] *Id.*

This means that although Islamic international criminal law places a heavy weight on the principles of proportionality and reciprocity, the implementation of these principles are not permitted in certain circumstances involving threat to the life of hostages.[8] The conclusion which may be reached is that Islamic international criminal law prohibits the killing of hostages for the purpose of revenge or retaliation and this principle is well consolidated in the second source of Islamic law *i.e. Sunnah.*[9]

[8] The most recent well known case of taking of hostages under Islamic regime is the occupation of the American Embassy in Teheran by Iranian students in 1979. They were later released after political negotiations between the American and Iranian authorities. See Malekian, International Criminal Law, Vol.II, pp.31-2.

[9] See chapter two.

Chapter Thirteen

Drug Offences

1. Criminalization in International Criminal Law

There are ample documents in the system of international criminal law that prohibit illegal trade in narcotic drugs. These documents come under the principles of conventional international criminal law.[1] Most of these

---

[1] Some of these conventions are: 1. International Opium Convention, Hague , 23 January 1912. 8 League of Nations Treaty Series, 187; 6 A.J.I.L. (1912), p.177.

2. Agreement Concerning the Suppression of the Manufacture of, Internal Trade in, and Use of Prepared Opium, Geneva, 11 February, 1925. 51 L.N.T.S, 337.

3. International Opium Convention, Geneva, 19 February 1925. 81 L.N.T.S, p.317; 23 A.J.I.L. (1929), p. 135.

4. Protocol to the International Opium Convention, Geneva, 19 February 1925. 81 L.N.T.S. 356; 23 A.J.I.L.(1923), p. 155.

5. Convention for Limiting the Manufacture and Regulating the Distribution of Narcotic Drugs, Geneva, 13 July 1931. 139 L.N.T.S, p.301; 28 A.J.I.L.(1934), p.21.

6. Agreement on the Suppression of Opium-Smoking, Bangkok, 27 November 1931. 177 L.N.T.S, p.373.

7. Convention for the Suppression of the Illicit Traffic in Dangerous Drugs, Geneva, 26 June 1936. 198 L.N.T.S, p.299.

8. Protocol amending the Agreements, Conventions and Protocols on Narcotic Drugs concluded at the Hague on 23 January 1912, at Geneva on 11 February 1925 and 19 February 1925, and 13 July 1931, in Bangkok on 27 November 1931 and at Geneva on 26 June 1936. 12 U.N.T.S, p.179.

9. Protocol Bringing under International Control Drugs Outside the Scope of the Convention of 13 July 1931 for Limiting the Manufacture and Regulating the Distribution of Narcotic Drugs, as Amended by the Protocol signed at Lake Success, New York on 11 December 1946, signed in Paris, on 19 November 1948. 44 U.N.T.S, p.277.

10. Protocol for Limiting and Regulating the Cultivation of the Poppy Plant, the Production of, International and Wholesale Trade in, and Use of Opium, New York, 23 June 1953. 456 U.N.T.S. 56.

11. Convention on the Territorial Sea and Contiguous Zone, Geneva, 29 April 1958. 516 U.N.T.S. 205.

12. Single Convention on Narcotic Drugs, New York, 30 March 1961. 520 U.N.T.S. 151.

13. Convention on Psychotropic Substances, Vienna, 21 February 1971. 10 I.L.M. (1971), p.261.

14. Protocol Amending the Single Convention on Narcotic Drugs, 1961, Geneva, 25 March 1972. 976 U.N.T.S; 11 I.L.M. (1972), p.804.

15. Convention on the Law of the Sea, Montego Bay, 10 December 1982. 1 I.L.M. (1982), p.1261.

conventions have permitted this trade for medical purposes use only and for other purposes which are emphasized in the conventions. It is on this basis that there are indeed a large number of rules and provisions prohibiting, preventing and criminalizing the cultivation, production, manufacture, possession, exportation, importation, distribution and numerous other acts relating to trade in narcotic drugs without a valid licence. Breaches of these rules and provisions constitute a very serious international crime.

The purpose of all these regulations has not only been to prevent illicit trade in narcotic drugs but also to bring the perpetrators of international crimes under an appropriate jurisdiction for prosecution and punishment.[2] As a general rule each party to these conventions is bound to adopt certain rules and

---

16. United Nations Convention Against Illicit Traffic in Narcotic Drugs and Psychotropic Substances, 1988. E/CONF. 82/15 and Corr. 1 and 2.

[2] For example Article 26 on Penal Provisions of the Single Convention on Narcotic Drugs 1961, reds that:

1. Subject to its constitutional limitations, each Party shall adopt such measures as will ensure that cultivation, production, manufacture, extraction, preparation, possession, offering, offering for sale, distribution, purchase, sale, delivery on any terms whatsoever, brokerage, dispatch, dispatch in transit, transport, importation and exportation of drugs contrary to the provisions of this Convention, and any other action which in the opinion of such Party may be contrary to the provisions of this Convention, shall be punishable offences when committed intentionally, and that serious offences shall be liable to adequate punishment particularly by imprisonment or other penalties of deprivation of liberty.

2. Subject to the constitutional limitations of a Party, its legal system and domestic law,

    (a) (i) Each of the offences enumerated in paragraph 1, if committed in different countries, shall be considered as a distinct offence;

        (ii) Intentional participation in, conspiracy to commit and attempts to commit, any of such offences, and preparatory acts and financial operations in connexion with the offences referred to in this article, shall be punishable offences as provided in paragraph 1;

        (iii) Foreign convictions for such offences shall be taken into account for the purposes of establishing recidivism; and

        (iv) Serious offences heretofore referred to committed either by nationals or by foreigners shall be prosecuted by the Party in whose territory the offence was committed, or by the Party in whose territory the offender was found if extradition is not acceptable in conformity with the law of the Party to which application is made, and if such offender has not already been prosecuted and judgement given.

    (b) It is desirable that the offences referred to in paragraph 1 and paragraph 2 *(a) (ii)* be included as extradition crimes in any extradition treaty which has been or may hereafter be concluded between any of the Parties, and as between any of the Parties which do not make extradition conditional on the existence of a treaty or on reciprocity, be recognized as extradition crimes; provided that extradition shall be granted in conformity with the law of the Party to which application is made, and that the Party shall have the right to refuse to effect the arrest or grant the extradition in cases where the competent authorities consider that the offence is not sufficiently serious.

3. The provisions of this article shall be subject to the provisions of the criminal law of the Party concerned on questions of jurisdiction.

4. Nothing contained in this article shall affect the principle that the offences to which it refers shall be defined, prosecuted and punished in conformity with the domestic law of a Party.

obligations which may be necessary under their domestic systems to criminalize the given conduct and especially to provide serious penalties for the production, manufacture, extraction, preparation, offering, offering for sale, distribution, sale, delivery in whatever way, brokerage, dispatch, dispatch in transit, transport, importation or exportation of any narcotic drugs and any other psychotropic substances.[3]

---

[3] For example Article 22 on Penal Provisions of the Convention on Psychotropic Substances, 1971, reads that:

1. *(a)* Subject to its constitutional limitations, each Party shall treat as a punishable offence, when committed intentionally, any action contrary to a law or regulation adopted in pursuance of its obligations under this Convention, and shall ensure that serious offences shall be liable to adequate punishment, particularly by imprisonment or other penalty of deprivation of liberty.

(b) Notwithstanding the preceding sub–paragraph, when abusers of psychotropic substances have committed such offences, the Parties may provide, either as an alternative to conviction or punishment or in addition to punishment, that such abusers undergo measures of treatment, eduction, after–care, rehabilitation and social reintegration in conformity with paragraph 1 of article 20.

2. Subject to the constitutional limitations of a Party, its legal system and domestic law,

(a)(i)   if a series of related actions constituting offences under paragraph 1 has been committed in different countries, each of them shall be treated as a distinct offence,

(ii)   intentional participation in, conspiracy to commit and attempts to commit, any of such offences, and preparatory acts and financial operations in connexion with the offences refer to in this article, shall be punishable offences as provided in paragraph 1;

(iii)   foreign convictions for such offences shall be taken into account for the purpose of establishing recidivism; and

(iv)   serious offences heretofore referred to committed either by nationals or by foreigners shall be prosecuted by the Party in whose territory the offence was committed, or by the Party in whose territory the offender is found if extradition is not acceptable in conformity with the law of the Party to which application is made, and if such offender has not already been prosecuted and judgement given.

(b) It is desirable that the offences referred to in paragraph 1 and paragraph 2 *(a) (ii)* be included as extradition crimes in any extradition treaty which has been or may hereafter to concluded between any of the Parties, and, as between any of the Parties which do not make extradition conditional on the existence of a treaty or on reciprocity, be recognized as extradition crimes; provided that extradition shall be granted in conformity with the law of the Party to which application is made, and that the Party shall have the right to refuse to effect the arrest or grant the extradition in cases where the competent authorities consider that the offence is not sufficiently serious.

3. Any psychotropic substance or other substance, as well as any equipment used in or intended for the commission of any of the offences referred to in paragraphs 1 and 2 shall be liable to seizure and confiscation.

4. The provisions of this article shall be subject to the provisions of the domestic law of the Party concerned on questions of jurisdiction.

5. Nothing contained in this article shall affect the principle that the offences to which it refers shall be defined, prosecuted and punished in conformity with the domestic law of a Party.

2. Prohibitions in Islamic International Criminal Law

The Islamic international criminal law does not provide, as does the system of international criminal law, provisions governing the prohibition of narcotic offences, but basically prohibits the use of narcotic drugs according to common Islamic purposes. The prohibition of narcotic drugs in Islamic law is based on the theory that social interests must be protected by the law and therefore any action which contradicts social development or creates civil or domestic problems between individuals, groups and the state is juridically wrong and must be punished according to the law. Moreover, the prohibition of narcotic drugs within Islamic law also rests on the theory that since narcotic drugs are harmful to the human body and may handicap physical growth and ability, any involvement in it must be recognized as criminal. One must remember that Islamic law has in one sense the function of a medical treatment of the body and for this reason it may even prohibit other substances in narcotic drugs which may be discovered in the future, on the condition that such substances are harmful to the human body. Permission for the use of narcotic drugs may be given under circumstances which are vital for the treatment of certain illnesses.

Narcotic offences under Islamic criminal law are penalized under the term *hudud* meaning fixed penalties. On a wider plane it means 'prevention, hindrance, restraint, prohibition, and hence a restrictive ordinance or statute of Allah, respecting things lawful and unlawful.'[4] In addition to this, *hudud* offences are against the fundamental principles of Islamic law and are considered acts against divine law and are therefore prosecutable and punishable by the state jurisdiction under which the given criminal conduct is committed.

It should be emphasized that according to the Islamic criminal law it is the intentional involvement in narcotic offences such as selling or possession of narcotic drugs which causes the application of criminal provisions and not unintentional elements. Thus, although Islamic criminal law has criminalized the possessions of narcotic drugs, it is against its equal standard of justice to punish those who are not intentionally guilty of the commission of such criminal conduct. In this way the Islamic criminal system attempts to safeguard the

---

[4] Iqbal Siddiqi, Muhammad., The Penal Law of Islam (Lahore: Kazi, 1979), p.50. Quoted in Matthew Lippman, Sean McConville, and Mordechai Yerushalmi., Islamic Criminal Law and Procedure: An Introduction (New York, Westport, Connecticut, London, 1988), p.38.

interests of the accused over whom Islamic criminal jurisdiction is exercised.[5]

The prohibition of narcotic drugs in Islamic law not only has national characterization but an international characterization also. This is because, according to the theory of Islamic law, acts by individuals or their state within their own territories should not harm other nations in the universal. This is on the grounds that all men must be treated equally before the law of God. Analogies in narcotic offences under Islamic international criminal law may therefore be made with similar prohibitions stated in the system of conventional international criminal law. These includes aspects such as production, manufacture, extraction, preparation, offering for sale, distribution, sale, delivery in whatever way, dispatch, transport, importation and exportation of any narcotic drugs. This conclusion is with the reservation that the system of international criminal law has regulated certain provisions for all these activities in conventional international criminal law, while the same conclusions in Islamic international criminal law are deduced from its purposes, functions and sources which forbid, prohibit and make any intentional involvement in narcotic drugs a prosecutable and punishable crime. Clear examples of this practice can be examined in the legislations of many states in which the Islamic law has influence, such as the legislation and practice of Iran. An involvement with any type of illegal narcotic drugs can be specified under the principle of *taboo*.

Although we do not deny that the procedure for jurisdiction over prosecution and punishment may differ in Islamic law from other systems, this does not preclude the comparative integration of both systems of international criminal law. As an acceptable general principle of the system of international criminal law, so long as there is not yet established a permanent international criminal court in order to exercise jurisdiction over the perpetrators of international crimes for the purpose of effective prosecution and punishment, the implementation and enforcement of the system remains the privilege of various select legal systems.

---

[5] It is useful to be noted here that Islamic criminal law does not punish those who are addicted to drugs while they attempt to stop their addiction. There will be inflicted *hudud* penalties, if after they have been cured of their dependency they become addicted again. Lippman, McConville and Yerushalmi, Islamic Criminal Law and Procedure, p.48.

Chapter Fourteen

Obscene Activities and Publications

1. Non-Effective Criminalization in International Criminal Law

Although the system of international criminal law has greatly developed in various fields of criminal law, the system still lacks certain effective provisions for the prohibition of certain activities which are harmful to individuals in general and the social interests of the international community in particular. For example the system of international criminal law has very limited provisions for the prohibition and prevention of obscene activities and publications. The relevant instruments applicable to this international crime are no longer useful in terms of the present epoch.[1] This is because there is still no effective movement(s) for the criminalization of obscene publications in the relevant legislations of states and governments are generally reluctant to adopt legal

---

[1] These instruments are: 1. Arrangement for the Suppression of the Circulation of Obscene Publications, 4 May 1910. 5 A.J.I.L. (1911), p.167.

2. International Convention for the Suppression of the Circulation of and Traffic in Obscene Publications, 12 September 1923. Hudson, II International Legislation, p.1051.

3. Protocol to Amend the Convention for the Suppression of the Circulation of and Traffic in Obscene Publications, concluded at Geneva on 12 September 1923, 1947. 46 U.N.T.S. 169.

4. International Convention for the Suppression of the Circulation of and Traffic in Obscene Publications, concluded at Geneva on 12 September 1923 and amended by the Protocol signed at Lake Success, New York, on 12 November 1947. 46 U.N.T.S. 201.

5. Protocol amending the Agreement for the Suppression of the Circulation of Obscene Publications, signed at Paris on 4 May 1910, 1949. 30 U.N.T.S. 3.

6. Agreement for the Suppression of the Circulation of Obscene Publications of 4 May 1910, amended by the Protocol of 4 May 1949, 1949, 47 U.N.T.S. 159, and

7. Convention on the Rights of the Child, 20 November 1989. Resolution 44/25, Adopted without a vote, Report: A/44/736 and Corr.1, U.N. Press Release, Department of Public Information, Press Release G.A/7977, 22 January 1990, Resolutions and Decisions Adopted by the General Assembly During the First Part of Its forty-fourth Session from 19 September to 29 December 1989. The 1910 Arrangement and the 1923 Convention regulate the most important provisions applicable to this international crime. Other instruments have only modified or adapted the provisions of the arrangement and the convention to the time.

measures to prohibit any type of obscene publications.[2] This is for two essential reasons. Firstly, governments do not see the publication of obscene materials as a threat to their national or international policies and secondly, publications of obscene material have become a great source of income for the economies of various countries.

Publications of obscene materials become more dangerous to the social structure of the national and international community when one considers that for the accomplishment of these publications many individuals and often families are used, whether by their own consent or through acts of force and slavery. This is especially notable in the countries which have no effective control over their populations and where prostitution and pornography have become an important aspect of their economies. Indeed, the pornography and prostitution of children has become one of the great problems facing various national authorities and the international community has not been successful in eliminating this form of abuse. A notorious example is Thailand and the involvement of its some of the younger generation in these activities.

We do not deny that states have taken legislative measures for the prevention and prohibition of certain activities and although the provisions of the 1910 Convention relating to the prohibition of the publication of obscene materials are updated by the establishment of the United Nations,[3] the provisions of

---

[2] The most effective international legislation for the criminalization of the publication of obscene materials is entered into the provisions of Article 1 of the International Convention for the Suppression of the Circulation of and Traffic in, Obscene Publications, concluded at Geneva on 12 September 1923 and Amended by the Protocol signed at Lake Success, New York on 12 November 1947. Article 1 reads that:

'The High Contracting Parties agree to take all measures to discover, prosecute and punish any person engaged in committing any of the following offences, and accordingly agree that:

It shall be a punishable offence:

(I) For purposes of or by way of trade or for distribution or public exhibition to make or produce or have in possession obscene writings, drawings, prints, paintings, printed matter, pictures, posters, emblems, photographs, cinematograph films or any other obscene objects;

(2) For the purposes above mentioned to import, convey or export or cause to be imported, conveyed or exported any of the said obscene matters or things, or in any manner whatsoever to put them into circulation;

(3) To carry on or take part in a business, whether public or private, concerned with any of the said obscene matters or things, or to deal in the said matters or things in any manner whatsoever, or to distribute them or to exhibit them publicly or to make a business of lending them;

(4) To advertise or make known by any means whatsoever, in view of assisting in the said punishable circulation or traffic, that a Person is engaged in any of the above punishable acts, or to advertise or to make known how or from whom the said obscene matters or things can be procured either directly or indirectly.'

[3] For example the provisions of the Agreement for the Suppression of the Circulation of Obscene Publications, signed at Paris on 4 May 1910, as Amended by the Protocol, signed at Lake Success, New York on 4 May 1949 are not seriously taken in the domestic legislations of states. Article 1 of the Agreement is in particular important for the criminalization of the given

these legislations are not sufficient in practice and in many regards the criminalization of the given conduct is not effective in the elimination of obscene activities and publications. One can easily obtain obscene publications including various types of pornographic videos in most European states. Since the publication, importation and exportation of obscene materials are legally permitted there is no effective international movement(s) for their prohibition. Although some states have provided for punishment in certain extreme cases, the penalties are very light and do no carry any effective weight in relation to the consequences of such criminal conduct.[4]

2. Prohibitions in Islamic International Criminal Law

Contrary to the basic weaknesses in the system of international criminal law, Islamic international criminal law criminalizes the publication of obscene materials and any involvement by a person or persons in acts of prostitution and/or pornography are prosecutable and punishable. Islamic law perceives the effect of published obscene materials from its fundamental social standards and believes that obscene materials is not only against family rights but also against the spiritual interests of human society. Islamic law tackles the issue of the publication of obscene materials on the basis of social structure and the harm which it may cause the social characterization of women – as the basic element of family unity. It is due to this theory that Islamic law criminalizes the given

conduct under the domestic systems of states. It reads that: 'Each one of the Contracting Powers undertakes to establish or designate an authority charged with the duty of
1. Centralizing all information which may facilitate the tracing and suppression of acts constituting infringements of their municipal law as to obscene writings, drawings, pictures or articles, and the constitutive elements of which bear an international character.
2. Supplying all information tending to check the importation of publications or articles referred to in the forgoing paragraph and also to insure or expedite their seizure all within the scope of municipal legislation.
3. Communicating the laws that have already been or may subsequently be enacted in their respective States in regard to the object of the present arrangement.
The Contracting Governments shall mutually make known to one another, through the Secretary–General of the United Nations, the authority established or designated in accordance with the present article.

[4] For example, under the relevant provisions of the Swedish legislation even Swedish courts until recently had the right to sell pornographic videos using children. This was occurring up to the end of May 1993. It should be noted however that such vidoes as evidence were sold under justifiable freedom of information acts, taking into consideration that the provisions of the relevant legislation were against the international obligations of the Swedish state as stated in the 1988 Convention on the Rights of Child. Many persons purchased pornographic videos using children from a court in Stockholm in particular, which was involved in the seizure of this obscene materials produced by Swedish citizens in Thailand.

conduct and makes its commission a punishable crime. This theory of Islamic law is also applicable in the Islamic system of international criminal law.

The element of Islamic international criminal law which is against the publication of obscene materials and prostitution is based on protecting the dignity and integrity of the human body. This is because the publication of obscene materials, in Islamic international criminal law, is against the legal and social personality of men and causes insecurity in family structure. This international crime can therefore be treated under the provisions of Islamic international human rights, protecting females and families from any type of violation including criminal ones. Islamic law examines almost all aspects of a violation in relation to the integrity of family values and its effect on the development, re–development and promotion of family dignity. It is on this basis that Islamic law emphasizes the internationalization of its principles and the criminalization of any act which violates the principles of family law in general and international social structure in particular.

One of the chief differences between Islamic international criminal law and the system of international criminal law with respect to the publication of obscene materials is that the given conduct is criminalized by the provisions of Islamic international criminal law while are clearly discover the non–existence of any effective international criminal convention applicable to various aspects of a comparable crime in the system of international criminal law. The existing conventions relating to the prohibition of the publication of obscene materials are very weak and it may be stated that their principles, because of present considerations in international relations, are not practical[5] and need to be re-

---

[5] For the effective criminalization of the publication of obscene materials I have suggested that 'Trafficking in obscene publications greatly damages the cultural, educational and ideological development of people in general and the young in particular. It is therefore of fundamental importance that states pay due attention to this international crime which is helping to destroy their cultural morality. It is particularly important to legislate against the open circulation of pornographic videos, which are not only harmful to national morality but are also harmful to the integrity of children, members of both sexes and the family itself. Consequently, it is recommended that the following measures be taken by states:

1. An international legal instrument dealing with all forms of trafficking in obscene publications must be adopted by the international legal community for the purpose of protection of national and international order.

2. States shall, in accordance with an international convention, agree that obscene publications constitute an international crime. They shall also undertake not to employ this category of international crime as a political tool.

3. In order to effectively prevent the publication of obscene materials, states shall undertake legal responsibility for all publications within their territorial jurisdiction.

4. States shall take necessary domestic legal measures in order to enforce the relevant laws for the prohibition of obscene publications, or shall formulate the requisite legislative measures for such purposes.

5. A lucid definition of what constitutes obscene materials must be agreed upon.

formulated in order to identify and criminalize the publication of obscene materials.

6. Regional and international cooperation of various kinds must be effected in order to bring about the elimination of traffic in obscene publications.

7. International and national provisions must not only recognize international trafficking in obscene publications as a crime, but also as a prosecutable and punishable crime.

8. National and international criminal responsibility must be applied to all those who have engaged in or participated in the trafficking of obscene publications.' Malekian, International Criminal Law, Vol.II, pp.416–7.

Chapter Fifteen

Crimes Against Natural Environments

1. Nature

Islamic law has broadly preserved the natural environment. It gives special respect to the natural environment, which not only includes natural phenomena such as water, gardens, agricultural fields and forests but also living creatures in the seas and land animals. The preservation and protection of natural environments under Islamic law must be regarded as one of the most significant values to be found in this law, especially when there was no protection for the natural environment at the time. The protection and preservation of the natural environment in Islamic international criminal law is essentially no different from the protection of the natural environment under international criminal law as recognized and criminalized under various international conventions.[1]

Under Islamic law the natural environment is basically protected by divine law for the purpose of preserving human life. It is for this reason that certain activities which harm or damage the natural environment are considered evil and strictly prohibited under Islamic law. As we have already mentioned elsewhere, under Islamic international criminal law the devastation and destruction of forests, agricultural fields and the unnecessary killing of animals is prohibited during war and armed attacks must not therefore be made upon certain natural objects. Similarly, Islamic law prohibits Muslims at all times from devastating the natural environment or any act which is against nature. One of the essential reasons for this is that under the law of *Qur'an* anything God has created in the human environment has a special purpose and therefore its principal natural characterization should not be disregarded or disabled by any means. This purpose is precisely what is now developing under the system of international criminal law for the purpose of protecting and preserving the international natural environment.

---

[1] See Malekian, International Criminal Law, Vol.II, pp.309-46.

2. Protection of Living Creatures

Special protection under Islamic law is given to living creatures and this protection should be regarded as one of the significant characterizations of Islamic law as revealed approximately fourteen hundred years ago.

According to the Prophet the use of animals must fit their nature.[2] The protection of animals in Islamic law also includes birds. According to one *hadith* when the Prophet saw a hummara which was separated from its two young he stated, 'Who has injured this bird by taking its young? Return them to her.'[3] The protection of birds in Islamic law is similar to the protection of birds in the system of international law, with the difference that the former protects birds on the ground of their natural rights and the latter mostly according to positive or conventional law. The value of the former is that it relies on both legal and moral aspects.

3. A Double Criminalization

Under Islamic international criminal law harm, injury, wrong or crime can be committed against any creature. This is regardless of the nature of such a creature, whether human, animal or otherwise.[4] All 'creatures' are considered an integral part of the inhabitants of our global life. Accordingly, it is recognized as 'a double crime: a crime against one's immediate victim, and also a crime against God, since the criminal conduct in question constitutes a violation of the Divine prescriptions. It is thus that, when there is an injustice or crime against another creature, one has not only to try to repair the damage, by restituting to the victim of one's violation the right which had been taken away from him, but he had also to beg pardon of God.'[5] This quotation

---

[2] Guillaume, Alfred., The Traditions of Islam: An Introduction to the Study of the Hadith Literature (Oxford, 1924), p.106.   According to one *hadith* of the Prophet, 'Do not use the backs of your beasts as pulpits, for God has only made them subject to you in order that they may bring you to a town you could only otherwise reach by fatigue of body.' This *hadith* can also be completed by another *hadith* stating 'Do not clip the forelocks of your horses, not their manes, not their tails; for the tail is their fly-whisk; the mane is their covering; and the forelock has good fortune bound within it.' Guillaume, p.107.

[3] *Id.*

[4] It was upon this philosophy of criminal law that the Prophet 'gave a warning, that on Doomsday, a certain person would be thrown in Hell because he had tied up a cat with a rope, giving it neither to eat nor to drink, thus causing the death of the poor animal.' Publications of Centre Culturel Islamique, p.79.

[5] *Id.*, p.79.

denotes the gravity of the crime and also the fact that all creatures are an important part of our natural environment and should not be harmed.

Thus not only activities against animals and the natural environment are criminalized under Islamic international criminal law but it also recognizes the compulsory duty of every person to protect and preserve natural environments.[6] Therefore 'Men should profit from what God has created, yet in an equitable and reasonable measure, avoiding all dissipation and waste.'[7] Islamic international criminal law also provides punishment against those who do not carry out their duties and obligations towards the natural environment.

[6] It is for instance prohibited to hew down trees unnecessarily. *Id.*, p.80.
[7] *Id.*, p.80.

Chapter Sixteen

Crimes Against Foodstuffs

In Islam the destruction of food is basically considered a sin and its protection is a great responsibility under divine law. All foodstuffs should consequently be preserved and should not therefore be devastated. This general rule in Islamic law is contrary to the system of international law and the general practices of modern states. This is because there is not any special rule in international law prohibiting the destruction of foodstuffs and therefore a huge amount of foodstuffs are destroyed *e.g.* in Europe every year. This is in order to keep prices monopolized and maintain artificial international standards. The *Qur'an* condemns the devastation of food by man who 'when he becomes a ruler, he runs about on earth greedily and his great effort everywhere is to make mischief and disorder in it and destroy the crops and the offspring of mankind.'[1]

Islamic law is originally against any monopolization of food and although it encourages commercial law in various economic aspects to protect individual and groups interests, it recognizes a great sin in destroying food for commercial purposes. According to *hadith*, 'He who monopolizes food ... may God smite with elephantiasis and grinding poverty.'[2] This statement of the Prophet should also be read in conjunction with another proclaiming that 'An importer is blessed, but a monopolist is accursed.'[3] This statement of the Prophet is strengthened by *another hadith* containing, 'He who monopolizes a commodity is a sinner.'[4] And a sin under *shari'ah* constitutes a crime against the divine jurisprudence.

Islamic law therefore recognizes any devastation of foodstuffs for the purpose of monopolizing prices as a great sin and therefore a violation of the law of Islam. This principle of Islamic law becomes stronger and more effective when foodstuffs are destroyed regardless of the starvation of certain people(s). Thus,

---

[1] The *Qur'an*, 2:205.

[2] Guillaume, The Traditions of Islam, p.102.

[3] *Id.*

[4] *Id.*

the destruction of foodstuffs under the orders of certain European states and others would be definitely recognized as crimes once treated under Islamic international criminal law. One of the important reasons for this is that Islamic law not only protects all mankind from all types of violations but also strongly supports the right to food for all men regardless of racial, ideological, political or religious differences. For this reason Islamic law has very broad principles regarding the division of wealth and protection of all humans from gradual starvation. Due to these legal and moral values in Islam a neighbour is responsible for other neighbours who are suffering and starving. This principle of Islam is internationally valid and Muslim nations should not destroy foodstuffs to monopolize prices and especially when there are already nations which have starving populations.

Chapter Seventeen

Criminalization of Alcoholic Drinks

The criminalization of alcoholic drinks is one of the well-known character-izations of Islamic law. The *Qur'an* does however refer to the usefulness of wine, but for the sake of an individual, group or nation drinking alcohol has been prohibited in order to strengthen ones resolution and control, as well as protecting family unities from destruction. The *Qur'an* therefore states the prohibition of drinking wine along with its utility and proclaims that 'They ask you concerning wine and gambling. Say: 'In both of them is great sin or great harm and some advantages for men but their disadvantage is greater than their advantage.'[1] Another verse reads that 'O you who have believed! do not offer your prayer when you are intoxicated until you know well what you utter...'[2] In another verse the *Qur'an* categorizes idolatry and alcoholic drinks as being on same level. It states that 'O you who have believed! intoxicants and gambling, set up stones (to worship, to sacrifice) and the divining arrows are an abomination, and are filthy deeds of the evil, insurgent, ignorant and satanic men, therefore refrain from such evil deeds so that you may be successful.'[3] 'The evil man or satan only desires to sow enmity and hatred among you, with intoxicants and gambling, and hinder you from the remembrance of God, and from prayer; will you not then abstain?'[4]

---

[1] The *Qur'an*, 2:219.
[2] The *Qur'an*, 4:43.
[3] The *Qur'an*, 5:90.
[4] The *Qur'an*, 5:91.

Chapter Eighteen

Piracy

1. Piracy in International Criminal Law

Piracy is one of the notorious international crimes recognized since the early conception of the regulation of the law of the sea.[1] Under the system of international criminal law it took a long period of time before states could prohibit piracy and not be allowed to support privateers for their own political purposes. One of the most profound controversies concerning the subject of piracy was the question of creating the right to visit and search vessels.

The term 'piracy' is employed in the system of international criminal law to indicate the illegal or unlawful nature of acts of plunder *animus furandi*.[2] One important characteristic of the international crime of piracy is that it is recognized as a crime against mankind and a pirate is considered as *hostes generis humani*.[3] For this reason any state which captures pirates has a recognized international right to bring them under its criminal jurisdiction for prosecution and punishment. This means that pirates can be prosecuted in accordance with the principle of universality under the system of international criminal law. In general some of the elements for the recognition of the crime of piracy under the customary and conventional international criminal law are intention, violation, plunder and the commission of the crime on the high seas.[4]

Piracy has not only been characterized as an international crime under customary international criminal law but there are also a number of international conventions which recognize piracy as a prosecutable and punishable international crime. Some of these conventions have mutual and others multilateral characters. Two of the most important of these conventions

---

[1] Malekian, International Criminal Law, Vol.I, p.489.

[2] *Id.*, p.490.

[3] *Id.*, p.500.

[4] For further clarifications, definitions and a comprehensive analysis of the international crime of piracy see *id.*, pp.489–seg.

are the 1958 and 1982 United Nations Conventions on the Law of the Sea. The latter convention modifies the former and is rather a modern comprehensive approach to the law of the sea compared with the former.

2. Land Piracy in Islamic International Criminal Law

The concept of piracy in the system of Islamic international criminal law is rather different from the concept of piracy in the system of international criminal law. This is because in the latter the term 'piracy' is employed in order to denote the commission of certain criminal activities on the open or upon the high seas. This is regardless of the fact that there are certain terminologies in the system of international criminal law such as brigandage, banditti, buccaneers, partisans and robbers which are assimilated or employed as synonyms for the term 'piracy'.[5] In Islamic international criminal law the status of the international crime of piracy is employed in connection with the term 'international highwaymen' or 'land piracy'.[6]. The original term 'piracy' is seldom employed. According to one writer 'The characteristics which the desert shares with the sea induced us to call the desert brigandage 'land piracy.'"[7]

In contrast to the system of international criminal law, which for a long period of time has had the problem of prohibiting and preventing the crime of piracy by a code of law, Islamic international criminal law has prohibited this international crime since the time of its revelation.[8]

It is essential to remember that the provisions of the *Qur'an* concerning the punishment of those who commit the crime of piracy were characterized close to fourteen hundred years ago and therefore their value should not be misinterpreted or diminished because of the modern codification of the law into the system of international criminal law. Moreover, these provisions and old methods of punishments are greatly adaptable to the modern codification of the

---

[5] Malekian, International Criminal responsibility of States, p.49.

[6] Al-Ghunaimi, The Muslim Conception of International Law and Western Approach, p.15.

[7] *Id.*

[8] The relevant law can be found in a valuable and significant verse of the *Qur'an*. Islamic lawyers are unanimous that the below provisions of a verse from the *Qur'an* obviously deals with the question of international highwaymen and pirates. It runs that: 'The punishment of those who wage war against God and His Apostle and strive to make mischief in the land is only this, that they should be slain or crucified, or their hands and feet should be cut off from opposite sides, or they should be exiled from the land; this shall be as a disgrace for them in this world, and in the Hereafter they shall have a grievous chastisement. (The *Qur'an*, 5:33.) Except those who repented and turned to the right Path but before they fell into your power, in that case, you know that God is Oft-forgiving, Most Merciful.' (The *Qur'an*, 5:34.)

law of piracy in the system of international criminal law.[9] In principle both systems condemn the unlawful or illegal character of plunder in international relations by certain individuals and therefore a prosecutable and punishable crime. More significantly, both systems support the universality of jurisdiction over pirates of all types (whether on land or at sea) and recognizes it the international duty and right of any state to punish the perpetrators of such international crimes.

The Islamic system of international criminal law especially recognized certain severe punishments to be inflicted upon criminals. Some of these crimes and their punishments were i) plundering which ended with murder and was punished through beheading followed by crucifixion, ii) beheading as inflicted for a murder, iii) amputation of hands or feet might be carried out if only plunder had been committed and iv) discretionary punishments might be imposed on those who intended committing a crime but had not yet done so, such as imprisonment and confinement to a border district.[10] According to modern Islamic international criminal law the prosecution and punishment of highwaymen and/or pirates must be carried out irrespective of their rank or position.

The severity of above punishments must however be understood from the fact that fourteen hundred years ago there was no law governing maritime navigation or the security of traders between two countries by land or upon the seas and further, the capacity of communication between states was in its absolute infancy. Consequently, from the perspective of conditions, capacities and abilities of states at the time, punishment was seen as a necessary element in preventing the commission of crimes. Moreover, punishment in the early practice of Islamic international criminal law was seen as a method of preventing other persons from committing the relevant international crime. This philosophy is still one of the essential reasons for the infliction of punishment in most modern societies at this time. It should also be noted that the above punishments may be entirely forgiven if the pirates or the highwaymen voluntarily submit themselves to the relevant state officials before they are able to arrest them for the commission of their crimes.[11] This means that the significance of punishment was not necessarily to harm the criminals but explicitly and implicitly to prevent others from involving themselves in behaviour which was theologically, morally and juridically wrong.

[9] See the above footnote.

[10] Hamidullah, Muslim Conduct of State, p.178.

[11] Id., p.179.

Chapter Nineteen

Limitations of Hostilities
in the
Conduct of States

1. Declaration of War

The Islamic system of international criminal law has considered the declaration of war as constituting one of the important elements within the institution of armed conflicts. For this reason Islamic law commands conflicting parties not to engage in an armed conflict before declaring their intentions to the enemy state. Islamic international criminal law does not however place particular emphasis on the declaration of war in certain situations and these are when i) a war is waged for the purpose of self-defence or is a defensive war, ii) a war with an enemy with whom there has been constant armed conflict and no treaty of peace is made, iii) a war against an absolute threat of aggression or a preventative war[1] and iv) a war of retaliation or a punitive war against a state which has violated its treaties' obligations.[2] In the above situations there is no need to give notification or a declaration to the conflicting party(s) regarding armed conduct.

In other situations Islamic international criminal law obliges a Muslim state not to engage in war without a clear notification or declaration. This rule must be especially respected regarding states with whom treaties are concluded. Declaration must also be made to those who are non-Muslim and for this reason a declaration of war in the Islamic system of international criminal law is inevitable. Yet, a declaration of war against non-Muslim states can only be made when all the necessary peaceful channels are already exhausted such as arbitrations, negotiation and diplomatic consultation.

---

[1] The examples of this are Banu'l-Mustaliq, Khaibar, Hunain.

[2] The examples of this are attacks on Banu-Quraizah and Mecca. Hamidullah, Muslim Conduct of State, pp.181-2.

2. Contraband of War and Trade

A declaration of war suspends most relations between the belligerent states and therefore diplomats are recalled to their home states and persons under the jurisdiction of the conflicting parties are prohibited from sending information about the activities of their home states regarding the strategies of the war. Analogous to the system of international criminal law, in Islamic international criminal law one may also find certain sanctions prohibiting commercial relations between the belligerent states and such trade is called 'contraband of war and trade.' In general it is to be noted that the enforcement of some of the prohibitive rules broadly depends on the political policies of the conflicting parties and it seems that prohibitive sanctions concerning foodstuffs are very difficult to entirely respect. In practice Muhammad – the Prophet of Islam – has lifted certain bans and it has been told that on one occasion when hostilities were enacted between Mecca and Madinah, he himself send a quantity of dates from Madinah to the Magnate, Abu-Sufyan and required animal hides in return.[3]

One must emphasize that although Islamic international criminal law places heavy weight on the actual conditions of hostilities, it simultaneously mitigates the effect of hostilities on humanitarian grounds.[4] This is because in Islamic international criminal law the institution of war is combined with humanitarian considerations and in other words, war cannot be made against the spirit of man, which is equal in all human beings.

3. Self-Defence

Islamic international criminal law recognizes self-defence as the natural and legal right of an individual, group and state. This right has been established in

---

[3] Hamidullah, Muslim Conduct of State, p.187.

[4] Of course we do not deny that the provisions of the Islamic international criminal law may not be respected by the conflicting parties and be severely violated – even by those who carry the banner of Islamic law and culture. For example, the Islamic law of armed conflict has been violated by Iraq not only during the eight years war between Iran and Iraq but also during the occupation of Kuwait in 1990. Similarly, the provisions of the system of international criminal law may not be respected by those same parties who consider themselves the most essential reasons for the development and consolidation of a number of international criminal law conventions. Examples of this type of double morality are numerous. A clear recent example is the selling of weapons by the Swedish authorities to the conflicting parties during the war between Iran and Iraq. A similar habit was also shown to be true of other European countries such as France, the United Kingdom and in other parts of the world by the United States and Canada.

the Islamic law since the early time of its revelation. In order for self–defence to be recognized, certain conditions are required by law. These conditions more or less coincide with the conditions found in the system of international criminal law governing the status of self–defence.[5] This is because both legal systems have limited the resort to the right of self–defence in order to prevent abuses in employing the right of self–defence in international relations. It must however be admitted that there is controversy in the system of international criminal law regarding the methods and degree of right of self–defence which can be employed.[6]

Islamic international criminal law lays down the following basic conditions in order that self–defence be recognized as proper.[7] These are the following:

i) There must be a definite sign of action which clearly constitutes a serious internationally wrongful conduct jeopardizing the security of a state.[8]

ii) It must be definitely impossible for a state which resorts to exercising the right of self–defence to obtain protection through another legal status such as opening negotiations and/or arbitrations. In the case of an individual or a group exercising the right of self–defence, there must not be any possibility of reporting the commission of wrongful conduct by the perpetrator(s) to independent legal authorities.

iii) The principle of proportionality must be fully respected.[9] This principle constitutes a basic element in the Islamic law of self–defence and has an important function identifying whether or not an act constitutes an act of self–defence.

iv) An attack must not be continued where a wrongful conduct has already been prevented or corrected.

v) A reprisal should not be considered an integral part of the right of self–defence. This is because the right of self–defence automatically comes into

---

[5] See Article 51 of the Charter of the United Nations.

[6] Generally see Kunz, Josef Laurenz., Individual and Collective Self–Defence in Article 51 of the Charter of the United Nations, 41 A.J.I.L. (1947), pp.872–9; Bowett, D.W., Self–Defence in international Law (1958); Brownlie, Ian, The Use of Force in Self–Defence, 37 British Year Book of International Law (1961), pp.254–7; Brownlie, International Law and the Use of Force by States (Oxford, 1963), pp.251–80; Malekian, International Criminal Responsibility of States, pp.118–20; Malekian, International Criminal Law, Vol.I, pp.65–8; Malekian, Condemning the Use of Force in the Gulf Crisis, pp.24–31; See also Lin, F.S., Self–Defense – A Permissible Use of Force Under the U.N. Charter, 13 De Paul Law Review (1963), pp.43–72.

[7] See *also* section 6 below.

[8] The Prophet 'always laid emphasis on the point that Muslims should never be the first to attack; they should on the other hand fight only for defence.' Allahdin, Extracts from the Holy Qur'an and Sayings of the Holy Prophet Mohammad, p.193.

[9] See *also* section 5 below.

force against a crucial act of attack which is obvious and not an act which has already been committed.

These five principles of Islamic international criminal law governing the status of self–defence may be compared with the status of self–defence under customary international criminal law and the provisions of Article 51 of the United Nations Charter. In order for self–defence to be recognized as legitimate under the Charter an armed attack must occur against a member of the United Nations and secondly, 'Measures taken by Members in the exercise of this right of self–defence shall be immediately reported to the Security Council and shall not in any way affect the authority and responsibility of the Security Council under the present Charter to take at any time such action as it deems necessary in order to maintain or restore international peace and security.'[10]

Islamic international criminal law places heavy weight on the principle of proportionality and a state should not resort to the use of excessive force in exercising the right of self–defence.[11] In other words the use of force must be equivalent to the force which is obviously needed and therefore should not be aggressive. The status of this principle is however not clarified in the system of international criminal law and the principle has been differently interpreted in the practice of states.[12]

4. Reprisals

Islamic international criminal law, in contrast to the system of international criminal law, forbids acts of reprisal in any form and for any reason. The term 'reprisal' in the system of Islamic international criminal law can be compared with the term 'reprisal' or *lex talionis* under the system of international criminal law. The concept of treatment of reprisal in Islamic law is one of the significant characterizations of Islamic international criminal law governing the humanitarian law of armed conflicts and because of this humanitarian purpose both acts of hostility and armed reprisal are prohibited. By and through this important principle Islamic international criminal law promotes pacific settlements of international disputes and effectively prevents killing, destruction, devastation and bloodshed.

---

[10] Article 51.

[11] See sub–section five.

[12] See Malekian, Condemning the Use of Force in the Gulf Crisis (2nd ed., Uppsala, 1994), pp.29–30.

In this connection the *Qur'an* states that 'All prohibited things are under the Law of Retaliation; if then any one acts aggressively against you, inflict injury on him according to the injury he has inflicted on you, and fear God, and know that God is with those who refrain from doing evil deeds and are righteous ones.'[13] This statement in the *Qur'an* must be regarded as a significant principle in the system of legislation of Islam in the effective extinguishing of bloodshed. The verse has vividly stated that 'All prohibited things are under the Law of Retaliation.' This theory encourages the conflicting parties to conclude peace treaties and not to engage in activities which extend or prolong hostilities.

A similar principle can also be found in other verses of the *Qur'an* which promote the stages of peace, even when a wrongful act has already occurred. According to one verse,

And the recompense of evil is punishment like it, but he who forgives and reforms the offenders or makes reconciliation, his reward is with God, surely God does not love the unjust tyrants.[14]

But indeed those who with the help of others after being oppressed take their revenge, these are they against whom there is no way to blame.[15]

The way to blame is only against those who oppress people transgressively and revolt in the earth unjustly, for them is a grievous chastisement.[16]

A modern interpretation of the above principles means that a state should not involve itself for any reason in acts of terrorism, the taking of hostages or the temporary detention of internationally protected persons on the grounds of reprisal.

5. The Principle of Proportionality

The principle of proportionality constitutes one of the important principles of Islamic law and must always be respected by Muslims in their social conduct. The principle also has an important function in the system of Islamic international criminal law and is treated broadly by the followers of the Prophet

---

[13] The *Qur'an*, 2:194. In another verse, the *Qur'an* reads that 'Whoever does the evil deeds, he is only recompensed with the like of it, and whoever does good, whether male or female and he is a believer these enter the Garden, in which they are provided sustenance without measure.' 40:40.

[14] The *Qur'an*, 42:40.

[15] The *Qur'an*, 42:41.

[16] The *Qur'an*, 42:42.

of Islam. For instance Imam Ail Ben Abi Talb, who is considered the first of twelfth leaders of Islam (by *Shi'a*) after the death of the Prophet, has given special respect to the principle of proportionality in the actual relations of Muslims. For instance, 'when Ali the successor to the prophet of Islam was stabbed in the back with a dagger by one of his enemies while praying, he gave advice to his followers that one should forgive one's attacker. If one cannot, one should not use any weapon other than that used against oneself and one should not strike one's attacker more times than one has been struck by him. If he does not die as a result, he should be released as soon as possible. Thus, even in cases of revenge, there were certain restrictions in the use of weapons.'[17]

The principle of proportionality must be respected at times of war.[18] According to the Islamic international criminal law a war should not be made unlimited and the conflicting parties must take into account certain rules and provisions governing an armed conflict.[19] The principle of proportionality is thus considered one of the important elements of the law of armed conflicts. This is of particular and prominent importance in cases of armed attack by a state against another state constituting individual or collective self–defence. In this regard the *Qur'an* – the main source of Islamic international criminal law – states 'if then any one acts aggressively against you, inflict injury on him according to the injury he has inflicted on you, and fear God, and know that God is with those who refrain from doing evil deeds and are righteous ones.'[20] This statement means that Islamic international criminal law places very significant respect on the principle of proportionality at all times and especially for the maintenance of the international humanitarian law of armed conflicts.[21]

[17] Malekian, International Criminal Law, Vol.I, pp.151–2.

[18] According to one opinion the principle of proportionality 'requires that no more force has to be used than is necessary for the purpose. There must be proportionality between the means chosen and the end in view.' Singh, J.N., Use of Force Under International Law (New Delhi, 1984), p.22.

[19] See chapter 4.

[20] The *Qur'an*, 2:194. In another verse, the *Qur'an* reads that 'Whoever does the evil deeds, he is only recompensed with the like of it, and whoever does good, whether male or female and he is a believer these enter the Garden, in which they are provided sustenance without measure.' 40:40.

[21] The position of the principle of proportionality is not however clear in the system of international criminal law. 'Although the criterion of the principle is notoriously difficult to apply, the measures for the restoration of the territorial integrity and political independence of a nation must of course be in conformity with the principles of justice and positive international law documented in the 1949 Geneva Conventions and 1977 Protocols governing the international humanitarian law of armed conflicts.' Malekian, Condemning the Use of Force in the Gulf Crisis, 2nd ed., p.30.

6. Self-determination

The principle of self-determination under Islamic international criminal law constitutes one of the most significant principles for the development of international equality between all nations struggling for their inalienable right of independence. This principle has especially been supported by those states exercising the provisions of Islamic law.[22] These states have voted for resolutions of the General Assembly adopted for the political, juridical, religious, economic or territorial independence of groups or nations having been colonized, monopolized or occupied by the military power of a third state in one way or another.

In a comparative respect the principle of self-determination has not only been greatly supported under the system of international criminal law but has also been encouraged and supported under the spirit of the United Nations Charter. One of the chief purposes of the United Nations Organization is 'To develop friendly relations among nations based on respect for the principle of equal rights and self-determination of peoples, and to take other appropriate measures to strengthen universal peace.'[23] This means that the principle of self-determination supported by Islamic international criminal law is not in contradiction with the system of international criminal law.

One of the basic reasons for the development of the principle of self-determination in Islamic international criminal law can be seen in the Charter of the Organization of the Islamic Conference established in 1972.[24] Participating states demonstrated a strong tendency towards re-establishing of

---

[22] According to one writer, 'Arab and Islamic countries insist that each country has the right to self-determination and on the principle of non-alignment. But in fact they offer military bases to Western countries. These are used by Western countries for their own interests.' Abu-Sahlieh, Sami A. Aldeeb., Muslims Human Rights: Challenges and Perspectives, in Schmale, Wolfgang Wolfgang (ed.)., Human Rights and Cultural Diversity: Europe. Arabic-Islamic World. Africa. China (Germany, 1993), pp.239-68, p.253.

[23] Article 1 (2) of the Charter. Although the principle of self-determination which is supported in the Charter is juridically very important in the development and promotion of the principle of equality of all nations, its scope of application is strongly limited by the other articles of the Charter yielding the most juridical and political power of the Organization to certain politically powerful states in the Security Council.

[24] Organization of the Islamic Conference, Jeddah, Saudi Arabia, the text of the Charter as amended; see also UNTS 914, 111-6. Members of the Organization of the Islamic Conference are Afghanistan, Algeria, Bahrain, Bangladesh, Benin, Brunei, Cameroon, Chad, Comoros, Djibouti, Egypt, Gabon, Gambia, Guinea, Guinea-Bissau, Indonesia, Iran, Iraq, Jordan, Kuwait, Lebanon, Libyan Arab Jamahiriya, Malaysia, Maldives, Mali, Mauritania, Morocco, Niger, Nigeria, Oman, Pakistan, Palestine, Qatar, Saudi Arabia, Senegal, Sierra Leone, Somalia, Sudan, Syrian Arab Republic, Tunisia, Turkey, Uganda, United Arab Emirates, Upper Volta (Burkina-Faso), Yemen - Arab Republic, Yemen -People's Democratic Republic.

the rights of oppressed peoples. According to this Charter the objectives and principles of the Conference are:

(A) Objectives
The objectives of the Islamic Conference shall be:
1. to promote Islamic solidarity among member States;
2. to consolidate co-operation among member States in the economic, social, cultural, scientific and other vital fields of activities, and to carry out consultations among member States in international organizations;
3. to endeavour to eliminate racial segregation, discrimination and to eradicate colonialism in all its forms;
4. to take necessary measures to support international peace and security founded on justice;
5. to co-ordinate efforts for the safeguard of the Holy Places and support of the struggle of the people of Palestine, and help them to regain their rights and liberate their land;
6. to strengthen the struggle of all Moslem peoples with a view to safeguarding their dignity, independence, and national rights;
7. to create a suitable atmosphere for the promotion of co-operation and understanding among member States and other countries.

(B) Principles
The member States decide and undertake that, in order to realize the objectives mentioned in the previous paragraph, they shall be inspired and guided by the following principles:
1. total equality between member States;
2. respect of the right of self-determination, and non-interference in the domestic affairs of member States;
3. respect of the sovereignty, independence and territorial integrity of each member States;
4. settlement of any conflict that may arise by peaceful means such as negotiation, mediation, reconciliation or arbitration;
5. abstention from the threat or use of force against the territorial integrity, national unity or political independence of any member State.[25]

One of the important aims of the principle of self-determination and its support under Islamic international criminal law is build on the protection of the rights of peoples who are the victims of various violations. One of these

---

[25] Article 2.

peoples are the Palestinians.[26] They struggle in order to achieve their right of independence.[27] The protection of the rights of Palestinians to political and

[26] See, for instance, The United Nations Special Committee to Investigate Israeli Practices Affecting the Human Rights of the Populations of the Occupied Territories; Report of the National Lawyers Guild 1977 Middle East Delegation, Treatment of Palestinians in Israeli-Occupied West Bank and Gaza (1978); 1988 Report of the National Lawyers Guild, International Human Rights Law and Israel's Efforts to Suppress the Palestinian Uprising (1989). Meron Benvenisti., The West Bank Data Base Project 1987 Report (1987); Playfair, Emma., Administrative Detention in the Occupied West Bank, Al Haq/Law in the Service of Man (1986); Al-Haq/Law in the Service of Man, Briefing Papers on Twenty Years of Israeli Occupation of the West Bank and Gaza (1987); Al Haq/Law in the Service of Man, Punishing a Nation: Human rights Violations During the Palestinian Uprising, December 1987 – December 1988 (1988); Lawyers Committee for Human Rights, an Examination of the Detention of Human Rights Workers and Lawyers from the West Bank and Gaza and Conditions of Detention at Ketziot (1988); Physicians for Human Rights, the Casualties of Conflict: Medical Care and Human Rights in the West Bank and Gaza Strip (1988). See also the B'Tselem which is an independent Jerusalem-based organization founded in 1989 by Israeli lawyers and others to report violations of human rights in occupied territories. See, for instance, B'Tselem/the Israeli Information Center for Human Rights in the Occupied Territories, Annual Report 1989: Violations of Human Rights in the Occupied Territories (1989) and B'Tselem/the Israeli Information Center for Human Rights in the Occupied Territories, the Military Judicial System in the West Bank (1989); B'Tselem/the Israeli Information Center for Human Rights in the Occupied Territories, the Use of Firearms by the Security Forces in the Occupied Territories (1990); B'Tselem/the Israeli Information Center for Human Rights in the Occupied Territories, the System of Taxation in the West Bank and the Gaza strip: As an Instrument for the Enforcement of Authority During the Uprising (1990); Amnesty International, Israel and the Occupied Territories – Excessive Force: Beatings to Maintain Law and Order (1988); Amnesty International, Israel and the Occupied Territories – The Misuse of Tear Gas by Israeli Army Personnel in the Israeli Occupied Territories (1988); Amnesty International, Israel and the Occupied Territories – Administrative Detention During the Palestinian Intifada (1989); Resolution 44/48, Report of the Special Committee to Investigate Israeli Practices Affecting the Human Rights of the Population of the Occupied Territories, U.N. Press Release, Department of Public Information, Press Release G.A/7977, 22 January 1990, Resolutions and Decisions Adopted by the General Assembly During the First Part of Its forty-fourth Session from 19 September to 29 December 1989; Roberts, Adam., Prolonged Military Occupation: The Israeli-Occupied Territories since 1967, 84 American Journal of International Law (1990); Falk, Richard., The Relevance of International Law to Palestinian Rights in the West Bank and Gaza, 32 Harvard International Law Journal (1991); Hiltermann, Joost., Israel's Deportation Policy in the Occupied West Bank and Gaza, Al Haq/law in the Service of Man (1986).

[27] "Palestine was historically an Arabic land, an Arab nation and above all ideologically and politically dependent on the Islamic system. Later, Palestine came under the control of the Turkish Ottoman Empire. In 1917-18 Palestine was occupied by the British and in 1920 the Palestine Mandate was given by the League of Nations to the British. According to the provisions of the Mandate, Britain was supposed to give *administrative advice* until Palestine was able to stand alone. However, in 1897 the idea of creating a Jewish state was presented through the World Zionist Organisation by T. Herzl. In 1917 the British Foreign Secretary, A.J. Balfour stated that Britain would support a Jewish national home in Palestine providing that 'nothing shall be done which may prejudice the civil and religious rights of existing non-Jewish communities in Palestine.'(Morphet, Sally., The Palestinians and their right of self-determination, in Vincent, R.J., Foreign Policy and Human Rights (London, 1986), pp.85-103, at pp.85-6.) However, Palestinian Arabs objected to Zionism in 1920 and in the following years, especially

territorial independence has been constantly supported under General Assembly resolutions, without any practical effect however.[28] There have recently been some relevant negotiations for the political and territorial independence of Palestinians. An agreement for the independence of some parts of Palestine was concluded between Israel and the PLO in September 1993,[29] and the first form of Palestinian self–rule was signed in May 4, 1994.

Although respect for the principle of self–determination of peoples has been constantly supported in the United Nations,[30] this principle has not been respected in the actual practice of states.[31] The United Nations Security Council has for instance adopted a number of resolutions governing the political and territorial independence of the Muslims in Bosnia–Herzegovina in 1993 and 1994, the Organization has not however been successful in the implementation and enforcement of the resolutions.[32] This is also a fact even after the Nato air strike ultimatum to Serbs in April 1994.

when the British Peel Commission suggested the partition plan for Palestine in 1937. After World War II a suggestion was passed to the United Nations, which finally resulted in a resolution in 1947. According to this resolution by the General Assembly of the United Nations Palestine was to be divided into eight parts. Three to constitute an Arab state, three a Jewish state, a seventh, Jaffa, an Arab enclave in Jewish territory and the eighth part Jerusalem, which is a *corpus separatum* controlled by an international regime. Israel declared its independence in 1948. The partition resolution and the independence of Israel created a difficult situation which is still not resolved today. Palestinians are now demanding self–determination. This was one of the essential reasons for the establishment of a Palestinian National Council and subsequently the Palestine Liberation Organization. This organizations struggles for the re–establishment of Palestinian rights." Malekian, International Criminal Law, Vol.II, pp.90–1.

[28] Although Muslim populations have supported the General Assembly resolutions concerning the principle of self–determination, they have not been in the favour of partition plan which was recommended by the General Assembly of the United Nations in the early years of its establishment. They were in a state of solidarity from the early days of political conflicts in Palestine with the Palestinian peoples in order to eliminate political conspiracy and intrigues and also to reject the Balfour Declaration and the League of Nations mandate over Palestine. Moinuddin, The Charter of the Islamic Conference and Legal Framework of Economic Co-Operation among its Member States, p.80.

[29] Malekian, Farhad., The Monopolization of International Criminal Law in the United Nations, A Jurisprudential Approach (Uppsala, 1993), p.166.

[30] For example, Article 1 (2) of the Charter of the United Nations reads the purposes of the Organization are ... 'To develop friendly relations among nations based on respect for the principle of equal rights and self–determination of people, and to take other appropriate measures to strengthen universal peace.'

[31] Abu-Sahlieh, Muslims Human Rights: Challenges and Perspectives, p.253.

[32] See the following letters by Malekian, Farhad., An Inquiry into the Severe Violations of International Criminal Law in Bosnia–Herzegovina, (A letter to the Members of the Security Council of the United Nations and the General Secretary of the Organization, 27/May/1993), 12 pp.; A letter to the Members of the Security Council of the United Nations and the General Secretary of the Organization, July 7, 1993, 5 pp.

7. Humanitarian Help

The system of Islamic international criminal law has recognized the institution of humanitarian help when necessary in order to give particular assistance to a nation which has become the object of criminal operations by another regime(s). The scope of this humanitarian help may however vary largely from case to case and also depends on the conditions of those to whom such humanitarian help is assumed to aid. Two verses of the *Qur'an* basically deal with the reasons for and scope of humanitarian aid (and asylum) which should be granted to a nation which has asked for it. According to one verse:

> Those who believed and took flight and made hard exertion in God's Way with their wealth and their persons, and those who gave asylum and aid – these are guardians, friends and protectors of one another; and those who believed but did not flee, you owe no duty of protection to them until they take flight; and if they seek aid from you in the matter of religion, then it is your duty to help them, except against a people between you and whom there is a treaty of mutual alliance, and God watches what you do.[33]

There are therefore two important conditions under which the institution of humanitarian help may be granted in order to save a nation from certain criminally inflicted. These conditions should not necessarily be treated in conjunction with one another. Each one of them has an independent characterization.

The *first* condition being that a nation has asked for humanitarian help based on a 'matter of religion'. This means that it is the moral and legal duty of a nation to help other nations of the same religion.[34]

The *second* condition is that humanitarian help cannot be granted as long as there is a treaty between the regime of a nation requesting help and the regime of a nation requested to help which contains contrary provisions.[35]

Thus, as we have mentioned elsewhere, Islamic international criminal law places heavy weight on respecting the obligations of a treaty between two nations and therefore such obligations should not be violated between

---

[33] The *Qur'an*, 8:72.

[34] A far reaching interpretation of the verse in accordance with modern circumstances is that a nation can give humanitarian help to a requesting nation if both nations hold common concepts, beliefs or are parties to a treaty, the provisions of which treat all contracting parties by the same degree. Members of an international organization may give humanitarian help to one another under the conditions of its charter or constitution if there are provisions for that purpose.

[35] The *Qur'an*, 8:72.

contracting parties.[36] This conclusion should not however be interpreted as meaning that the provisions of a treaty must be respected when a particular regime or government has illegally come into power, has been judged illegal on the grounds of its criminal activities or practices political tyranny over its own or other nations. Humanitarian help can be requested for deliverance from danger or freedom from criminal conditions and this is irrespective of whether or not the authorized government under which a Muslim nation is suffering is Muslim. The *Qur'an* reads that 'And those who, when they are oppressed revolt against the oppressors, and ask other powers for help to defend themselves.'[37] Moreover, treaty obligations may lose their legal validity when the situation is one of inevitable necessity or extreme emergency. In other words, obligations of a treaty must be respected, 'Except one who is driven by necessity, neither craving nor transgressing, it is no sin for him.'

Humanitarian help must be especially given to all minors, children and females who are suffering for one reason or another from unjustified, immoral or unnecessary use of force by others. Accordingly,

> And what reason have you and why should you not fight in the cause of God and for the weak among the men and the women and the children who pray: 'Our Lord! rescue us from this town, whose people are tyrants, and raise for us from thee defender, guardian and raise for use from Thee a protector, helper.'[38]

The above provisions must be seen in the light of their revelation, at a time when no international organization or entity existed which could give humanitarian help or assistance to those who were attacked and plundered immorally and illegally by other nations. The Islamic law by its very notion of universality and significant humanitarian purposes aims to function as a universal organization for the prevention of war. It is for this reason that Islamic law provides full humanitarian support for the poor, victims and the oppressed. Its provisions do not encourage war; They provide legal grounds for those who are already under attack to seek humanitarian help from other nations.

More or less similar provisions to those in Islamic international criminal law can be found in the system of international criminal law. The system of

---

[36] See chapter one.

[37] The *Qur'an*, 42:39.

[38] The *Qur'an*, 4:75. 'Those who have believed battle for the cause of God, and those who disbelieved battle for the cause of devil, therefore battle against the friends of the devil leader, surely the cunning schemes, evil plots, and the stratagems of devil are weak.' The *Qur'an*, 4:76.

international criminal law generally prohibits states from intervening in the political affairs of other states and the Charter of the United Nations indicates this also.[39] Accordingly, the provisions of both these legal systems legitimate humanitarian help. The relevant provisions of Islamic international criminal law and the system of international criminal law regarding the giving of assistance to those who are the victims of international crimes can be especially examined in light of the conclusions of the International Court of Justice regarding the Case Concerning Application of the Convention on the Prevention and punishment of the Crime of Genocide in Bosnia–Herzegovina.[40]

---

[39] 'Nothing contained in the present Charter shall authorize the United Nations to intervene in matters which are essentially within the domestic jurisdiction of any state or shall require the Members to submit such matters to settlement under the present Charter; but this principle shall not prejudice the application of enforcement measures under Chapter VII.' Article 2 (7).

[40] It reads that: '4. That under the current circumstances, the Government of Bosnia and Herzegovina has the right to seek and receive support from other States in order to defend itself and its people, including by means of immediately obtaining military weapons, equipment, and supplies. 5. That under the current circumstances, the Government of Bosnia and Herzegovina has the right to request the immediate assistance of any State to come to its defence, including by means of immediately providing weapons, military equipment and supplies, and armed forces (soldiers, sailors, airpeople, etc.) 6. That under the current circumstances, any State has the right to come to the immediate defence of Bosnia and Herzegovina – at its request – including by means of immediately providing weapons, military equipment and supplies, and armed forces (soldiers, sailors, and airpeople, etc.); ...' See Case Concerning Application of the Convention on the Prevention and Punishment of the Crime of Genocide (8 April, 1993, Order), p.7.

Chapter Twenty

Institution of Protections

1. Overview

By the term 'institution of protections' we mean all forms of protection which may be sought, granted or given under the Islamic jurisprudence of national and international law to those soliciting protection or to those to whom it is granted without any form of soliciting also. These protections under Islamic law are not only broad but also have a certain significance in the development of Islamic human rights and the Muslim humanitarian law of armed conflicts. These protections include asylum, refuge, extradition, hospitalities for foreigners and internationally protected persons, aliens, shipwreck victims and quarter. We have not however dealt with the scope and perspective of all these institutions and protections here, since each one of them has its own broad philosophical, theological and juridical characterization and cannot therefore be completely studied in one volume. Some of these legal protections are studied below.

2. Refugees

Rules governing the status of refugees constitute an important institution in the system of Islamic international criminal law. The *Qur'an* reads that 'And if anyone of the polytheists seeks asylum, grant him asylum, till he has heard the message of God, then escort him to his place of security...'[1] This institution has been recognized since the creation of Islamic law and been considered an important principle for the promotion of the concept of Islamic human rights and the Muslim humanitarian law of armed conflicts. The *Qur'an* (constituting the main source of Islamic international criminal law) provides a number of verses dealing directly with both the concept and questions concerning the condition of refugee. Some of the relevant verses from the *Qur'an* are:

---

[1] The *Qur'an*, 9:6. See also section 4 below.

The wealth left by enemy is for the poor who fled, those who were expelled from their homes and from their property, who seek grace of God and His pleasure, and supporting God and His apostle they are indeed the sincere and truthful ones.[2]

And those who before them took refuge into the homes and the faith impressed their hearts, they love and show their affection to those who have fled to them, and entertain no desire in their hearts for those things which are given to the latter, and give them preference over themselves even though poverty may afflict them on account of their entertaining, and whoever is preserved from the niggardliness of his soul, so they are the successful ones.[3]

Under Islamic law there is no difference between persons who are refugees or those who take asylum under the territorial jurisdiction of an Islamic state. Refugees from all classes of religion, race, language, colour, ideological or political view or ethnic origin are welcome and treated fairly and equally in accordance with the system of Islamic international law. Historically, 'The victims of racial, religious, political and other persecutions have always found refuge and shelter in the land of Islam.'[4]

The Islamic institution of refugee gives special consideration to those persons who have been considered slaves and a slave who has escaped and come under the territorial jurisdiction of Islamic states should be immediately considered as free. Slaves can also be freed if they seek refuge in a Muslim army camp active in a war which is not in a home state. This is because a Muslim camp in the territory of a conflicting party is regarded as a temporary Muslim territory.[5] Moreover, according to Islamic law the state of resident for aliens has a duty to protect their rights and it is also incumbent upon such states, where Muslims have encampments in enemy territory, to help resident aliens and assist them if they are taken prisoners by the state(s) at war with the relevant Muslim state.[6] Islamic human rights, in contrast to the Western institution of human rights governing the rules of refuge (the rules of which are conditional), commands the state of asylum to provide the necessary aid from the public

---

[2] The *Qur'an*, 59:8.

[3] The *Qur'an*, 59:9.

[4] Publications of Centre Culturel Islamique, p.135.

[5] Hamidullah, Muslim Conduct of State, p.128.

[6] *Id.*

wealth of the state for such refugees.[7]

It may also be useful to note that in the system of international law to seek refuge is not a right and must be determined in accordance with the legal and political factors of each state. In contrast to this, to seek refuge under the Islamic system of law is considered the right of any person who, for one reason or another, comes under Islamic jurisdiction.

3. Extradition

The principle of extradition is also dealt with in the system of Islamic international criminal law. The principle of extradition in the Islamic system, like the system of international criminal law, has different aspects governing the extradition of those who are requested to be returned to their country of origin. The institution of extradition in the Islamic system of international criminal law limits the scope of protections which may be granted to certain persons who have sought refuge or taken asylum. This is because according to Islamic international criminal law when there is an agreement of extradition its provisions must be fully respected. For example, there are agreements from the time of Muhammad, the Prophet of Islam, which clarify the scope of extradition in the practice of Islamic law. Sometimes the provisions of an agreement could only represent the interests of one of the conflicting parties. Nevertheless, the provisions of such an agreement could still be fulfilled. One early example is the agreement of Hudaibiyah concluded between Muhammad and the city–state of Mecca in 6 Hegery. According to this pact, 'Whoever from among the Quraishites went to Muhammad without permission of his superior ... Muhammad shall extradite him to them; yet whoever from among the partisans of Muhammad went to the Quraishites, they will not extradite him.'[8]

Islamic international criminal law also recognizes the extradition of those who are subjects of a Muslim state and have committed highway robbery under the

---

[7] In one instance in my own memory the Islamic system *has* even given asylum to a person who seriously violated its regulations and committed crimes against the common values of Islamic society. This occurred in the early twentieth century when certain Russian envoys raped some Persian women and because of the anger of the public took asylum in one of the religious tombs situated close to Teheran, the capital of Persia. They had closed themselves into the vaults of the tomb in order to receive amnesty (a tradition to receive mercy or amnesty). Their crimes were not however forgiven and they were not juridically given amnesty but they were safely returned to their country. This example displays the high level of humanitarian support under the system of Islamic international criminal law. It also proves the high level of respect which can be given to the institution of asylum under the Islamic system as well as municipal legislation.

[8] Hamidullah, p.132.

jurisdiction of another form of state but have escaped to the jurisdiction of a Muslim state. Such persons should not be tried under Islamic jurisdiction and should be extradited to the relevant state for prosecution and punishment. This rule is valid even though their criminal conduct has basically been committed against Muslim subjects. Extradition is however granted according to the terms of any relevant extradition treaty.[9]

4. Quarter

Quarter constitutes one of the largest institutions of protection under Islamic law and therefore we shall only consider its certain aspects. Quarter in the system of Islamic international criminal law means the act of giving life to a defeated enemy. This means that quarter is normally granted to enemy persons and therefore when one speaks of giving quarter in Islamic international criminal law one means specifically persons who are enemies and have come for one reason or another under Islamic jurisdiction during an armed conflict;[10] This is regardless of the social position or religious status of such a person. The source of quarter in the Islamic system of international criminal law arises from its basic constitution *i.e.* the *Qur'an*. The relevant verse in the *Qur'an* reads, 'And if anyone of the polytheists seeks asylum, grant him asylum, till he has heard the message of God, then escort him to his place of security...'[11] The above verse contains the basic provisions of Islamic international criminal law governing the statute of quarter and also implies that

---

[9] *Id.*, p.178.

[10] It was a recognized practice in the tradition of the Prophet to give amnesty to those who had violated their peace treaty with Muslims. For example when the pagans of Mecca violated their peace treaty the Prophet occupied Mecca in a bloodless diplomacy and ordered the defeated population to assemble. He reminded them of their treaty violations, their ill-deeds towards Muslims, the devastation of their properties and especially their prolonged hostilities against Muslims during a twenty year period. He asked them, 'What do you expect of me?' They lowered their heads with shame. The Prophet therefore proclaimed, 'May God pardon you; go in peace; there shall be no responsibility on you today; you are free.' This statement by the Prophet created a profound psychological transformation. After this amnesty by the Prophet of Islam, the Meccan leader accessed to the Prophet and declared his acceptance of Islam. The Prophet appointed him as governor of Mecca. The Prophet retired to Medina without leaving a single soldier in Mecca and consequently the whole population of the city, due to this great generosity on the part of the Prophet and arising from the Islamic principles, became Muslims within a few hours. Publications of Centre Culturel Islamique., Introduction to Islam (Park Lane, Secunderabad, 1376 H/ 1957 A.C.), p.12.

[11] The *Qur'an*, 9:6. This verse has been also translated as 'And if anyone of the Associators seek thy protection (O Muhammad), then protect him so that he may bear the Word of God and afterwards convey him to his place of safety.' See also section 2 above.

quarter is only given to those who do not hold faith with the divine law, in other words those considered non-Muslims.

There are two different forms of quarter in the system of Islamic international criminal law. One is requested by the relevant person(s) from the official authorities of the state and the other is considered by the same authorities without any need for prior request. In both cases it is the relevant state department which decides whether or not to grant quarter. Quarter can be conditional or temporary. Conditional quarter is granted in order for persons to receiving quarter in the fulfilment of certain conditions such as certain payment. Temporary quarter means a limited period of time granted for a person receiving quarter to fulfil a definite requirement.[12]

Quarter granted by an individual Muslim is regarded valid if it is not contradicted by the superior or commander of the Muslim army. Moreover, both forms of quarter may also be granted by the lowest Muslims, combatants, persons incapable of fighting, the sick, blind, slaves and women and still be binding upon the whole Muslim state. The right of granting quarter is exclusively given to Muslims but quarter granted by a non-Muslim who is fighting for a Muslim army may also be regarded valid if such a person is authorized by a competent Muslim.[13]

There are several differences between quarter, refugee and asylum regulations. One basic difference is that the former must be solicited by the relevant persons while the latter two do not need to be solicited as long as a person comes under the jurisdiction of an Islamic state in order to seek refuge or asylum. The reason for this is that a person who is given quarter is an enemy who has been surrounded, captured, arrested or detained for reasons of war, while a refugee does not necessarily need to come from a place of war and can be anyone who has taken asylum for one reason or another in an Islamic state. The second difference is that a refugee does not necessarily need to be a non-Muslim person and therefore may be a Muslim who has come from the jurisdiction of one Islamic state to another. The third difference is that refugees are protected persons in most cases and according to their own will usually ask for asylum in the Islamic regions. In contrast to this, persons given quarter have no right of choice and are considered belligerents. The fourth difference is that to seek refuge is usually considered a spiritual right of protection in the Islamic system of international criminal law, while quarter is a form of protection which

[12] Hamidullah, Muslim Conduct of State, pp.200-2.
[13] *Id., pp.201-2.*

must be decided in accordance with the circumstances in each instance.[14] According to the fifth difference to seek asylum or refuge is a right of a person while quarter is not.

[14] Taking these differences into consideration, one must always remember that all these statutes may finally be considered relative to political and economic factors and may therefore be ignored by the relevant authorities within Islamic systems.

Chapter Twenty One

Humanitarian Protections
of
Prisoners of War

1. Prisoners of War in International Criminal Law

There have until recently been very few regulations governing the treatment of
prisoners of war under the system of international criminal law. Attempts at
such regulations have been very weak and have not been internationally
binding. Most of the earlier rules in international criminal law dealing with
armed conflicts are without any especially effective regulations relating to the
status of prisoners of war. These rules were formulated during the second half
of the nineteenth century and did not give prisoners of war any special legal
protection.[1]

The events of the First and the Second World Wars and especially the mass
killings of Jew prisoners in the Second World War were strong proof of a lack
of regulations under the international legal system. A single agreement was
however in force. This was the 1929 Convention concerning the Treatment of
Prisoners of War and was applicable between the major Western states. This
Convention was also the development of the Hague Regulations of 1899 and
1907 governing the law of war or armed conflicts, but none of these agreements
could provide the necessary support to appropriately consolidate the legal
situation of prisoners of war. This was for several reasons; Firstly, these
agreements mostly had regional rather than international effects. Secondly, the
legal scope of applicability of the 1899 and 1907 regulations were very narrow
and indeed from a political aspect impractical. Thirdly, at the time of the
drafting of the Regulations and the 1929 Convention many states of the world
were under colonial domination and were not therefore free to express their
own legal consent. Thus, these agreements were formulated in accordance with

---

[1] Malekian, International Criminal Law, Vol.I, p.100-seq.

the will of colonial and powerful states and their allies. Fourthly, the legal framework of the system of international criminal law was not recognized as it is recognized today and therefore the characterization of the law of armed conflicts was more or less a matter of formality, not of implementation and enforcement. The International Military Tribunals in Nuremberg and Tokyo to some extend implemented the system of international criminal law but according to the will and interests of the victorious states.

The third Geneva Convention Relative to the Treatment of Prisoners of War, 1949, has however converted the unstable and irregular situation of prisoners of war and a large number of states are parties to this Convention, which basically aims at harmonizing and humanizing the status of prisoners of war. The Convention contains a number of humanitarian provisions in order to eliminate acts which may, in one way or another, cause various forms of harm to prisoners of war. Accordingly, parties have undertaken to take necessary measures for the implementation of the provisions of the Convention. In particular the 1949 Convention, among many other provisions governing the protection of prisoners of war, states that its provisions must be fully respected by the conflicting parties and any unlawful acts against a prisoner by the detaining power causing his death or endangering the health of the prisoner is not only prohibited but can also be regarded as a serious violation of the provisions of the Convention. The Convention also protects prisoners from any act against their dignity, exercise of religious duties, right to food or any other necessity, medical treatment, personal honour, insults and public curiosity.

As a whole, the provisions of the convention today have the effect of customary international criminal law, which means that they must be respected by all means by the conflicting parties in an armed conflict. This means that the provisions of the convention are binding upon all those who are involved in armed conflicts regardless of whether or not they are parties to the convention. Respect for the provisions of the convention are so important that they should not be denied by any state. The convention is also strengthened by the provisions of the 1977 Geneva Protocol I, Relating to the Protection of Victims of International Armed Conflicts and the 1977 Geneva Protocol II, Relating to the Protection of Victims of Non-International Armed Conflicts, both of which are Additional to the Geneva Conventions of 12 August 1949. Despite this, the provisions of the 1949 Convention Relative to the Treatment of Prisoners of War and the additional Protocols have been violated, for example, in the Yugoslavia war.

2. Prisoners of War in Islamic International Criminal Law

2.1. Definition of Prisoners of War

In Islamic international criminal law prisoners of war are those who have been captured by one means or another during a state of hostility in actual armed conflicts between the conflicting parties and are consequently considered enemy combatants.[2]

In the early practice of Islamic international criminal law prisoners of war could be enslaved due to the prevailing practice of the Middle Ages and in accordance with the wrong interpretation of one of the verses of *Qur'an* to save individuals from further killing.[3] The verse reads that 'So when you encounter the unbelievers in a battle, smite at their necks until when you have slaughtered them and consequently have overcome them, then you imprison them, and afterwards either set them free as a favour or taking some ransom until they lay down their arms, this is a just Law of God for war mongers; and if God had pleased, He would have taken revenge from them Himself (some other way), but (He lets you fight) that He may try some of you by the others; and those who are slain in the Way of God, so He never let their deeds to go in vain.'[4] For this reason one cannot deny that Islamic international criminal law did not permit prisoners of war to be reduced to the status of slavery.

In certain situations the practice was however different, as prisoners were divided among those who had conducted the war. Prisoners of war could therefore be enslaved in situations considered proportionate to the hostile activities of the enemy state. In connection with the above verse and the position of the prisoners of war it is rightly asserted that ' ... the Islamic state has the choice only between two alternatives; either to set free the prisoners of war gratuitously or to claim ransom. The verse unequivocally does not entitle the Muslims to enslave their prisoners of war since it does not contemplate such right. Moreover, it – *a contrario* – forbids enslavement.'[5] It should be further stated that 'the permission of enslaving the prisoners of war is given as a measure of retaliation and not as a right *ab initio*. Therefore, the Muslims are not entitled to enslave their prisoners of war whenever they like but only when

---

[2] According to one writer, 'The prisoners of war are the enemy combatants who, in a legitimate war declared by a Muslim sovereign, were made prisoners by Muslims.' Al-Ghunaimi, The Muslim Conception of International Law and Western Approach, p.148.

[3] The *Qur'an*, 47:4.

[4] The *Qur'an*, 47:4.

[5] Emphasis added. Al-Ghunaimi, The Muslim Conception of International Law and Western Approach, p.190.

their enemy enslaves the Muslim prisoners of war. In other words the Islamic law of war does not contain enslavement as one of its tenets but as a sanction that could be inflicted on a basis of *reciprocity.*[6] It must therefore be emphasized that the *Qur'an* does not support enslavement of prisoners of war and although it was sometimes practiced during the early days of Islamic law (close to fourteen hundred years ago), the practice should definitely be regarded as abolished.

The Prophet of Islam as much as was possible prevented this practice and actively encouraged its abolition.[7] This means that the relevant verse of the *Qur'an* was practiced by the Prophet and the second source of Islamic international criminal law i.e. *Sunnah* was strongly interpreted as a means of promoting its abolition. Thus, it is certainly incorrect to state that in Islamic law enslavement of prisoners was an absolute right of the military commanders or superiors and that there was no tendency towards its abolition. This is irrespective of the fact that there are a number of cases documenting the enslavement of prisoners of war in the early practice of the Muslim states. In any event, enslavement did not constitute a right but an amnesty to mitigate further killings and family unity suffering. Because of the development of international relations and according to the modern interpretation of Islamic law, enslavement is considered a grave violation of the Islamic international humanitarian law of armed conflicts.[8]

2.2. Protections of Prisoners of War

The system of Islamic international criminal law lays down a number of humanitarian principles in order to protect those who have been captured as prisoners during a regional or an international armed conflict. These principles must be regarded as the earliest and most consolidated principles of international humanitarian law of armed conflicts which have been achieved in the history of civilization. They provide certain basic guarantees for prisoners which have only recently been codified in the modern legislations of the system

---

[6] *Id.,* pp.190-1.

[7] See chapter seven.

[8] That is why international conventions prohibiting slavery are signed by states with Muslim populations. For data see Bassiouni, The Islamic Criminal Justice System, pp.48-53.

of international criminal law.[9]

According to Islamic international criminal law the following principles must be fulfilled with respect to prisoners who have been captured during an Islamic (even non-Islamic) state military action.[10] These are:

1. Prisoners should not be held responsible for the cause of hostilities between the conflicting parties.

2. Prisoners who have acted in accordance with the law of war during an armed conflict should not be held responsible for whatsoever damages caused to the conflicting parties.

3. Food and any other necessities such as clothes must be provided for all prisoners and they should not be charged to that effect.

4. A conflicting party who holds prisoners should provide appropriate shelter for their protection.

5. The dignity and integrity of prisoners should not be disregarded.

6. Any cause of human suffering must be avoided. This includes torture and the humiliation of prisoners.

7. Superiors must be equally respected.

8. The cultural attitudes of prisoners must be fully respected.

9. Females should especially be respected.

10. No person should be raped.

11. Females, minors, disable persons and families must be given special respect because of their particular status.

12. Family unity should be respected.

13. Mothers should not be separated from their children.

14. Close relatives should not be separated from one another.

15. In all procedures prisoners should be fairly treated by the conflicting parties.

16. Communications by letter or other forms of this type should be handed over to the relevant enemy authorities.

17. Prisoners who suffer from special discomfiture or a special condition should as much as possible be given help to that effect.

18. Sick and wounded must be given medical services where possible.

---

[9] Some important traditions may be useful to be mentioned here. i) A prisoner could generally be released upon a ransom; ii) A non-Arab origin prisoner could be released only for half of that ransom in (i); iii) A prisoner could be released on the ground of teaching knowledge to others; iv) Poverty of a prisoner could be a basic reason for one's immediate unconditional release; v) Transportation of prisoners should be carried out on the best possible facilities. Hamidullah, The Battlefields of the Prophet Muhammad, p.17.

[10] Hamidullah, Muslim Conduct of State, pp.205-8.

19. Compulsory work should not be imposed on prisoners.

20. Prisoners should not be forced to fight against their own will.

21. Capital punishment should not be carried out on prisoners of war.[11]

22. Any forms of retaliation or revenge on prisoners is prohibited.

23. Prisoners who have escaped to their own country and are again captured during an armed conflict should not be punished for a previous escape(s). They may only be punished if they have already committed other crimes.

24. Prisoners who violate discipline may be punished accordingly.

25. A prisoner of war who is accused of having committed activities beyond the rights, rules and regulations of belligerency may be brought before a tribunal for the purpose of prosecution and if so, found guilty for punishment.

26. The above provisions are a duty of the conflicting parties and therefore parties should not expect prisoners to be grateful for the fulfilment of such a duty.

Islamic law also recognizes certain duties for Islamic states to negotiate for the release of Muslim soldiers captured by enemy states as soon as possible. According to the main source of Islamic law – the *Qur'an* – certain incomes from a Muslim state must be specified and administrated for that purpose.[12] Similarly, ransom is legalized by the *Qur'an* for the release of prisoners of war and simultaneously recommends the gratuitous release of prisoners of war when hostilities have ceased.[13] Prisoners of war should also be exchanged between conflicting parties whenever possible.

With all these provisions Islamic international criminal law diminishes the risk of killing prisoners of war through acts of revenge, hostility or reprisals and harmonizes the activities of conflicting parties in order to achieve peaceful settlements of disputes.

---

[11] An exception to this principle is to be found in extreme situations of military necessity for the interests of a conflicting party. It has however been demonstrated that the companions of the Prophet were unanimous that death penalty should not be carried out on prisoners of war. *Id.*, pp.208–9.

[12] The *Qur'an*, 9:60.

[13] The *Qur'an*, 47:4. See the previous sub-section.

Chapter Twenty Two

The Principles of Human Rights in Both Systems

1. Human Rights in International Criminal Law

The creation and development of the principles of human rights in the system of international law are basically the result of the criminal events of the Second World War. Although the 1948 Declaration of Human Rights is not a law-making treaty, its principles are considered an integral part of international customary law. It is upon the development of the principles of this Declaration that many international criminal conventions have been regulated under the authority of the United Nations Organization. The most illustrative examples are the 1948 Convention on Genocide, the 1949 Geneva Conventions on the law of armed conflicts, the 1952 Protocol relevant to the 1926 Convention on Slavery, the 1956 Supplementary Convention on the Abolition of Slavery, the Slave trade, and the Institutions and Practices Similar to Slavery, the 1973 Convention on Apartheid, the 1975 Declaration on the Protection of All Persons from being subjected to Torture and Other Cruel, Inhuman or Degrading Treatment or Punishment, the 1977 Protocols addition to the four Geneva Conventions of 1948 and the 1984 Convention against Torture and Other Cruel, Inhuman or Degrading Treatment or Punishment.[1]

---

[1] For a brief examination of most of these conventions see the relevant chapters. Generally speaking, certain principles of the system of international human rights have the effect of customary rules of international law and should therefore be respected in the national and international relations of individuals, groups, governments or states. Some other instruments on human rights are the 1953 Convention on the Political Rights of Women, the 1960 Declaration on the Granting of Independence to Colonial countries and People, the 1966 International Covenant on Economic, Social, and Cultural Rights, the 1966 International Covenant on Civil and Political Rights, the 1966 International Convention on the Elimination of All Forms of Racial Discrimination, the 1975 Declaration on Protection from Torture, the 1979 Convention on the Elimination of All Forms of Discrimination against Women, the 1989 United Nations Convention on the Rights of the Child and a number of other international instruments contributed by the International Labour Organization and other international bodies on the principles of human rights.

All these instruments in the field of international human rights represent certain core principles of social structure. Some of these instruments deal especially with those consolidated principles of criminal jurisdiction which should be respected by all legislations.[2] They have not only emphasized the right of every individual to security and liberty but also that all rights integrated in the instruments are applied to everyone without distinction of any kind, such as race, colour, sex, language, religion, political or other ethnic background.[3] Moreover, the instruments guarantee that no one shall be subjected to arbitrary arrest, detention, exile or retroactive law.[4] This also means that 'Everyone is entitle in full equality to a fair and public hearing by an independent and impartial tribunal, in the determination of his rights and obligations and of any criminal charge against him.'[5]

The essence of all these instruments in the field of international human rights is that they guarantee certain rights for all and these rights are granted to all irrespective of social or racial status. As we have demonstrated elsewhere, the rights provided by the system of international human rights are strongly protected by the provisions of the system of international criminal law. In particular a number of international criminal conventions are regulated to prevent and prohibit the commission of certain crimes in the national and international conduct of governments and/or states.[6] However, we cannot deny that the provisions of the instruments on international human rights and the relevant international criminal conventions have often been violated in the official and unofficial conduct of states.[7] These violations have occurred under the jurisdiction of most states and must be analyzed in other volumes.

[2] On the whole, the core principles of these instruments, whether legal or philosophical, have integrated the chief principles of Islamic law into the protection of humans according to the principles of brotherhood, equality and justice.

[3] Article 2 of the 1948 Universal Declaration of Human Rights.

[4] *Id.*, Articles 9 and 11.

[5] *Id.*, Article 10.

[6] See the first paragraph of this section.

[7] As with Islamic international criminal law, many international crimes in the system of international criminal law are today considered crimes against humanity and a number of resolutions of the General Assembly denote this fact. Moreover, an analysis of the system of international criminal law demonstrates that within the system, most crimes including war crimes have on many occasions been considered crimes against humanity and this was especially proven by the procedures of the Nuremberg Tribunal, which had much difficulty distinguishing between war crimes and crimes against humanity specified in its constitution.

2. Human Rights in Islamic International Criminal Law

2.1. Basis

The whole notion of the Islamic philosophy of jurisdiction rests on the creation and the establishment of a universal or international standard of equality between all races irrespective of any distinction based on race, colour, sex, language, religion, political or other ethnical background.[8] Although Islamic law encourages all men to enter into the Islamic sovereignty of God and fulfil their theological (moral) duties towards the divine law, the Islamic philosophy of law (contrary to its understanding in some societies) does not compel a person to enter into a religion as it is contrary to the law of God and is therefore basically prohibited. Islam 'prohibits all compulsion in the matter of religious beliefs; ... Islam is under the self-imposed religious dogmatic duty of giving autonomy to non-Muslims residing on the soil of the Islamic State. The Qur'an, the *Hadith* and the practice of all time demand that non-Muslims should have their own laws, administrated in their own tribunals by their own judges, without any interference on the part of the Muslim authorities, whether it be in religious matters or social.'[9] It is therefore stated that 'Not a single instance can be quoted to show that the Holy Prophet ever brought the pressure of the sword to bear on *one individual, let alone a whole nation,* to embrace Islam. What was not permissable in the case of the Holy Prophet, could not be permissable in that of any one acting in his name and on his behalf.'[10]

Islamic law has therefore promoted its principles, rules, regulations and traditions through the Islamic sources of law but emphasizes that the key principles of co-existence are brotherhood, equality, liberty and justice. Islamic law has also strongly encouraged two other important principles for the promotion of human dignity and the development of other related principles; These are the principles of mercy and compassion. It is on the basis of these

---

[8] It cannot be denied however that classical Islamic law has distinguished between Muslim and non-Muslim residents under the territorial jurisdiction of Islamic states. This has occurred historically for several important reasons, *inter alia* the superiority of divine law and to guarantee the security of the Islamic state against any internal and external intervention. This practice of classical Islamic internal law must be seen from a political perspective, during a time in which all religions were rivals in order to control the political power of a sovereign state(s). One must however emphasized that according to Islamic international law, 'the Muslims and non-Muslims are equal (sawa') with regard to the sufferings of this world.' Publications of Centre Culturel Islamique, p.94.

[9] *Id.,* p.40.

[10] Ali, Maulana Muhammad., The Call of Islam, 2nd ed. (Lahore, 1926), p.21.

important principles that the Islamic law presents a universal union of human rights, much broader and effective than the enumerated human rights presented by the modern philosophy of international human rights.

2.2. Functions

The chief principles of Islamic law are for the purpose of protecting people(s) from all types of tyranny and crime which may be committed by individuals, groups, governments or states. It is therefore upon the basis of protecting and promoting the principles of brotherhood, equality and justice that the whole philosophy of the Islamic international criminal law is build.

The observation of the principles of Islamic human rights under the Islamic law is a basic legal and moral duty of the political structure of a state.[11] The State should not refuse to fulfil these duties, primarily regulated by the divine law in order to establish the core principles of the Islamic law i.e. brotherhood, equality and justice.[12] Human rights must be respected by every individual and this includes self-inflicted abuses also. It is for this reason that suicide is considered an act against the principles of human rights in Islamic jurisprudence.[13] Political authorities are especially responsible in the fulfilment of Islamic human rights concerning all social conduct under their jurisdiction – including criminal ones.[14] Similar protection is also provided for by the Islamic law for those who have other religions. Thus, Islamic law does not place any restrictions on the freedoms and practices of other groups and minorities. They can fulfil their religious obligations without restrictions.

[11] Publications of Centre Culturel Islamique, p.87.

[12] One of the strongest reasons for this is that Islamic international law is not necessarily a positive law arising from international human rights conventions, the policies of which are based on acceptance, adherence and ratification by states. Although the automatic legal characterization of Islamic international human rights is of significant importance, it does not necessarily mean that Islamic human rights or the system of international human rights are superior or inferior to one another. The former is based on moral-legal autonomy while the latter has a conventional ratified characterization. It is axiomatic that in practice the human rights principles, norms, provisions, rules and other regulations of modern international human rights should be entirely respected and fulfilled by states having been affected by Islamic human rights provisions. For some views on human rights practices in Islamic states see, generally, Mayer, Ann Elizabeth., Islam & Human Rights: Tradition and Politics (London, 1991).

[13] But for exceptional suicide see the *Qur'an*, 22:11-22 'Suicide is unlawful for those people who cannot bear a slight suffering or confusion and commit suicide; that is a great ... sin.' The Glorious Holy Quran, Translated by Jullundri, part 17, p.19, note 15.

[14] But see Warberg, Lasse A., Shari'A: Om den Islamiske Strafferetten (Uqûbât), 80 (4) Nordisk Tidsskrift for Kriminalvidenskab (1993), pp.260-83.

According to the classical practices of Islam, the Islamic state is not only responsible for the fulfilment of its own specific duties but also has a great responsibility for the protection of the life, liberty, property and other social affairs of those who are resident under its jurisdiction.[15] Therefore, if a Muslim state is attacked by belligerent armed forces the state must protect all residents irrespective of their religion, political view, colour, language etc. It must be possible for an alien to benefit from the protection of their state of residence[16] and the state in question must also protect the rights of its minorities. The reason for this is that Islamic human rights strongly advocate equal rights and it makes no difference whether such rights are violated by the majority of the population or by minorities.

[15] The following provisions have been recognized by a number of Islamic jurists (*Ulama*) in 1951 and should be contained within the Constitution of an Islamic State. These principles are considered the Basic Principle of an Islamic State. These are: '...
'Citizens' Rights
7.   The citizens shall be entitled to all the rights conferred upon them by the Islamic *Law i.e.* they shall be assured within the limits of the law, of full security of life, property and honour, freedom of religion and belief, freedom of worship, freedom of person, freedom of expression, freedom of movement, freedom of association, freedom of occupation, equality of opportunity and the right to benefit from public services.
8.   No citizen shall, at any time, be deprived of these rights, except under the law and none shall be awarded any punishment of any charge without being given full opportunity of defence and without the decision of a court of law.
9.   The recognized Muslim schools of thought shall have, within the limits of the law, complete religious freedom. They shall have the right to impart religious instruction to their adherents and the freedom to propagate their views. Matters coming under the purview of Personal Law shall be administrated in accordance with their respective codes of jurisprudence (*fiqh*), and it will be desirable to make provision for the administration of such matters by judges (*Qadis*) belonging to their respective schools of thought.
10.   The non-Moslim citizens of the State shall have, within the limits of the law, complete freedom of religion and worship, mode of life, culture and religious education. They shall be entitled to have all their matters concerning Personal Law administrated in accordance with their own religious code, usages and customs.
11.   All obligations assumed by the State, within the limits of the *Shari'ah*, towards the non-Muslim citizens shall be fully honoured. They shall be entitled equally with the Muslim citizens to the rights of citizenship as enunciated in paragraph 7 above.
12.   The Head of the State shall always be a male Muslim in whose piety, learning and soundness of judgment the people or their elected representatives have confidence.
13.   The responsibility for the administration of the State shall primarily vest in the Head of the State although he may delegate any part of his powers to any individual or body.
...' Appendixed in Maududi, Sayyid Abul A'la., The Islamic Law and Constitution (Islamic Publication Ltd, Lahore, 7th ed. 1980), pp.333-4.
[16] Hamidullah, Muslim Conduct of State, p.128.

2.3. Judicial Criminal Autonomy

The Islamic criminal justice system also provides equal principles of criminal jurisdiction for all individuals irrespective of their social status. These include questions of arbitrary arrest, remand in custody, detention, equality before public hearing, the principle of not guilty until proven otherwise before an impartial criminal jurisdiction and equality in all procedures of prosecution and punishment.[17] However, during a criminal proceeding there may be slight differences in the procedure of the jurisdiction between those who are and those who are not Muslims. The reason for this is that because of the strong faith given to the Islamic philosophy an Islamic court may rely heavily on an oath taken from the accused, while this method is not reliable for those who are

---

[17] According to one writer, 'Islam has also laid down the principle that no citizen can be imprisoned unless his guilt has been proved in an open court. To arrest a man only on the basis of suspicion and to throw him into a prison without proper court proceedings and without providing him a reasonable opportunity to produce his defense is not permissible in Islam. It is related in the *Hadith* that once the Prophet was delivering a lecture in the Mosque, when a man rose during the lecture and said: "O Prophet of God, for what crime have my neighbours been arrested?" The Prophet heard the question and continued his speech. The man rose once again and repeated the same question. The Prophet again did not answer and continued his speech. The man rose for a third time and repeated the same question. Then the Prophet ordered that the man's neighbours be released. The reason why the Prophet had kept quiet when the question was repeated twice earlier was that the police officer was present in the Mosque and if there were proper reasons for the arrest of the neighbours of this man, he would have got up to explain his position. Since the police officer gave no reasons for these arrests the Prophet ordered that the arrested persons should be released. The police officer was aware of the Islamic law and therefore did not get up to say: "the administration is aware of the charges against the arrested men, but they cannot be disclosed in public. If the Prophet would inquire about their guilt *in camera* I would enlighten him." If the police officer had made such a statement, he would have been dismissed then and there. The fact that the police officer did not give any reasons for the arrests in the open court was sufficient reason for the Prophet to give immediate orders for the release of the arrested men. The injunction of the Holy *Quran* is very clear on this point. "Whenever you judge between people, you should judge with (a sense of) justice" (4:58). And the Prophet has also been asked by God: "I have been ordered to dispense justice between you. "This was the reason why the Caliph Umar said: "In Islam no one can be imprisoned except in pursuance of justice." The words used here clearly indicate that justice means due process of law. What has been prohibited and condemned is that a man be arrested and imprisoned without proof of his guilt in an open court and without providing him an opportunity to defend himself against those charges. If the Government suspects that a particular individual has committed a crime or he is likely to commit an offense in the near future then they should give reasons of their suspicion before a court of law and the culprit or the suspect should be allowed to produce his defense in an open court so that the court may decide whether the suspicion against him is based on sound grounds or not and if there is good reason for suspicion, then he should be informed of how long he will be in preventive detention. This decision should be taken under all circumstances in an open court, so that the public may hear the charges brought by the Government, as well as the defense made by the accused and see that the due process of law is being applied to him and he is not being victimized.' Maududi, A., Human Rights in Islam (1977), pp.25–6.

non–Muslim.[18] Nevertheless, there should not be any practical differences between Muslims and non–Muslims under the territorial jurisdictions of Muslim states.[19]

Islamic law provides many rights for the defence procedure. Under the Islamic criminal justice system and according to its theory of 'protected interests', both plaintiff and accused have the right to present evidence.[20] They also have the right to access counsel during pre–trial interrogation, at trial and in the case of conviction at the execution of the sentence.

The right to counsel emanates from the Islamic theory of 'protected interests'.[21] These include and guarantee freedom of religion for all types of religious practitioners in the practice of their beliefs; the right of self preservation and self–protection; freedom of mind including expression of thought, acquisition of education and developing and increasing knowledge; the right to have a family through marriage; and the right to obtain property including movable and immovable property and their preservation and disposition.[22] Needless to say, a person has the right to obtain legal assistance for the protection of their rights. The Islamic criminal justice system penalizes violations of 'protected interests'.[23] This means that the principle of preservation in the Islamic criminal jurisdiction has been given a broader definition. For more clarification:

> The preservation of the self according to Islamic jurists implies the preservation of the right to live with dignity. It includes both the preservation of physical well–being and certain moral aspects such as the maintenance of dignity and the freedom from humiliation. It also includes freedom to work, freedom of conscience and freedom to live where one chooses. It assumes that in a civilized society, liberty is the cornerstone of human life, which in turn

[18] Bassiouni, M. Cherif., Sources of Islamic Law and the Protection of Human Rights in the Islamic Criminal Justice System in Bassiouni (ed.) The Islamic Criminal Justice System (London, Rome, New York, 1982), p.23.

[19] This is in fact one of the basic principles of Islamic international human rights governing the protection of non–Muslims and essentially promotes the principle of equality between all men. The only difference between Muslims and Non–Muslims from the point of view of Islam are philosophical and celestial theories and these should not qualify any nation over another. This significant characteristic of Islam concerning full respect for non–muslims is also stated by the *Qur'an*. Publications of Centre Culturel Islamique (No.1), pp.139 and 143.

[20] Abd–el–Malek al–Saleh, Osman., The Right of the Individual to Personal Security in Islam, in Bassiouni, the Islamic Criminal Justice System, pp.55–90, p.83.

[21] *Id.*

[22] *Id.*

[23] *Id.*

ensures the security of the individual. It is clear that the principle of preservation of self is enhanced by extension of the right to counsel to those accused of crimes, as it provides the accused with the means to establish innocence and to defend himself.[24]

The importance of the principle of preservation especially appears in the Islamic criminal justice system when its norms are examined from the perspective of the Islamic international criminal laws, which basically have universal functions and purposes. This principle can be especially compared with those principles of international human rights which are for the preservation of individual rights and are to be found within certain specific instruments. The relevance of the principles of Islamic international criminal law governing the protection of individuals from unlawful and illegal acts by any type of administration, group, government or state can also be examined by noting a scholarly resolution on the principles of the Islamic criminal justice system of 1979. This resolution presents a number of principles of the Islamic theory and philosophy of justice with respect to the principles of international human rights instruments. According to it, 'Any departure from (the below) ... principles would constitute a serious and grave violation of Shariah Law, international human rights law, and the generally accepted principles of international law reflected in the constitutions and laws of most nations of the world.' The basic principles of the Islamic human rights applicable under the Islamic criminal jurisdiction are *inter alia*:

(1)   the right of freedom from arbitrary arrest, detention, torture, or physical annihilation;

(2)   the right to be presumed innocent until proven guilty by a fair and impartial tribunal in accordance with the Rule of Law;

(3)   the application of the Principle of Legality which calls for the right of the accused to be tried for crimes specified in the Qur'an or other crimes whose clear and well-established meaning and content are determined by Shariah Law (Islamic Law) or by a criminal code in conformity therewith;

(4)   the right to appear before an appropriate tribunal previously established by law;

(5)   the right to a public trial;

(6)   the right not to be compelled to testify against oneself;

(7)   the right to present evidence and to call witnesses in one's defense;

---

[24] *Id.* Footnotes omitted.

(8)   the right to counsel of one's own choosing;
(9)   the right to decision on the merits based upon legally admissible evidence;
(10) the right to have the decision in the case rendered in public;
(11) the right to benefit from the spirit of Mercy and the goals of rehabilitation and resocialization in the consideration of the penalty to be imposed;
      and
(12) the right to appeal.[25]

Strictly speaking the above provisions are not a new innovation in the Islamic system of criminal jurisdiction. They have always existed in the main sources of Islamic law, but have not always been appropriately exercised within the political structure of Islamic states and their constitutions – which have integrated some of the Islamic legal philosophies into their provisions but have exercised them negatively for political purposes.[26]

2.4. Human Rights within the Sunnah

The principles of human rights under the second source of Islamic international criminal law i.e. *Sunnah* have indeed the highest degree of philosophical and human rights jurisprudence documented in the earliest traditions of various

---

[25] For the complete text of the resolution see Bassiouni, pp.249–50.

[26] See, generally, Rosenthal, Franz., The Muslim Concept of Freedom Prior to the Nineteenth Century (Leiden, 1960); Abdul Hakim, Khalifa., Fundamental Human Rights (Lahore, 1952); Ahmad, Muhammed Khalafalla., Islamic Law, Civilization and Human Rights, 12 Egyptian Review of International Law (1956); Anderson, J.N.D., Islamic Law in the Modern World (New York University Press, 1959); Allahdin, Abdullah., Decision by Majority in Islamic Law (Berlin, 1973); Anderson, J.N.D., Law Reform in the Muslim World (London, 1976); Coulson, N.J., Islamic Surveys: A History of Islamic Law (Edinburgh University Press, 1964); Brevli, Mahmud., Islam and the Contemporary Faiths (Karachi, 1965); Mawdudi, Abu'l A'la., Human Rights in Islam (Leicester, 1980); Diwan, Paras., Muslim Law in Modern India (Allahabad, 1977); Macdonald, D.B., Development of Muslim Theology, Jurisprudence, and Constitutional Theory (London, 1903); An–Na`im, Abdullahi., Toward an Islamic Reformation: Civil Liberties, Human Rights and International Law (Syracuse, 1990); An–Na`im, Abdullahi., A modern Approach to Human Rights in Islam: Foundations and Implications for Africa, in Claude Welch and Ronald Meltzer (eds.)., Human Rights and Development in Africa (Albany, 1984). See also Sharwani, Haroon Khan., Studies in Muslim Political Thought and Administration (Lahore, 1959); Shihata, Ibrahim., Islamic Law and the World Community, I, No.4 Harvard International Club Journal (1962); Bonderman, David., Modernization and Changing Perceptions of Islamic Law, 81 Harvard Law Review (1968)), pp.1169–93; Abu Sahlieh's, Sami Aldeeb., Les Droits de l'homme et l'Islam, 89 Revue general de droit international public (1985), 625–716.

nations.[27] These principles of Islamic human rights can be examined and compared with the principles of the Declaration of Human Rights in the system of international law.[28] These principles are specially presented in the 'Farewell Sermon of the Prophet' which provides one of the broadest principles of equality between peoples and eliminates all forms of inequality in the social life of men regardless of race, colour, language, religion, sex, culture, ethnic origin, all types of social position, physical ability or disability and the many superficial inequalities, the types of which have no substantive character in the social value of men.[29]

According to one of the statements of the Prophet:

Now to proceed, O people, listen to me; I would deliver a message to you. For I do not know whether I shall ever get an opportunity to meet you after this year in this place.

So he who has any trust with him he should restore it to the person who deposited it with him.

Be aware, no one committing a crime is responsible for it but himself. Neither son is responsible for the crime of his father nor father is responsible for the crime of his son.

Lo, O people, listen to my words and understand them. You must know that the Muslim is the brother of the Muslim and the Muslims are one brotherhood. Nothing of his brother is lawful for a Muslim except what he himself allows. So you should not oppress yourselves. O Allah, have I conveyed the message? ...

O people, do fear Allah concerning the women. You have taken them with the trust of Allah and you have made their private parts lawful with word of Allah.[30]

...

[27] For some examination see Watt,W. Montgomery., Muhammad, Prophet and Statesman (Oxford, 1961); Mawlawi, Muhammad Ali., The Religion of Islam (Lahore, 1936); Bukhush, Khuda, S., Contribution to the History of Islamic Civilization (Calcutta, 1930).

[28] Abu-Sahlieh, Sami A. Aldeeb., Muslims Human Rights: Challenges and Perspectives, in Schmale, Wolfgang (ed.)., Human Rights and Cultural Diversity: Europe. Arabic-Islamic World. Africa. China (Germany, 1993), pp.239-68, p.243.

[29] See below.

[30] Ubaidul Akbar, Mumtaz-Ul-Muhaddetheen Maulana A.M.G.M. Muhammad., The Orations of Muhammad (The Prophet of Islam, (Lahore, 1972), pp.84-6.

The Farewell Sermon reads that:

> 'O people, listen to my words; verily I do not know, I may not ever meet you after my this year at this place.[31]
>
> Behold, no criminal committing a crime is responsible for it but himself. No son is responsible for the crime of his father and no father is responsible for the crime of his son.
>
> Behold, the Muslim is the brother of the Muslim. So nothing is lawful for a man from his brother except what he gives him willingly. So you should not oppress yourselves. O Allah! have I conveyed? ...
>
> Take care of your slaves; take care of your slaves. Feed them from what you eat and clothe them from what you wear.
>
> If they commit any crime which you do not like to forgive, then sell the bonds of Allah and do not chastise them.
>
> O people, fear Allah; and (even) if a mangled Abyssinian slave becomes your chief hearken to him and obey as long as he executes the Book of Allah.[32] ...
>
> O people, verily your Lord is one and your father is one. All of you belong to Adam and Adam is (made) of earth. Behold, there is no superiority for an Arab over a non–Arab and for a non–Arab over an Arab; nor for a red-coloured over a black–coloured and for a black–skinned over a red–skinned except in piety. Verily the noblest among you is he who is the most pious.[33]
> ...
>
> I recommend you to do good to the First Emigrants and I recommend the Emigrants to do good among themselves.[34] ...
>
> Then he said: 'There may be some rights which I owe to you and I am nothing but a human being. So if there be any man whose honour I have injured a bit, here is my honour; he may retaliate.
>
> Whosoever he may be if I have wounded a bit of his skin, here is my skin; He may retaliate.
>
> Whosoever he may be, if I have taken anything from his property, here is may property; so he may take. Know that he, among you, is more loyal to me who has got such a thing and takes it or absolves me; then I meet my Lord while I am absolved.'[35]

---

[31] *Id.*, p.90.

[32] *Id.*, pp.92–4.

[33] *Id.*, pp.96–7.

[34] *Id.*, p.102.

[35] *Id.*, p.106.

The above principles obviously provide full juridical,theological and human rights support for Muslim and non–Muslim nations in all parts of the world. This is the real method of application of principle of equality for all men regardless of their theoretical, philosophical, theological or political opinions.

Chapter Twenty Three

International Criminal Responsibility

1. The System of International Criminal Law

The principle of international criminal responsibility constitutes one of the most important principles for the implementation and enforcement of the provisions of the system of international criminal law on the perpetrators of international crimes. This principle has been developed and enlarged from numerous international criminal conventions governing the law of armed conflicts and was particularly consolidated by the establishment of the International Military Tribunals after the Second World War and the creation of the United Nations Organization. The Tribunals were mostly effective in developing the concept of the international criminal responsibility of individuals and the prosecution and punishment of perpetrators of war crimes in connection with the Second World War. The legal effect of the law of the Tribunals can be particularly examined in the provisions of a number of international criminal instruments applicable to international crimes.[1]

The principle of international criminal responsibility of individuals is rather controversial when there is a question of superior order or the plea of superior order for individuals to evade prosecution and punishment. This is one of the reasons that the perpetrators of international crimes have normally been successful in avoiding the application of criminal sanctions. However, the International Criminal Tribunals after the Second World War strongly rejected the plea of superior order in order to escape prosecution and punishment.

---

[1] To note only a few: the Geneva Convention for the Amelioration of the Condition of the Wounded and Sick in Armed Forces in the Field, 12 August 1949, the Geneva Convention Relative to the Treatment of Prisoners of War, 12 August 1949, the Geneva Convention Relative to the Protection of Civilian Persons in Time of War, 12 August 1949, Protocol I Additional to the Geneva Conventions of 12 August 1949, 12 December 1977, Protocol II Additional to the Geneva Conventions of 12 August 1949, 12 December 1977, the Convention on the Prevention and Punishment of the Crime of Genocide, 9 December 1948, the International Convention on the Elimination of All Forms of Racial Discrimination, 7 March 1966, the International Convention on the Suppression and Punishment of the Crime of Apartheid, 30 November 1973 and the United Nations Convention on the Rights of Child, 20 November 1989.

Consequently a perpetrator of international crime cannot free himself from the application of criminal sanctions by reasoning that he has acted due to a superior order or government command. It is for this reason that all individuals bear a heavy criminal responsibility for any violation of the principles of international criminal law.

The principle of international criminal responsibility of individuals is originally based on the assumption that individuals are the most essential characters in the commission of international crimes and therefore liable to prosecution and punishment and this is regardless of their official position and includes heads of states and governments. Thus, in the system of international criminal law by the term 'international criminal responsibility of individuals' we mean all those who have participated in one way or another in the commission of certain acts constituting international crimes.

This principle also extends in certain circumstances to the concept of criminal responsibility of organizations and states. It is on the grounds of this legal extension that the 1973 Convention on Apartheid recognized the concept of criminal responsibility of Organizations involved in criminal activities constituting apartheid.

The principle of criminal responsibility in international criminal law is more controversial when attributed to states in cases of the commission of international crimes. The notion of international criminal responsibility of states has essentially developed since the early 1920's alongside the concept of criminal responsibility of individuals in international criminal law. The notion has been particularly extended by the work of the International Law Commission on the general subject of international responsibility of states and Article 19 on 'the International crimes and international delicts' of the Draft Articles on International Responsibility of States.

It is however important to emphasize that the principle of international criminal responsibility of individuals, organizations and states, because of a lack of juridical and political agreements, has rarely been employed in the system of international criminal law. Other factors such as the reluctance of states to yield their legal power to the jurisdiction of other states have also been effective in the non−implementation and non−enforcement of the provisions of the system of international criminal law.[2] This is one of the basic reasons why a great

---

[2] A report from the World Conference on the Establishment of an International Criminal Tribunal to Enforce International Criminal Law and Human Rights points out the following factors for the lack of establishment of an international criminal court. These are: '(a) Continuing conflict between national interests; (b) The reluctance of states to yield any part of their sovereignty; (c) Chauvinism in regarding one's own national laws as superior; (d) The dangers inherent in the establishment of yet another international bureaucracy with possibly minimum benefits to the world community; (e) The difficulty in agreeing on the subject−matter jurisdiction

number of international criminals have escaped from prosecution and punishment and there is not yet any international juridical organ or an international criminal court capable of bringing the perpetrators of international crimes under an effective criminal jurisdiction.[3]

2. Islamic International Criminal Law

2.1. The General Concept

The concept of responsibility in Islamic law is by itself a separate institution. This is because the provisions of Islamic law cannot properly be enforced without the concept of responsibility upon its subjects. Thus, responsibility in Islamic law constitutes the core principle of the implementation and application of the principles of Islamic jurisdiction. Islamic law recognizes various types of responsibility for its subjects including moral, civil, contractual, brotherhood, family, neighbourhood, social, economic, taxation, international or universal and criminal responsibility. The concept for all these types of responsibilities is essentially based on breaches of the Islamic code of behaviour.

Islamic law attributes the concept of criminal responsibility to individuals and therefore recognizes the responsibility of the offender according to their intentional or deliberate abuse of the freedom of choice in their social or international conduct.[4] It is upon this theory that Islamic law rejects any other

of an international tribunal; (f) Concerns about the selection of an international judiciary; (g) The conflict of an international system of criminal justice with national jurisdictions; (h) The remoteness of an international criminal justice system from the peoples of the world; (i) The difficulty of agreeing on a general part; (j) The difficulty of agreeing on procedural rules; (K) The role which individual states should play in the international criminal justice process; (l) The problem of invoking (initiating) the international criminal justice process; (m) The cost to the international community; (n) The lack of enforcement power of an international criminal tribunal, and above all, (o) The concern that the International Criminal Court might dispense 'victor's justice." World Conference on the Establishment of an International Criminal Tribunal to Enforce International Criminal Law and Human Rights, in Cooperation with the United Nations, A Satellite Conference to the 1993 World Human Rights Conference, Siracusa, December 2-5, 1992, 49 pp., p. 6.

[3] The commission of serious international crimes, especially the international crimes of genocide, crimes against humanity, war crimes and torture in the former Yugoslavia against the Muslim nationals by Serbians are an effective reason for the establishment of a temporary international criminal tribunal for the prosecution and punishment of the perpetrators of international crimes. Such a tribunal will no doubt be established in the near future.

[4] Moreover, 'The concept of personal responsibility is associated with the principle of equality and uniformity in punishment. It is a fundamental Islamic belief that every adult offender is responsible and should be punished for his crime. Moreover, penalties are to be inflicted equally

opinions regarding the concept of criminal responsibility of individuals. For example, one of the chief differences between the Islamic concept of criminal responsibility and other criminal systems has been that Islamic jurisprudence totally contradicts the opinions of those earlier European writers who advocated that certain persons may habitually commit crimes and are therefore 'born criminals.' Such an assumption is totally rejected by the Islamic jurisprudence of criminal law and according to it all crimes are essentially avoidable and not inevitable whether committed socially, generally or in the international conduct of individuals. In other words, the soul spirit of all individuals is free of sin and sin is the result of the actual conduct of a person in his/her temporary life and is not therefore substantive in the spirit of man.

It must however be added that Islamic law places much emphasis on the philosophical and spiritual idea that God is aware of the nature of man including his will, thoughts and desires and therefore God knows the fate of man. In spite of all this, it is still the person alone who decides their destiny, actions, will, good deeds and evil deeds. The reason for this is that an individual generally has the capacity of thinking, choosing and understanding. God has given man the ability to be good and do good and whatever action a person may therefore take is their own desire and choice, although God is already omniscient of all actions during a lifespan; God is omnipotent.

The concept of criminal responsibility in Islamic law may be mitigated or even deleted under certain circumstances. This is when an action by a person is carried out without deliberation or unintentionally and the principle of freedom of choice is lacking in those actions. This includes such conditions as duress, immaturity and mental disability including insanity. In these cases the concept of criminal responsibility cannot be attributed to an accused who has unintentionally violated the law. However, in the cases of disability a guardian may be accountable before the Islamic criminal jurisdiction.

2.2. International Aspects

The concept of criminal responsibility of individuals in the system of Islamic international criminal law is more or less similar to the concept of criminal responsibility in positive international criminal law. This is because Islamic international criminal law bases the concept of criminal responsibility of persons on the element of intention and consequently intention constitutes one of the

on all, regardless of distinctive characteristics such as race, religion, colour sex, language, ethnic background or social class.' Lippman, Matthew, Sean McConville, and Mordechai Yerushalmi., *Islamic Criminal Law and Procedure*, p.81.

essential elements for the imputation of the concept of criminal responsibility to the perpetrators of international crimes. Unintentional acts are not therefore classified under the concept of responsibility. For example, in time of war 'Muslim soldiers have to take care that they do not fire directly on neutrals, women and minors and other non-combatants, yet if any damage is done to them unintentionally, no responsibility is to be placed on the Muslim army.'[5]

In Islamic international criminal law only the perpetrators of international crimes bear the concept of international criminal responsibility and this responsibility is applicable to all persons who participate in the commission of international crimes regardless of their legal and political position within the state system. Some of these international crimes involving the concept of international criminal responsibility of individuals for violations of Islamic provisions of international criminal law include war crimes, crimes against humanity, mass killing or systematic destruction (genocide), drug offences and involvement in activities concerning obscene materials.[6]

One important point in the application of international criminal responsibility under Islamic international criminal law is that violated legal provisions must be *de lege lata* and in all aspects of criminal jurisdiction the principle of legality must always be respected by judges.[7] This is an important point in the protection of the criminally accused before the process of any criminal jurisdiction.

It must be emphasized that since all international crimes in Islamic international criminal law are treated under the principle of universality, because of their effects on mankind, all Muslim states are (according to the Islamic principles) authorized to prosecute and punish the perpetrators of international crimes which have come under their jurisdiction. This theory may not be respected however by Islamic states in practice on the grounds of political considerations. The consolidation of the theory is nevertheless a fact under the Islamic jurisprudence of law. The theory is originally based on the assumption that all Muslim states are equal before divine law and that a serious violation of Islamic international criminal law can be regarded as a serious violation against all Muslims. In contrast to this, in the system of international criminal law all international crimes cannot be treated at the present time under the principle of universality and there are only a few international crimes which are considered crimes against mankind and treated with the universality

---

[5] Hamidullah, Muslim Conduct of State, p.194.

[6] For an examination of these international crimes under the system of Islamic international criminal law see the relevant chapters.

[7] See chapter one.

principle. These are such crimes as piracy, war crimes, genocide and narcotic offences.

2.3. Superior Order

Islamic international criminal law has basically promoted the concept of fear and appropriate justice in relations between superior or higher officials and others who come under their supervision. For example, the earlier practice of Islamic international criminal law provided full instruction concerning the decisions of commanders in the course of war. It requested that they should, in all situations, fulfil the humanitarian provisions of Islamic international criminal law and fear God regarding the treatment of those who accompany them. Some of these instructions can be found in the second source of Islamic law i.e. the *Sunnah* or exclusively in the traditions of the Prophet of Islam. Their provisions may adapt themselves to the circumstances of the present time governing the activities of superiors and the treatment of those who are at war with Muslims. According to one instruction by the Prophet, 'Fight ye all in the path of God and combat those who do not believe in God. Yet never commit breach of trust nor treachery nor mutilate anybody nor kill any minor or woman. This is the pact of God and the conduct of His Messenger for your guidance.'[8] This type of significant instruction by Muhammad the Prophet of Islam to commanders, superiors or high ranking officials of armed forces or government departments continued during his lifespan and can now be regarded one of the chief reasons for the promotion of Islamic humanitarian regulations during armed conflicts.

The successors of the Prophet commanded the high ranking officials or superiors of armed forces to 'remember... 'Souvenez-vous, disait-il à ses généraux, que vous êtes toujours sous les regards de Dieu et à la veille de la mort; que vous rendrez compte au dernier jour ... Lorsque vous combattrez pour la gloire de Dieu, conduisez-vous comme des hommes, sans tourner le dos, mais que le sang des femmes, ou de celui des enfants et des vieillards, ne souille pas votre victoire. Ne détruisez pas les palmiers, ne brûlez pas les habitations, les champs de blé, n'abattez jamais les arbres fruitiers, et ne tuez le bétail que lorsque vous serez contraints de le manger. Quand vous accordez un traité ou une capitulation, ayez soin d'en remplir les clauses. A mesure que vous avancerez, vous rencontrerez des personnes religieuses qui vivent dans des monastères (moines) et qui servent Dieu dans la retraite: laissez-les seuls, ne

---

[8] Hamidullah, Muslim Conduct of State, p.299.

les tuez point, et ne détruisez pas leurs monastères...[9],[10]

The model of instructions for commanders must be read in conjunction with chapter four, which lists the prohibited acts during an armed conflict and recognizes their violations as constituting war crimes and giving rise to the concept of international criminal responsibility of the perpetrators. This means that the activities of high ranking officials are limited during war and must conform to the humanitarian principles of Islamic international criminal law. It also means that a person acted pursuant to an order of a superior does not relieve him of criminal responsibility for the violation of the law of armed conflicts.

In a comparative analogy the provisions of Islamic international criminal law concerning the limitation of the scope of activities of superiors and the system of international criminal law are parallel and the scope of their applicability may, in many aspects, overlap each others provisions.

---

[9] 'Siyer. t. I, pp.30–38; – Ockley, La Conquête de la Syrie, de la Perse et de l'Egypte par les Sarrasins, t.I, p.22–27, etc.; Gibbon, The Decline and fall of the Roman Empire, trad. france. Buchon, Paris, 1837), Vol.II, p.449.'

[10] Quoted in Rechid, L'Islam et le Droit des Gens, pp.451–2.

Chapter Twenty Four

Comparative Conclusions

An examination of the preceding chapters proves that Islamic international criminal law is a very flexible law and its rules and provisions are undoubtedly adaptable to the provisions of the modern system of international criminal law arising from a great number of international criminal conventions applicable to international crimes. The scope of Islamic international criminal law is characterized under the principle of *nulla poena sine lege* or *nullum crimen sine lege*.

Undoubtedly a brief examination of the system of international criminal law and Islamic international criminal law demonstrates that both systems have certain consolidated principles, rules and regulations prohibiting a number of acts in national and international conflicts and recognizing their commission as constituting international crimes. In most instances the provisions of conventions such as genocide, apartheid and those on the law of armed conflicts overlap with the provisions of Islamic international criminal law. The Islamic law has in principle prohibited mass killing or genocide. It has recognized that it is against its basic principles to discriminate on the basis of race, language, ethnic origin or political view – including apartheid. It has also criminalized the commission of certain acts during armed conflicts. In the modern system of law these are called war crimes. One of the chief differences between these two systems is the category of international crime called crimes against humanity, as specified in the Charter of the International Military Tribunal. This is because Islamic international criminal law does not distinguish (as does the system of international criminal law slightly) between two categories of international crimes, namely crimes against humanity and war crimes. The reason for this is that in Islamic international criminal law both concepts define the same criminal conduct more or less to the same extent. According to Islamic law all men are considered an integral part of one family unit and therefore the commission of any crime is considered a crime against family unity and a crime against humanity.

The relevant provisions of Islamic international criminal law especially overlap with those provisions of the 1977 Protocols governing the international humanitarian law of armed conflicts. One of the serious differences between these two legal systems is that the rules and provisions of Islamic international criminal law applicable to armed conflicts have the character of universal international criminal law, in contrast to this most of the rules of the system of international criminal law applicable to the law of armed conflicts must be accepted by the positive contribution of all states involved. This means that states must ratify the relevant conventions on the law of war. Although we cannot deny that the relevant rules of the system of international criminal law have the character of customary international criminal law and must therefore be respected by all states, this statement has proven controversial as long as certain practices in international criminal jurisdictions do not exist confirming this fact. According to the philosophy of Islam the rules of the Islamic international criminal law are by themselves the expression of the positive law and therefore do not need to be ratified in relations between states. This philosophy is based on the universality of divine law. This must be respected at all times irrespective of whether a conflict is between Muslims or non-Muslims. This philosophy also arises from the assumption that all man must respect certain rules in the course of war in order to mitigate the horrors of war and make it more humane.

The chief principles of both systems in their recognition of international crimes emanate from considerations concerning the core principles of criminal law, including legalization, prosecution and penalization of certain criminal conducts. With the difference that the criminalization of certain acts in the Islamic international criminal law arise from divine law, whereas penalization in the system of international criminal law arises from customary and conventional law. Nevertheless, these differences cannot effect or diminish the values common to both systems towards the promotion of mutual aims.

Appendixes

Universal Islamic
Declaration of Human Rights

Islamic Council
19 September 1981

Preamble

Whereas the age-old human aspiration for a just world order wherein people could live, develop and prosper in an environment free from fear, oppression, exploitation and deprivation, remains largely unfulfilled;

Whereas the Divine Mercy unto mankind reflect in its having been endowed with super-abundant economic sustenance is being wanted, or unfairly or unjustly withheld from the inhabitants of the earth;

Whereas Allah has given mankind through His revelations in the Holy Qur'an and the *Sunnah* His of his Blessed Prophet Mohammad and abiding legal and moral framework within which to establish and regulate human institutions and relationships;

Whereas the human rights decreed by the Divine law aim at conferring dignity and honour on mankind and are designed to eliminate oppression and injustice;

Whereas by virtue of their Divine source and sanction these rights can neither be curtailed, abrogated nor disregarded by authorities, assemblies or other institutions, nor can they be surrendered or alienated;

Therefore we, as Muslims, who believe
- (a) in God, the Beneficent and Merciful, the Creator, the Sustainer, the Sovereign, the sole Guide of mankind and the Source of all Law;
- (b) in the Vicegerency (Khilafah) of man who has been created to fulfil the Will of God on earth;
- (c) in the wisdom of divine guidance brought by the Prophets, whose mission found its culmination in the final Divine message that was conveyed by the Prophet Mohammad (Peace be upon him) to all mankind;
- (d) that rationality by itself without the light of revelation from God can

neither be a sure guide in the affairs of mankind nor provide spiritual nourishment to the human soul, and knowing that the teachings of Islam represent the quintessence of Divine guidance in its final and perfect form, feel duty–bound to remind man of the high status and dignity bestowed on him by God;

(e)   in inviting all mankind to the message of Islam;

(f)   that by the terms of our primeval covenant with God, our duties and obligations have priority over our rights, and that each one of us is under a bounden duty to spread the teachings of Islam by word, deed, and indeed in all gentle ways, and to make them effective not only in our individual lives but also in the society around us;

(g)   in our obligation to establish an Islamic order;

  (i)   wherein all human beings shall be equal and none shall enjoy a privilege or suffer a disadvantage or discrimination by reason of race, colour, sex, origin or language;

  (ii)   wherein all human beings are born free;

  (iii) Wherein slavery and forced labour are abhorred;

  (iv)   wherein conditions shall be established such that the institution of family shall be preserved, protected and honoured as the basis of all social life;

  (v)   wherein the rulers and the ruled alike are subject to, and equal before, the Law;

  (vi)   wherein obedience shall be rendered only to those commands that are in consonance with the Law;

  (vii) wherein all worldly power shall be considered as a sacred trust, to be exercised within the limits prescribed by the Law and in a manner approved by it, and with due regard for the priorities fixed by it;

  (viii) wherein all economic resources shall be treated as Divine blessings bestowed upon mankind, to be enjoyed by all in accordance with the rules and the values set out in the Qur'an and the *Sunnah*;

  (ix)   wherein all public affairs shall be determined and conducted, and the authority to administer them shall be exercised after mutual consultation (*Shura*) between the believers qualified to contribute to a decision which would accord well with the Law and the public good;

  (x)   wherein everyone shall undertake obligations proportionate to his capacity and shall be held responsible pro rata for his deeds;

  (xi)   wherein everyone shall, in case of an infringement of his rights, be assured of appropriate remedial measures in accordance with the Law;

(xii) wherein no one shall be deprived of the rights assured to him by the Law except by its authority and to the extend permitted by it;

(xiii) wherein every individual shall have the right to bring legal action against anyone who commits a crime against society as a whole or against any of its members;

(xiv) wherein every effort shall be made to

    (a) secure into mankind deliverance from every type of exploitation, injustice and oppression.

    (b) ensure to everyone security, dignity and liberty in terms set out and by methods approved and within the limits set by the Law;

    Do hereby, as servants of Allah and as members of the Universal Brotherhood of Islam, at the beginning of the Fifteenth century of the Islamic Era, affirm our commitment to uphold the following inviolable and inalienable human rights that we consider are enjoined by Islam.

I. Right to Life

(a) Human life is scared and inviolable and every effort shall be made to protect it. In particular no one shall be exposed to injury or death, except under the authority of the Law.

(b) Just as in life, so also after death, the sanctity of a person's body shall be inviolable. It is the obligation of believers to see that a deceased person's body is handled with due solemnity.

II. Right to Freedom

(a) Man is born free. No inroads shall be made on his right to liberty except under the authority and in due process of the Law.

(b) Every individual and every people has the inalienable right to freedom in all its forms – physical, cultural, economic and political – and shall be entitled to struggle by all available means against any infringement or abrogation of this right; and every oppressed individual or people has a legitimate claim to the support of other individuals and/or peoples in such a struggle.

III. Right to Equality and Prohibition Against Impermissible Discrimination

(a) All persons are equal before the Law and are entitled to equal opportunities and protection of the Law.

(b) All persons shall be entitled to equal wage for equal work.

(c) No person shall be denied the opportunity to work or be discriminated against in any manner or exposed to greater physical risk by reason of religious belief, colour, race, origin, sex, or language.

IV. Right to Justice

(a) Every person has the right to be treated in accordance with the Law, and only in accordance with the Law.

(b) Every person has not only the right but also the obligation to protest against injustice; to recourse to remedies provided by the Law in respect of any unwarranted personal injury or loss; to self-defence against any charges that are preferred against him and to obtain fair adjudication before an independent judicial tribunal in any dispute with public authorities or any other person.

(c) It is the right and duty of every person to defend the rights of any other person and the community in general (*Hisbah*).

(d) No person shall be discriminated against while seeking to defend private and public rights.

(e) It is the right and duty of every Muslim to refuse to obey any command which is contrary to the Law, no matter by whom it may be issued.

V. Right to fair Trial

(a) No person shall be adjudged guilty of an offence and made liable to punishment except after proof of his guilt before an independent juridical tribunal.

(b) No person shall be adjudged guilty except after a fair trial and after reasonable opportunity for defence has been provided to him.

(c) Punishment shall be awarded in accordance with the Law, in proportion to the seriousness of the offence and with due consideration of the circumstances under which it was committed.

(d) No act shall be considered a crime unless it is stipulated as such in the clear wording of the Law.

(e) Every individual is responsible for his actions. Responsibility for a crime cannot be vicariously extended to other members of his family or group, who are not otherwise directly or indirectly involved in the commission of the crime in question.

VI. Right to Protection Against Abuse of Power

Every person has the right to protection against harassment by official agencies. He is not liable to account for himself except for mankind a defence to the charges made against him or where he is found in a situation wherein a question regarding suspicion of his involvement in a crime could be *reasonably* raised.

VII. Right to Protection Against Torture

No person shall be subject to torture in mind or body, or degraded, or threatened with injury either to himself or to anyone related to or held dear by him, or forcibly made to confess to the commission of a crime, or forced to consent to an act which is injurious to his interests.

VIII. Right to Protection of Honour and Reputation

Every Person has the right to protect his honour and reputation against calumnies, groundless charges or deliberate attempts at defamation and blackmail.

IX. Right to Asylum

(a) Every persecuted or oppressed person has the right to seek refuge and asylum. This right is guaranteed to every human being irrespective of race, religion, colour and sex.

(b) *Al Masjid Al Haram* (the sacred house of Allah) in Mecca is a sanctuary for all Muslims.

X. Rights of Minorities

(a) The Qur'anic principle 'There is no compulsion in religion' shall govern the religious rights of non–Muslim minorities.

(b) In a Muslim country, religious minorities shall have the choice to be governed in respect of their civil and personal matters by Islamic Law or by their own laws.

XI. Right and Obligation to Participate in the Conduct and Management of Public Affairs

(a) Subject to the Law, every individual in the community *(Ummah)* is entitled to assume public office.

(b) Process of free consultation *(Shura)* is the basis of the administrative relationship between the government and the people. People also have the right to choose and remove their rulers in accordance with this principle.

XII. Right to Freedom of Belief, Thought and Speech

(a) Every person has the right to express his thoughts and beliefs so long as he remains within the limits prescribed by the Law. No one, however is entitled to disseminate falsehood or to circulate reports which may outrage public decency, or to indulge in slander, innuendo or to cast defamatory aspersions on other persons.

(b) Pursuit of knowledge and search after truth is not only a right but a duty of every Muslim.

(c)   It is the right and duty of every Muslim to protest and strive (within the limits set out by the Law) against oppression even if it involves challenging the highest authority in the State.

(d)   There shall be no bar on the dissemination of information provided it does not endanger the security of the society or the State and is confined within the limits imposed by the Law.

(e)   No one shall hold in contempt or ridicule the religious beliefs of others or incite public hostility against them; respect for the religious feelings of others is obligatory on all Muslims.

XIII. Right to Freedom of Religion

Every person has the right to freedom of conscience and worship in accordance with his religious beliefs.

XIV. Right to Free Association

(a)   Every person is entitled to participate individually and collectively in the religious, social cultural and political life of his community and to establish institutions and agencies meant to enjoin what is right (*ma'roof*) and to prevent what is wrong (*munkar*).

(b)   Every person is entitled to strive for the establishment of institutions whereunder an enjoyment of these rights would be made possible. Collectively, the community is obliged to establish conditions so as to allow its members full development of their personalities.

XV. The Economic Order and the Rights Evolving Therefrom

(a)   In their economic pursuits, all persons are entitled to the full benefits of nature and all its resources. These are blessings bestowed by God for the benefit of mankind as a whole.

(b)   All human beings are entitled to earn their living according to the Law.

(c)   Every person is entitled to own property individually or in association with others. State ownership of certain economic resources in the public interest is legitimate.

(d)   The poor have the right to a prescribed share in the wealth of the rich, as fixed by *Zakah*, levied and collected in accordance with the Law.

(e)   All means of production shall be utilised in the interest of the community (*Ummah*) as a whole, and may not be neglected or misused.

(f)   In order to promote the development of a balanced economy and to protect society from exploitation, Islamic Law forbids monopolies, unreasonable restrictive trade practices, usury, the use of coercion in the making of contracts and the publication of misleading advertisements.

(g) All economic activities are permitted provided they are not detrimental to the interests of the community (*Ummah*) and do not violate Islamic laws and values.

XVI. Right to Protection of Property

No property may be expropriated except in the public interest and on payment of fair and adequate compensation.

XVII. Status and Dignity of Workers

Islam honours work and the workers and enjoins Muslims not only to treat the workers justly but also generously. He is not only to be paid his earned wages promptly, but is also entitled to adequate rest and leisure.

XVIII. Right to social Security

Every person has the right to food, shelter, clothing, education and medical care consistent with the resources of the community. This obligation of the community extends in particular to all individuals who cannot take care of themselves owing to some temporary or permanent disability.

XIX. Right to Found a Family and Related Matters

(a) Every person is entitled to marry, to found a family and to bring up children in conformity with his religion, traditions, and culture. Every spouse is entitled to such rights and privileges and carries such obligations as are stipulated by the Law.

(b) Each of the partners in a marriage is entitled to respect and consideration from the other.

(c) Every husband is obliged to maintain his wife and children according to his means.

(d) Every child has the right to be maintained and property brought up by its parents, it being forbidden that children are made to work at an early age or that any burden is put on them which would arrest or harm their natural development.

(e) If parents are for some reasons unable to discharge their obligations towards a child, it becomes the responsibility of the community to fulfil these obligations at public expense.

(f) Every person is entitled to material support, as well as care and protection, from his family during his childhood, old age or incapacity. Parents are entitled to material support as well as care and protection from their children.

(g) Motherhood is entitled to special respect, care and assistance on the part of the family and the public organs of the community (*Ummah*).

(h) Within the family, men and women are to share in their obligations and responsibilities according to their sex, their natural endowments, talents and inclinations, bearing in mind their common responsibilities towards their progeny and their relatives.

(i) No person may be married against his or her will, or loss or suffer diminution of legal personality on account of marriage.

XX Rights of Married Women

Every married women is entitled to:

(a) live in the house in which her husband lives;

(b) receive the means necessary for maintaining a standard of living which is not inferior to that of her spouse, and, in the event of divorce, receive during the statutory period of waiting *(Iddah)* means of maintenance commensurate with her husband's resources, for herself as well as for the children she nurses or keeps, irrespective of her own financial status, earnings, or property that she may hold in her own right;

(c) seek and obtain dissolution of marriage *(Khul'a)* in accordance with the terms of the Law. This right is in addition to her right to seek divorce through the courts;

(d) inherit from her husband, her parents, her children and other relatives according to the Law;

(e) strict confidentiality from her spouse, or ex-spouse if divorced, with regard to any information that he may have obtained about her, the disclosure of which could prove detrimental to her interests. A similar responsibility rests upon her in respect of her spouse or ex-spouse.

XXI. Right to Education

(a) Every person is entitled to receive education in accordance with his natural capabilities.

(b) Every person is entitled to a free choice of profession and career and to the opportunity for the full development of his natural endowments.

XXII. Right of Privacy

Every person is entitled to the protection of his privacy.

XXIII. Right to Freedom of Movement and Residence

(a) In view of the fact that the World of Islam is veritably *Ummah Islamia*, every Muslim shall have the right to move freely in and out of any Muslim country.

(b) No one shall be forced to leave the country of his residence, or be arbitrary deported therefrom, without recourse to due process of law.

Explanatory Notes

1. In the above formulation of Human Rights, unless the context provides otherwise:

(a) the term 'person' refers to both the male and female sexes.

(b) the term 'Law' denotes the *Shari'ah*, *i.e.* the totality of ordinances derived from the Qur'an and the *Sunnah* and any other laws that are deduced from these two sources by methods considered valid in Islamic jurisprudence.

2. Each one of the Human Rights enunciated in this Declaration carries a corresponding duty.

3. In the exercise and enjoyment of the rights referred to above, every person shall be subject only to such limitations as are enjoined by the law for the purpose of securing the due recognition of, and respect for, the rights and the freedom of others and of meeting the just requirements of morality, public order and the general welfare of the Community *(Ummah)*.

4. The Arabic text of this Declaration is the original.

Glossary of Arabic Terms

Sunnah	The example or way of life of the Prophet (peace be upon him), embracing what he said, did or agree to.
Khilafah	The vicegerency of man on earth or succession to the Prophet, transliterated into English as the Caliphate.
Hisbah	Public vigilance, an institution of the Islamic State enjoined to observe and facilitate the fulfilment of right norms of public behaviour. The *Hisbah* consists in public vigilance as well as an opportunity to private individuals to seek redress through it.
Ma'roof	Good act.
Munkar	Reprehensible deed.
Zakah	The 'purifying' tax on wealth, one of the five pillars of Islam obligatory on Muslims.
Iddah	The waiting period of a widowed or divorced women during which she is not to re-marry.
Khul'a	Divorce a women obtains at her own request.
Ummah Islamia	World Muslim community.
Shari'ah	Islamic law.

Bibliography on Islamic Law[*]

Abd-el-Malek al-Saleh, Osman., The Right of the Individual to Personal Security in Islam, see Bassiouni, pp.55-90.

Abdul Hakim, Khalifa., Fundamental Human Rights (Lahore, 1952).

– – The Natural Law in the Moslem Tradition, 5 Natural Law Institute Proceeedings (1951).

Abul-Fazl, M., Sayings of the Prophet Muhammad (New Delhi, 1980).

Aghnides, Nicolas P., Mohammedan Theories of Finance with an Intorduction to Mohammedan Law and a Bibliography (Columbia University, New York, London, 1916).

El-Ahdab, Abdul Hamid., Arbitration with the Arab Countries (Denver, Boston, 1990).

Ahmad, Muhammed Khalafalla., Islamic Law, Civilization and Human Rights, 12 Egyptian Review of International Law (1956).

Ali, Maulana Muhammad., Muhammad the Prophet (Lahore, 1924).

– – The Call of Islam, 2nd ed. (Lahore, 1926).

– – Back to the Qur'an, Back to Muhammad, Rise! Advance! (Lahore, 1926).

Ali, Maulvi Muhammad., Islam the Religion of Humanity (1926).

Ali, Muhammad., Islam or the Natural Religion of Man: A Brief Sketch of Its Principles as given in the Holy Quran (Lahore, 1912).

– – A brief Sketch of the Life of the Prophet of Islam (Lahore, 1928).

Ali, S. A., The Spirit of Islam (London, 1896, second publication Delhi 1981).

– – The Ethics of Islam (Calcutta, 1893).

Allahdin, Abdullah., Extracts from the Holy Quran and Sayings of the Holy Prophet Mohammad, 7th ed. (India, 1933).

Al-Amir, Muhammad., Kitab al-Iklil Sharh Muktasar Khalil (Cairo, A.H. 1224).

Al-'Awwa, Muhammad Salim., The Basis of Islamic Penal Legislation, in Bassiouni, pp.127-47.

Anderson, J.N.D., Islamic Law in the Modern World (New York University Press, 1959).

– – Decision by Majority in Islamic Law (Berlin, 1973).

– – Law Reform in the Muslim World (London, 1976).

Arabi, Abdel Rahman, L'Islam et la guerre à l'Epoque du Prophète Mahomet

---

[*] It must be clarified that the references and bibliography, due to the profound development and evolution of Islamic law, are far from being exhausted.

(Ambilly, 1954).

Arkoun, Mohammad., The Death Penalty and Torture in Islamic Thought in Bockle and Pohier, pp.75–82.

Armanazi, Najib., Les Principes Islamiques et les Rapports Internationaux en Temps de Paix et de Guerre (Paris, 1929).

Arnold, Sir T.W., The Peaching of Islam (London, 1913).

Ubaidul Akbar, Mumtaz–Ul–Muhaddetheen Maulana A.M.G.M. Muhammad., The Orations of Muhammad (The Prophet of Islam, (Lahore, 1972).

Azami, M.M., Studies in Hadith Methodology and Literature (Indianapolis, 1977).

– – Studies in Early Hadith Literature (Indianapolis, 1978).

Bassiouni, M. Cherif (ed.), The Islamic Criminal Justice System (London, Rome, New York, 1982).

– – Sources of Islamic Law, and the Protection of Human Rights in the Islamic Criminal Justice System, see Bassiouni, pp.3–53.

– – Islam: Concept, Law and Word Habeas Corpus, 2 Rutgers Camden Law Journal (1970).

– – Protection of Diplomats under Islamic Law, 74 American Journal of International Law (1980), pp.609–33.

Bell, Richard., Introduction to the Qur'an (Edinburgh University Press, 1953).

Bockle, F. and Pohier, J. (ed.)., The Death Penalty and Torture (New York, 1979).

Bosworth–Smith, R., Mohammed and Mohammedanism (London, 1889).

Brevli, Mahmud., Islam and the Contemporary Faiths (Karachi, 1965).

Bryce, J., Studies in History and Jurisprudence, Vol.2 (Oxford, 1901).

Bukhush, Khuda, S., Contribution to the History of Islamic Civilization (Calcutta, 1930).

Chiragh, Ali, A Critical Exposition of the Popular Jihad (1885).

Cheragh Ali., A Critical Exposition of the Popular Jihad (Calcutta, 1988).

Coulson, N.J., Islamic Surveys: A History of Islamic Law (Edinburgh University Press, 1964).

– – Conflict and Tensions in Islamic Jurisprudence (University of Chicago Press, 1969).

– – The State and the Individual in Islamic Law, 6 International and Comparative Law Quarterly (1957).

Diwan, Paras., Muslim Law in Modern India (Allahabad, 1977).

Donnelly, J., Human Rights and Human Dignity: An Analytic Critique of Non–Western Conceptions of Human Rights, 76 American Political Science Review (1982).

Fyzee, A.A.A., Outlines of Muhammadan Law (London, 1955).

Al–Ghunaimi, Mohammad, Talaat., The Muslim Conception of International

Law and Western Approach ((Netherlands, 1968).

The Glorious Holy Quran, Translated by Jullundri, L.A.A.K., (Pakistan, 1962).

Guillaume, Alfred., The Traditions of Islam: An Introduction to the Study of the Hadith Literature (Oxford, 1924).

- - The Summa Philosophiae of Al-Shahrastani, Kitab Nihayatu 'L-Iqdam fi `Ilmi 'L-Kalam, edited with a translation from manuscripts in the Libraries of Oxford, Paris and _Berlin (Oxford University Press, London, 1934).

- - New Light on the Life of Muhammad, Monograph 1 Journal of Semitic Studies (Manchester University Press, 1960).

Hamidullah, Muhammad., The Battlefields of the Prophet Muhammad (England, 1953).

- - Muslim Conduct of State (Lahore - India, 1945).

- - Le Prophète de l'Islam (Paris, 1959), Vols.I-II.

- - See also Publications of Centre Culturel Islamique.

- - The First Written Constitution in the World, 2nd. edn. (Lahore, 1968).

Hamilton, Charles., The Hedaya, or A Commentary on the Mussulman Laws (London, 1791).

Hasan, Ahmad., Analogical Reasoning in Islamic Jurisprudence - A Study of the Juridical Principle of Qiyas (Islamic Research Institute, Islamabad, Pakistan, 1986).

Hilli, Tabsirat al-Muta`allimin (Damascus, A.H. 1342).

Iqbal, Afzal., Diplomacy in Islam, An Essay on the Art of Negotiation as Conceived and Developed by the Prophet of Islam (Lahore, 1965).

Iqbal Siddiqi, Muhammad., The Penal Law of Islam (Lahore: Kazi, 1979).

Jafary Langaroody, Muhammad Jafar., Islamic Law (in Persian language, Tehran, 1978).

Jarrett, H.S., History of the Caliphs (Calcutta, 1881).

Johnson Bo, Islamisk rätt: Studier i den islamiska rätts- och samhällsordningen (Stockholm, 1975).

Jullundri, Ali, Ahmad Khan., Translation of the Glorious Holy Qur'an (Lahore, 1962).

Khadduri, Majid (ed.)., Law in the Middle East (1955).

- - War and Peace in the Law of Islam (Baltimore, 1955).

- - Islam and the Modern Law of Nations, 50 American Journal of International Law (1956), pp.358-72.

- - (translator) The Islamic Law of Nations: Shaybani's Siyar (Tanslated with an introduction, notes and appendices, Baltimore, 1966).

- - The Islamic Theory of International Relations and Its Contemporary Relevance, see Proctor, 24-ff.

Lippman, Matthew, Sean McConville, and Mordechai Yerushalmi., Islamic Criminal Law and Procedure: An Introduction (New York, Westport,

Connecticut, London, 1988).

Macdonald, D.B., Development of Muslim Theology, Jurisprudence, and Constitutional Theory (London, 1903).

Mallat, Chibli., The Renewal of Islamic Law, Muhammad Baqer as-Sadr, Najaf and the Shi'i International (Cambridge, University Press, 1993).

Margoliousth, D. S., The Early Development of Muhammadanism (London, 1914).

Maududi, Sayyid Abul A'la., The Islamic Law and Constitution (Islamic Publication Ltd, Lahore, 7th ed. 1980).

Mawdudi, Abu'l A'la., Human Rights in Islam (Leicester, 1980).

Mawlawi, Muhammad Ali., The Religion of Islam (Lahore, 1936).

Mayer, Ann Elizabeth., Islam & Human Rights: Tradition and Politics (London, 1991).

De Menasce Dominican, Pierre Jean., Bibliographische Einführungen in das Studium der Philosophie: G, Arabische Philosophie (Bern, 1948).

Moinuddin, Hasan., The Charter of the Islamic Conference and Legal Framework of Economic Co-Operation among its Member States: A study of the Charter, the General Agreement for Economic, Technical and commercial Co-operation and the Agreement for Promotion, Protection and Guarantee of Investements among Member States of the OIC (Oxford, 1987).

Morland, Samuel., History of the Evangelical Churches of the Valleys of Piedmont (London, 1658).

Muhammad, Ali., Religion of Islam (Lahore, 1936).

An-Na`im, Abdullahi., Toward an Islamic Reformation: Civil Liberties, Human Rights and International Law (Syracuse, 1990).

– – A modern Approach to Human Rights in Islam: Foundations and Implications for Africa, in Claude Welch and Ronald Meltzer (eds.)., Human Rights and Development in Africa (Albany, 1984).

Nawaz, M.K., The Doctrine of 'Jihad' in Islamic Legal Theory and Practice, 8 The Indian Year Book of International Affairs (1959), pp.32-ff.

Proctor, J. Harris(ed)., Islam and International Relations (New York, 1965).

Publications of Centre Culturel Islamique (No.1)., Introduction to Islam (Park Lane, Secunderabad, 1376 H/ 1957 A.C.). This book is also mentioned under Hamidullah, Muhammad.

Rechid, Ahmed., L'Islam et le Droit des Gens, 2 Recueil des Cours, Académie de Droit International (1937), pp.371-506.

Rosenthal, Franz., The Muslim Concept of Freedom Prior to the Nineteenth Century (Leiden, 1960).

Abu-Sahlieh, Sami A. Aldeeb., Les Droits de l'homme et l'Islam, 89 Revue general de droit international public (1985), 625-716.

Abu-Sahlieh, Sami A. Aldeeb., Muslims Human Rights: Challenges and

Perspectives, in Schmale, Wolfgang (ed.)., pp.239–68.

Schmale, Wolfgang (ed.)., Human Rights and Cultural Diversity: Europe. Arabic–Islamic World. Africa. China (Germany, 1993).

Sharwani, Haroon Khan., Studies in Muslim Political Thought and Administration (Lahore, 1959).

Shihata, Ibrahim., Islamic Law and the World Community, I, No.4 Harvard International Club Journal (1962).

Singh, Nagendra, India and International Law, Vol.I (New Delhi, 1973).

Smith, R. Bosworth., Muhammad and Muhammedanism, Lectures delivered at the Royal Institute of Great Britain, 2nd ed. (London, 1876).

Warberg, Lasse A., Shari'A: Om den Islamiske Strafferetten (Uqûbât), 80 (4) Nordisk Tidsskrift for Kriminalvidenskab (1993), pp.260–83.

Watt,W. Montgomery., Free Will and Predestination of Early Islam (London, 1948).

– – Muhammad at Medina (Oxford, 1956).

– – Islam and the Integration of Society (London, 1961).

– – Muhammad, Prophet and Statesman (Oxford, 1961).

– – Islamic Philosophy and Theology (Edinburgh, 1962).

– – The Formative Period of Islamic Thought (Edinburgh, 1973).

Weeramantry C.G., Islamic Jurisprudence: An International Perspective (1988).

Bibliography on International Criminal Law[*]

Ahluwalia, Kuljit., The Legal Status, Privileges and Immunities of the Specialized Agencies of the United Nations and Certain other International Organizations (Hague, 1964) and (1971).

Akehurst, Michael., Hijacking, 14 I.J.I.L. (1974), pp.81–9.

Al–Haq/Law in the Service of Man, Briefing Papers on Twenty Years of Israeli Occupation of the West Bank and Gaza (1987).

Al Haq/Law in the Service of Man, Punishing a Nation: Human rights Violations During the Palestinian Uprising, December 1987 – December 1988 (1988)

Alexander, Glover G., International Criminal Law, III Journal of Comparative Legislation (1921), pp.237–44.

Amnesty International, Israel and the Occupied Territories – Administrative Detention During the Palestinian Intifada (1989).

Amnesty International, Israel and the Occupied Territories – Excessive Force: Beatings to Maintain Law and Order (1988).

Amnesty International, Israel and the Occupied Territories – The Misuse of Tear Gas by Israeli Army Personnel in the Israeli Occupied Territories (1988).

Amnesty International: Report on Torture (1975).

Anonym, The Declaration of Geneva, 1948: A 1971 Reappraisal, 2 The Medical Journal of Australia (1971), No 15, pp.735–6

Anonymous, The Nyon Arrangements – Piracy by Treaty? 19 B.Y.I.L (1938), pp.198–208.

Appleman, Alan John., Military Tribunal and International Crimes (Indianapolis, 1954).

Aroneanu, Eugéne., Le Crime Contre L'Humanité (Paris, 1961).

Awad, Mohamed., Report on Slavery (United Nations, New York, 1966).

Ayala Balthazar., De Jure et Officiis Bellicis et Disciplinac Militari Libri, Vol.II, The Classics of International Law edited by Scott, James Brown., (1919).

Bailey, H.S., The Anti–Drug Campaign, an Experiment in International Control (London, 1935).

Ballis, William., The Legal Position of War: Changes in its Practice and Theory From Plato to Vattel (Hague, 1937).

Bar, L., Das Internationale Private– und Strafrecht (Hannover, 1862),

---

[*] Mention here does not necessarily mean that it is also mentioned in the context of the book.

pp.523–ff.

Barrow, R.H., Slavery in the Roman Empire (London, 1928).

Bassiouni, M. Cherif., The Definition of Aggression in International Law: The Crime Against Peace in Bassiouni and Nanda (1973).

–– An appraisal of the growth and developing trends of international criminal law, 45 Revue Internationale de Droit Pénal (1974).

–– (ed.) International Terrorism and Political Crimes (Illinois, 1975).

–– Unlawful Seizure of Persons by States as Alternatives to Extradition, in Bassiouni (1975), pp.343–73.

–– International Law and the Holocaust, 9 California Western International Law Journal (1979), pp.202–70.

–– International Criminal Law: A Draft International Criminal Code (The Netherlands, 1980).

–– International Criminal Law (The Netherlands, 1980).

–– A Draft International Criminal Code and Draft Statute for an International Criminal Tribunal (Netherlands, 1th ed 1981, 2th ed. 1986).

–– The Proscribing Function of International Criminal Law in the International Protection of Human Rights, – Yale Stud. World Public Order – (1983).

–– Reflections on Criminal Jurisdiction in International Protection of Cultural Property, 10 Syracuse Journal of International Law & Commerce (1983), pp.281–322.

–– I, II International Criminal Law: Crimes (New York, 1986).

–– Characteristics of International Criminal Law Conventions, in Bassiouni, Vol.I (1986), pp.1–13.

–– Introduction to Genocide, in Bassiouni, Vol.I (1986), pp.281–86.

–– Regulation of Armed Conflicts, in Bassiouni, Vol.I (1986), pp.201–7.

–– The International Narcotic Control Scheme, in Bassiouni, Vol.I (1986), pp.507–24.

– – The Time Has Come for an International Criminal Court, 1 Indiana International & Comparative Law Review (1991), pp.1–43;

Bassiouni, M. Cherif and Ved P. Nanda., Vols. I, II A Treatise on International Criminal Law: Crimes and Punishment (Illinois, 1973).

Baumann, Carol. Edler., The Diplomatic Kidnappings, A Revolutionary Tactic or Urban Terrorism (Hague, 1973).

Baxter, R.R., The Municipal and International Basis of Jurisdiction over War Crimes, in Bassiouni and Nanda, Vol.II (1973), p.65–ff.

Bedau, Hugo, Adam., Genocide in Vietnam, 53 Boston University Law Review (1973).

–– Genocide in Vietnam, 53 Boston University Law Review (1973); Bryant, Comment, Part I: Substantive Scope of the Convention, 16 Harvard

International Law Journal (1975).

Bello, Emmanuel., Shared Legal Concepts Between African Customary Norms and International Conventions on Humanitarian Law, 21 I.J.I.L. (1981), pp.79–95.

van Bemmelen, J.M., Reflections and Observations on International Criminal Law, in Bassiouni and Nanda, Vol.1 (1973), pp.77–94.

Berber, F.J., Some Thoughts on the Laws of War and the Punishment of a War Crimes, in Nawaz, pp.260–65.

Bindschedler–Robert, Denise., Biological and Chemical Weapons, in Bassiouni, International Criminal Law (1973), pp.351–6.

–– Problems of the Law of Armed Conflicts, in M. Cherif. Bassiouni and V.P. Nanda, eds., Vol. I (1973), pp.295–319.

Blischenko, Igor, P., Modern International Law and Genocide, Nos. 16–7 Etudes Internationales de Psycho–sociologie Criminelle (1969).

Bowett, D.W., Self–Defence in International Law (New York, 1958).

A Brief History of the Creation by UNESCO of an Intergovernmental Committee for Promoting the Return of Cultural Property to its Countries of Origin or its Restitution in Case of Illicit Appropriation, in Return and Restitution of Cultural Property (special issue), 31 Museum 59, No.1 (1979).

Browne, Edward. G., The Reign of Terror at Tabriz. England's Responsibility (Manchester, 1912).

Brownlie, Ian., International Law and the Use of Force by States (Oxford, 1963).

–– Principles of Public International Law (Oxford, 1979).

–– Basic Documents on Human Rights (Oxford, 1981).

B'Tselem/the Israeli Information Center for Human Rights in the Occupied Territories, Annual Report 1989: Violations of Human Rights in the Occupied Territories (1989).

B'Tselem/the Israeli Information Center for Human Rights in the Occupied Territories, the Military Judicial System in the West Bank (1989).

B'Tselem/the Israeli Information Center for Human Rights in the Occupied Territories, the Use of Firearms by the Security Forces in the Occupied Territories (1990).

B'Tselem/the Israeli Information Center for Human Rights in the Occupied Territories, the System of Taxation in the West Bank and the Gaza strip: As an Instrument for the Enforcement of Authority During the Uprising (1990).

Buchheit, Lee C., The Use of Nonviolent Coercion: A Study in Legality Under Article 2(4) of the Charter of the United Nations, 122 University of Pensylvania Law Review (1974).

Buergenthal, Thomas., Implementing the UN Racial Convention, 12 Texas International Law Journal (1977), pp.187–221.

Burwell, David G., Civilian Protection in Modern Warfare: A Critical Analysis of the Geneva Civilian Convention of 1949, 14 Virginia Journal of International Law (1973), pp.123–50.

van Bynkershoek, Cornelius., Quaestionum Juris Publici Libri duo, The Classics of International Law., edited by Scott James Brown., Vol.II (1930).

Carlton, David and Schaerf, Carlo., International Terrorism and World Security (London, 1975).

Castel, J.G., Polish Treasures in Canada – 1940–1960: A Case History, in International Reciprocity and Cultural Imperialism: Art Treasures–Media–Data Transfer, 69 American Society of International Law (1974), pp.117–37.

Chatterjee., S.K., Legal Aspects of International Drug Control (Hague, Boston, London, 1981).

Clark, Roger. S., The Crime of Apartheid, in I Bassiouni International Criminal Law (1986), pp.299–323.

Clarke, Edward., A Treatise upon the Law of Extradition (London, 1888).

Clarkson, Thomas., An Essay on the Slavery and Commerce of the Human Species, particularly the African, 2th ed. (London, 1788).

Command Responsibility for War Crimes, 82 Yale L. J. (1973), pp.1274–304.

Commentary on the Convention on Psychotropic Substances, done at Vienna on 21 February 1971 (United Nations publication, New York, 1976).

Commentary on the Protocol Amending the Single Convention on Narcotic Drugs, 1961 (United Nations, New York, 1976).

Commentary on the Single Convention on Narcotic Drugs, 1961 (Prepared by the Secretary–General in accordance with paragraph 1 of Economic and Social Council resolution 914 D (XXXIV) of 3 August 1962), United Nations (New York, 1973).

Crelinsten, Ronald and Denis Szabo., Hostage–Taking (Toronto, 1979).

Dautricourt, 'The International Criminal Court: The Concept of International Criminal Jurisdiction – Definition and Limitation of the Subject' in Bassiouni and Nanda, Vol. I (1973).

Derby, Daniel H., A Framework for International Criminal Law, in Bassiouni, Vol.I (1986), pp.33–58.

Dinstein, Yoram., Criminal Jurisdiction Over Aircraft Hijacking, 7 Israel Law Reviw (1972), pp.195–206.

Donnedieu de Vabres, H., Introduction a l'Étude du Droit Pénal International (Paris, 1922).

Draper, G.I.A.D., Human rights and the Law of War, 12 Virginia Journal of International Law (1972), pp.326–56.

Drost, Peter., The Crime of State: Genocide, Vols. I, II (London, 1959).

Duffett, J., Against the Crime of Silence (New York, London, 1968).

Dugard, John., International Terrorism: Problems of Definition, 50 International Affairs (1974), pp.67–81.

Dupuy Trevor. N., and Gay. M. Hammerman, A Documentary History of Arms Control and Disarmament (New York, London, 1973).

Durham, W. Cole, Law of War: Humanitarian Law in Armed Conflicts, 14 H.I.L.J. (1973), pp.573–84.

Edwards, Contribution of the Genocide Convention to the Development of International Law, 8 Ohio Northern University Law Review (1981), pp.300–ff.

Explanatory Report on the European Convention on the International Validity of Criminal Judgments (Council of Europe– Strasbourg, 1970).

Falk, Richard, A., Six Legal Dimensions of the United States Involvement in the Vietnam, in Falk, The Vietnam War and International Law, pp.216–59.

-- The Beirut Raid and the International Law of Retaliation, 63 A.J.I.L. (1969), pp.415–43.

-- The Vietnam War and International Law (Princeton, 1969), 2 vols.

-- Government Accountability 40 Years after Nuremberg, 3 the Journal of World Peace (Spring 1986), No.1, pp.11–5.

Falk, Richard, A, Lee Meyrowitz and Jack Sanderson., Nuclear Weapons and International Law, 20 I.J.I.L. (1980), pp.541–95.

-- and Saul Mendlovitz., Toward a Theory of War Prevention (New York, 1966), pp.307–59.

-- and Burns, H. Weston., The Relevance of International Law to Palestinian Rights in the West Bank and Gaza: In Legal Defense of the Intifada, 32 Harvard International Law Journal (1991), pp.129–57.

Faulkner, Stanley., War Crimes: Responsibility of Individual Servicemen and Superior Officers, 31 Guild Practitioner (1974), pp.131–44.

Feimpong, J.K & S Azadon Tiewel., Can Apartheid Successfully Defy the International Legal System? 5 The Black Law Journal (1977), pp.287–311.

Ferencz, Benjamin B., Compensating Victims of the Crimes of War, 12 Virjinia Journal of International Law (1972), pp.343–56.

-- Defining International Aggression – The Search for World Peace, Vols. I, II (1975).

Finch, Georg A., The Nürenberg Trial and International Law, 41 A.J.I.L. (1947), pp.20–37.

-- The Genocide Convention, 43 A.J.I.L. (1949), pp.732–8.

FitzGerald, Gerald F., The Development of International Rules Concerning Offences and Certain Other Acts Committed on Board Aircraft, 1 The Canadian Yearbook of International Law (1963), pp.230–51.

Friedlander, Robert A., The Foundation of International Criminal Law: A Present–Day Inquiry, 15 Case Western Reserve Journal of International Law (1983), pp.13–25.

Friedman, Leon, ed., I, II The Law of War: A Documentary History, (New York, 1972).

Fundamental Rules of International Humanitarian Law Applicable in Armed Conflicts,, ICRC and League of Red Cross Societies, Geneva, 1979.

Genocide as a Crime Under International Law, 41 A.J.I.L. (1947), pp.145–51.

Glaser, Stefan., Introduction à l'étude du droit international pénal (1954).

-- Infraction Internationale (1957).

-- Le droit international penal, 43 Revue de Droit Pénal et de Criminologie (1962–3), pp.748–53.

-- Droit International Pénal, Son origine, son État Actuel et son développement, L'indice Pénale (1968), pp.297–318.

-- Droit International Pénal Conventionnel, Vol.I (Bruxelles, 1970).

-- Droit International Pénal Conventionnel, Vol.II (Bruxelles, 1978).

Goldenberg, Sydney., Crimes Against Humanity – 1945–1970: A study in making and unmaking of international criminal law, 10 Western Ontario Law Review (1971), pp.1–55.

Gottlieb, Gidon., International Assistance to Civilian Populations in Armed Conflicts, 4 New York University Journal of International Law & Politics (1971).

Gracia–Amador, F. V., State Responsibility in the Light of the New Trends of International Law, 49 A.J.I.L (1955).

Graefrath, Bernhard., Convention Against the Crime of Apartheid, Vol. XI German Foreign Policy (1972), pp.395–402.

-- The Crime of Apartheid: Responsibility and Reparations, Review of Contemporary Law (1981), pp.31–8.

Grahl-Madsen, Atle., Territorial Asylum (Uppsala, 1980).

Graven, Jean., "les crimes contre l'humanité", Académie de droit international de la Haye, Recueil des cours, 1950, Vol.I.

Grebing, Gerhardt., La création d'une Cour pénale internationale: bilan et perspectives, 45 Revue Internationale de Droit Pénal (1974), pp.435–52.

Grotius, Hugo., The Rights of War and Peace (translated by A.C. Campbell, A.M.) Mr. Walter Dunne (Washington, London, 1901).

-- De Juri Belli ac Pacis Libri Tres: Classics of International Law, Vol.II, Translated by Kelsey, Francis W., (1925).

Gulbrandsen, Perry., A Commentary on the Geneva Conventions of August 12, 1949, in Bassiouni and Nanda, Vol.I (1973) pp.368–400.

Herman, Edward. S., The Real Terror Network (Boston, 1984).

Higgins, Rosalyn., The Legal Limits to the Use of Force by Sovereign States: United Nations Practice, 37 British Year Book of International Law (1961).

Hiltermann, Joost., Israel's Deportation Policy in the Occupied West Bank and

Gaza, Al Haq/law in the Service of Man (1986).

Historical Survey, of the Question of International Criminal Jurisdiction (United Nations–General Assembly, International Law Commission, New York, 1949).

History of the United Nations War Crimes Commission (1948).

Holton, Thomas., An International Peace Court, Design for Move from State Crime Toward World Law (Hague, 1970).

Horlick, Gary N., The Developing Law of Hijacking, 12 Harvard International Law Journal (1971), pp.33–70.

Hutchinson, Martha Crenshaw., The Concept of Revolutionary Terrorism, 16 The Journal of Conflict Resolution (1972), pp.383–96.

Indian antiques on display in the Los Angeles County Museum of Art (stolen 1966, display 1971) in The Protection of the Artistic and Archaeological Heritage: A View from Italy and India (United Nations Social Defence Research Institute, Rome, 1976).

International Military Tribunal, Trial of the Major War Criminals Before the International Military Tribunal in Nuremberg, Germany, Vol.XXII (1947).

Jardine, David., A Reading on the Use of Torture in the Criminal Law of England (London, 1837).

Jescheck, Hans–Heinrich., International Criminal Law: Its Object and Recent Developments, in 1 Bassiouni and Nanda (1973), pp.49–76.

Johnson, D.H.N., The Draft Code of Offences Against Peace and Security of Mankind, 4 International and Comparative Law Quarterly (1955).

–– Piracy in Modern International Law, 43 Trans. Grot. Soc. 63 (1957).

The Judgment of the International Military Tribunal for the Trial of German Major War Criminals, Nuremberg 1946, H.M. Stationary Office Cmd. 6964.

Kapoor, K.J.S.R., The International Convention Against the Taking of Hostages, 1979: An Evaluation, 21 I.J.I.L. (1981), pp.253–78.

Kelsen, Hans., Peace Through Law (New York, 1944).

–– The Law of the United Nations: A Critical Analysis of its Fundamental Problems (London, 1950).

Khare, Subhas C., Use of Force Under United Nations Charter (New Delhi, 1985).

Kidd, John., Torture and International Law: A Note on Recent Developments, 15 Law Journal (University of Queensland, 1989), pp.228–38.

Kimminich, Otto., The Present International law of Asylum, 32 Law and State, A Biannual Collection of Recent German Contributions to These Fields (1985), pp.25–46.

–– A "Federal" Right of Self-Determination?, in C. Tomuschat (ed.) Modern Law of Self-Determination (1993), pp.83–100.

Kohler, Josef., Internationales Strafrecht (Stuttgart, 1917).

Kröger, Herbert., Responsibility under International Law for Crimes of Aggression and War - An Important Instrument for Consolidating International Security, XI German Foreign Policy (1972), pp.171–5.

Kuhn, Arthur. K., The Genocide Convention and State Rights, 43 A.J.I.L. (1949), pp.498– 501.

Kunz, Josef. L., The United Nations Convention on Genocide, 43 A.J.I.L. (1949), pp.738–46.

Kuper, Leo., Genocide: Its Political Use in the Twentieth Century (New Haven and London; Yale University Press, 1981).

Lande, Adolf., The Single Convention on Narcotic Drugs, 1961, 16 International Organization (1962), pp.776–97.

Langbein, John. H., Torture and the Law of Proof, Europe and England in the Ancient Régime (Chicago and London, 1977).

Laqueur, Walter., Terrorism (London, 1977).

Lauterpacht, H., The Law of Nations and the Punishment of War Crimes, 21 B.Y.I.L. (1944), pp.58–95.

Law Reports of Trials of War Criminals, Vol.VII (1948).

Lawyers Committee for Human Rights, an Examination of the Detention of Human Rights Workers and Lawyers from the West Bank and Gaza and Conditions of Detention at Ketziot (1988).

LeBlance, Lawrence., The Intent to Destroy Groups in the Genocide Convention: The Proposed U.S. Understanding, 78 no. 2 A.J.I.L. (1984), pp.369–385.

Lee, Andrew., International Suppression of Hijacking, in Bassiouni, International Terrorism and Political Crimes (1975), pp.248–56.

Lemkin, Raphael., Genocide as a Crime under International Law, 41 A.J.I.L (1947), pp.145–51.

Leningrad, Smolensk, Stalingrad and Novgorod. 1 International Military Tribunal, Trial of the Major War Criminals Before the International Military Tribunal (1947).

Lerner, Natan., The U.N. Convention on the Elimination of all Forms of Racial Discrimination (Netherlands, 1980).

Levie, Howard S., Criminality in the Law of War, in Bassiouni, International Criminal Law, Vol.I, 1986, pp.233–42.

Levner, Natan., The U.N. Convention on the Elimination of all forms of Racial Discrimination (Netherlands, 1980).

Lewis, Edward., Responsibility for Piracy in the Middle Ages, XIX Journal of Comparative Legislation and International Law (1937), pp.77–89.

Livingston, Marius H, Kress, Bruce Lee and Wanek Marie G., International Terrorism in the Contemporary World (London, 1978).

Lombois, Claude., Droit Pénal International (France, 1971).

MacDermot, Nial, Q.C., Crimes Against Humanity in Bangladesh, 7 The International Lawyer (1973), pp.476–84.

Malekian, Farhad., International Criminal Responsibility of States – A Study on the Evolution of State Responsibility with Particular Emphasis on the Concept of Crime and Criminal Responsibility (Stockholm, 1985).

– – The System of International Law: Formation, Treaties, Responsibility (Uppsala, 1987).

– – International Criminal Law: The Legal and Critical Analysis of International Crimes, 2 voles. (Uppsala, 1991).

– – Condemning the Use of Force in the Gulf Crisis (Uppsala, 1992, Second Edition 1994).

– – The Principal Function of an International Criminal Tribunal, Paper submitted to the World Conference on the Establishment of an International Criminal Court to enforce International Criminal Law and Human Rights, Associated with the United Nations, International Institute of Higher Studies in Criminal Sciences (Siracusa, Italy, November 2–5, 1992), 16 pp.

– – An Inquiry into the Severe Violations of International Criminal Law in Bosnia–Herzegovina, (A letter to the Members of the Security Council of the United Nations and the General Secretary of the Organization, 27/May/1993), 12 pp.

– – A letter to the Members of the Security Council of the United Nations and the General Secretary of the Organization, July 7, 1993, 5 pp.

– – The Monopolization of International Criminal Law in the United Nations, A Jurisprudential Approach (Uppsala, 1993).

Mallison, W.T. and Mallison, S.V., The Juridical Characteristics of the Palestinian Resistance: An Appraisal in International Law, Vol.II (No.2) Journal of Palestine Studies (1973), pp.64–78.

–– The Concept of Public Purpose Terror in International Law, IV (no 2, Issue 14), Journal of Palestine Studies (1975), pp.36–51.

––The Concept of Public Purpose Terror in International Law: Doctrines and Sanctions to Reduce the Destruction of Human and Material Values, in Bassiouni, International Terrorism and Political Crimes (1975), pp.67–85.

Manner, George., The Legal Nature and Punishment of Criminal Acts of Violence Contrary to the Laws of War, 37 A.J.I.L (1943).

McCaffrey, Stephen. C., Crimes Against the Environment, in Bassiouni, Vol.I (1985), pp.541–61.

McKean, Warwick., Equality and Discrimination under International Law (Oxford, 1983).

Meron Benvenisti., The West Bank Data Base Project 1987 Report (1987).

Meron, Theodor., Enhancing the Effectiveness of the Prohibition of Discrimination Against Women, Vol.84 A.J.I.L. (1990), pp.213–17.

Merze Tate., The Disarmament Illusion: The Movement for a Limitation of Armaments to 1907 (New York, 1942) pp.167-9.

Meyer, E. Karl., The Plundered Past (London, 1973).

Minear, Richard H., Victors' Justice: The Tokyo War Crimes Trial (New Jersey, 1971).

Mitscherlich, Alexander and Mielke, Fred., Doctors of Infamy: the Story of the Nazi Medical Crimes (New York, 1949).

Mueller, G.O. W. and Besharov. Douglas J., Evolution and Enforcement of International Criminal Law, in Bassiouni, (1986), pp.59-80.

Mueller, G.O.W. and Wise, E. M., International Criminal Law (London, 1965).

Mugadu, Isabirye David., State Responsibility for Nationals Who Serve as Mercenaries in Armed Conflicts, 26 I.L.I.L. (1986), p.405-424.

Mushkat, Roda., "Technical" Impediments on the Way to a Universal Definition of International Terrorism, 20 I.J.I.L. (1980), pp.448-71.

Nafziger, James A.R., The New International Legal Framework for the Return, Restitution or Forfeiture of Cultural Property, 15 New York University Journal of International Law and Politics (1982), pp.789-812.

Nahlik, Stanislaw E., International Law and the Protection of Cultural Property in Armed Conflicts, 27 The Hastings Law Journal (1976), pp.1069-87.

Nawaz, M.K. (ed.), Essays on International Law (The Netherelands, 1976), pp.260-65.

Ndulo, Muna., The Developing Law of Air Hijacking, 3-4 Zambia Law Journal (1971), pp.125-142.

Noll, Alfons., Drug Abuse and Penal Provisions of the International Drug Control Treaties, 29 Bulletin on Narcotics (1977), pp.41-57.

Nordlöf, Kerstin., Straffprocessuella Tvångsmedel: Gripande, Anhållande och Häktning (Stockholm, 1987).

O'Brien, William V., The Law of War, Command Responsibility and Vietnam, 60 The Georgetown Law Journal (1972), pp.605-64.

Owen, David. Edward., British Opium Policy in China and India (London, 1934).

van Panhuys, Haro. F., Aircraft Hijacking and International Law, 9 Columbia Journal of International Law (1970) pp.1-22.

Pariente, M., L'approche Psychologique du génocide, Études Internationales de psycho-sociologie criminelle, No. 11, 12 and 13 (1967).

Parry, L. A., The History of Torture in England (London, 1934).

Parry, Clive., The Consolidated Treaty Series (1969 & Suppl., 231 Vols.)

Pella, Vespasien V., La Criminalite Collective des Etats et le Droit Penal de l'Avenir (2ed., 1925).

-- La Répression de la Piraterie, in Hague Academy, Recueil des Cours, 15 (1926) (V).

-- La répression des crimes contre la personnalité internationale de l'Etat (Paris, 1931).

-- Plan d'un Code Repressif Mondial, Revue Internationale de Droit Penal 12: 148 (1935).

-- La Guerre-Crime et les Criminels de Guerre (Genève, Paris, 1946).

-- Plan for World Criminal Code, 17 Revue Internationale de Droit Penal, (1946).

-- Fonctions Pacificatrices du Droit Pénal Supranational et Fin du Système Traditionnel des Traités de Paix, LI Droit International Public (1947), pp.1-27.

-- Towards an International Criminal Court, 44 A.J.I.L (1950), pp.37-68.

Perlman, Philip. B., The Genocide Convention, XXX Nebraska Law Review (1950, no.1), pp.1-10.

Peters, Edward., Torture (Great Britain, 1985).

Phillips, Orie L and Deutsch, Eberhard P., Pitfalls of the Genocide Convention, 56 American Bar Association Journal (1970), pp.641-6.

Physicians for Human Rights, the Casualties of Conflict: Medical Care and Human Rights in the West Bank and Gaza Strip (1988).

Plawski, Stanislaw., Etude des Principes Fondamentaux du Droit International Pénal (Paris, 1972).

Playfair, Emma., Administrative Detention in the Occupied West Bank, Al Haq/Law in the Service of Man (1986).

Poulantzas, Nicholas M., The Hague Convention for the Suppression of Unlawful Seizure of Aircraft (December, 1970), XVIII, Netherlands International Law Review (1971), pp.25-75.

The Protection of the Artistic and Archaeological Heritage: A View from Italy and India (United Nations Social Defence Research Institute, Rome, 1976), pp.226-41.

Pufendorf, Samuel., De Jure Naturae et Gentium Libri octo. The Classics of International Law., Edited by Scott, James Brown., Vol.II (1934).

Radin, Max., International Crimes, 32 Iowa Law Review (1946), pp.33-50.

Raymond, John M., Genocide: An Unconstitutional Human Rights Convention? 12 Santa Clara Lawyer (1972), pp.294-318.

Reddy, Enuga S., Apartheid: The United Nations and the International Community (New Delhi, 1986).

Reisman, W.M., Responses to Crimes of Discrimination and Genocide: An Appraisal of the Convention on Elimination of Racial Discrimination, I the Denver Journal of International Law and Policy (1971), pp.29-64.

Report of the National Lawyers Guild 1977 Middle East Delegation, Treatment of Palestinians in Israeli–Occupied West Bank and Gaza (1978).

1988 Report of the National Lawyers Guild, International Human Rights Law and Israel's Efforts to Suppress the Palestinian Uprising (1989).

Report of the Special Committee to Investigate Israeli Practices Affecting the Human Rights of the Population of the Occupied Territories, U.N. Press Release, Department of Public Information, Press Release G.A/7977, 22 January 1990, Resolutions and Decisions Adopted by the General Assembly During the First Part of Its forty–fourth Session from 19 September to 29 December 1989.

Richard (ed.)., Genocide in Paraguay (Temple University Press, Philadelphia, 1976).

Roberts, Adam., and Guelff, Richard., Documents on the Laws of War (Oxford, 1982).

Roberts, Adam., Prolonged Military Occupation: The Israeli–Occupied Territories since 1967, 84 American Journal of International Law (1990), pp.44–103.

Royse, Morton William., Aerial Bombardment and the International Regulation of Warfare (New York, 1928).

Rubin, L., Apartheid in Practice (1971), in Feimpong., pp.287–311.

Ryu, Paul K and Silving, Helen., International Criminal Law – Search for Meaning, in Bassiouni and Nanda, Vol.I (1973), pp.22–49.

Sandoz, Yves., Penal Aspects of International Humanitarian Law, in Bassiouni, 1 International Criminal Law (1986) pp.209–32.

Sarkar, L., The Proper Law of Crime in International Law, 11 International Law & Comparative Law Quarterly (1962).

Sartre, Jean–Paul., On Genocide (Boston, 1968).

–– On Genocide, in Duffett.

Schick, F.B., International Criminal Law – Facts and Illusions, 11 The Modern Law Review (1948), pp.290–305.

Schiller, Barry. M., Life in a Symbolic Universe: Comments on the Genocide Convention and International Law, 9 Southwestern University Law Review (1977), pp.47–83.

Schindler, Dietrich and Toman Jiri., The Laws of Armed Conflict (Leiden, Geneva, 1973 and 1981).

Schwarzenberger, Georg., The Problem of an International Criminal Law 3 Current Legal Problems (1950), pp.263–96.

–– Problem of an International Criminal Law, 3 Current Legal Problems (1950), pp.263–96.

–– International Law as Applied by International Court and Tribunals, vol. 2, The Law of Armed Conflicts (1968).

–– Neo–Barbarism and International Law, 22 Year Book of World Affairs

(1968), pp.191-ff.

Schwelb, Egon., Crimes Against Humanity, XXIII B.Y.B.I.L. (1946), pp.178-225.

Scott, George Ryley., The History of Torture Throughout the Ages (1954, London).

Sellin, J. Thorsten., Slavery and the Penal System (New York, Oxford, Amsterdam, 1976).

Seltzer, Garry., The Rule of the South Africa Criminal Code in Implementing Apartheid, 8 Georgia Journal of International and Comparative Law (1978), pp.176-94.

Shaalan, Mohammed., Psychological Aspects of Torture, Revue International de Droit Pénal (1977), N.os 3 et 4, pp.247-259.

Shaker, Mohamed I., The Nuclear Non-Proliferation Treaty: Origin and Implementation 1959-1979 (London, Rome, New York, 1980), Vols.I and II.

Shotwell, James., War as an Instrument of National Policy, and its Renunciation in the Pact of Paris (New York, 1929).

Singh, J.N., Use of Force Under International Law (New Delhi, 1984).

Sottile, Antoine., Le Terrorisme International, 65 Acadèmie de Droit International (1937).

Spencer Landsman, Provisions of National Constitutions Relevant to the Prevention or Prohibition of Torture, 48 Revue Internationale de Droit Pénal (1977), No. 3-4, pp.139-211.

Stone, Julius., Aggression and World Order (Berkeley and Los Angeles, London, 1958).

Stowell, Ellery C., Intervention in International Law (Washington, 1921).

Stuyt, A.M., Genocide, 23 Nederlands Juristenblad (1948), No.9 pp.125-51 and No.10 pp.157-163.

Sørensen, Max., Manual of Public International Law (Hong Kong, 1978).

Taylor, Telford., The Concept of Justice and the Laws of War, 13 Columbia Journal of International Law (1974), pp.189-207.

Tornaritis, Criton., The Individual as a Subject of International Law and International Criminal Responsibility, in 1 Bassiouni and Nanda, A Treatise on International Criminal Law: Crimes and Punishment (Illinois, 1973), pp.103-121.

Torture in the Eighties: An Amnesty International Report (Amnesty International Publications, 1984).

Trials of War Criminals Before the Nuremberg Military Tribunals under Control Council Law No. 10 (Nuremberg, 1946-1949), vol.II.

Tricaud, Martial., The Law of War and Weapons of Mass Destruction, in Bassiouni and Nanda, Vol.I (1973), pp.327-38.

Triffterer, Otto., Jurisdiction Over States for Crimes of State, in Bassiouni and Nanda, Vol.2 (1973), pp.86–96.

De Vabres, Les Principes Modernes du Droit Pénal International (Paris, 1928).

De Vattel, E., The Law of Nations (ed., by Chitty, London, 1844).

De Victoria, Francisco., De Indis et Ivre Belli Relectiones, The Classics of International Law, ed., by Scott, James Brown., (1917).

Ward, Robert., An Enquiry into the Foundation and History of the Law of Nations in Europe: from the time of the Greeks and Romans to the Age of Grotius (London, 1795).

Whitney, Vernon Cassin, and Kailes, Deberois Howard, and Thompson, Terence., The Definition of Aggression, 16 The Harvard International Law Club Journal (1975).

Wilkinson, Paul., Political Terrorism (New York, 1974).

Williams, Sharon A., The International and National Protection of Movable Cultural Property: A Comparative Study (New York, 1978).

–– The Draft Code of Offenses Against the Peace and Security of Mankind in Bassiouni, International Criminal Law (1985), pp.109–121.

Wolff, Christian., Jus Gentium Methodo Scientifica Pertractatum, The Classics of international Law, edited by Scott, James Brown., Vol.II. (1934).

Wright, Quincy., The Law of the Nuremberg Trial, 41 A.J.I.L (1947), pp.38–72.

–– The Scope of International Criminal Law: A Conceptual Framework, 15 Va. J. Int'l L. (1975), pp.561–ff.

Index

Abbassids, 7
Asylum, 144, 148, 149, 150, 151, 152
Canon Law, 9
Christian, 4, 58, 85
Communist, 4, 49
Countries and cities
  Afghanistan, 141
  Africa, 100
  Algeria, 141
  Bahrain, 141
  Bangladesh, 141
  Benin, 141
  Bosnia-Herzegovina, 28, 144, 147, 155
  Brunei, 141
  Cameroon, 141
  Canada, 136
  Chad, 141
  China, 54
  Comoros, 141
  Djibouti, 141
  Egypt, 141
  France, 42, 136
  Gabon, 141
  Gambia, 141
  Geneva, 25, 26, 36, 60, 66, 67, 68, 69, 76,
    81, 99, 155
  Greece, 2, 85
  Guinea, 141
  Guinea-Bissau, 141
  Hiroshima, 74
  Hudaibiya, 112, 150
  Indonesia, 141
  Iran (Persia), 29, 115, 136, 141, 150
  Iraq, 54, 91, 136
  Israel, 143, 144
  Jordan, 141
  Kuwait, 136, 141
  Lebanon, 141
  Libyan Arab Jamahiriya, 141
  Madinah, 1, 3, 136
  Malaysia, 141
  Maldives, 141
  Mali, 141
  Mauritania, 141
  Mecca, 60, 112, 135, 136, 150, 151
  Morocco, 141
  Nagasaki, 74
  Niger, 141
  Nigeria, 141
  Nuremberg, 22, 27, 42, 63, 66, 76, 77, 93,
    155, 161
  Oman, 141
  Oxford, 55
  Palestine, 142, 143
  Paris, 64
  Persia, see Iran
  Qatar, 141
  Rome, 2, 85
  Saudi Arabia, 141
  Senegal, 141
  Sierra Leone, 141
  Somalia, 141
  South Africa, 24
  Soviet Union, 42, 49, 113, 143
  Stockholm, 123
  Sudan, 141
  Sweden, 123, 136
  Syrian Arab Republic, 141
  Teheran, 115, 150
  Thailand, 122, 123
  Tibet, 54
  Tokyo, 27, 155
  Tunisia, 141
  Turkey, 54, 91, 141, 142, 143
  Uganda, 141
  United Arab Emirates, 141
  United Kingdom, 42, 85, 98, 136
  United States, 42, 79, 85, 100, 113, 115,
    136
  Upper Volta (Burkina-Faso), 141
  Vienna, 107
  Vietnam, 74
  Yemen - Arab Republic, 141
  Yemen -People's Democratic Republic,
    141
  Yugoslavia, 42, 54, 63, 155, 174
Crimes
  adultery, 39

against cultural property, 40
against foodstuffs, 129–30
against honour, 39
against humanity, 25, 33, 39, 76–8, 91, 93, 95, 96, 161, 174, 176, 179
against internationally protected persons, 40, 107–12
against peace, 25, 33
against property, 39
against the natural environment, 40, 126–8
aggression, 7, 15, 38, 39, 45–62, 71, 140
apartheid, 23, 24, 33, 36, 39, 76, 94–97, 108, 160, 172, 173, 174, 176, 179
discrimination, 23, 24
drug offences, 33, 39, 40, 116–20, 176
falsification, 40
fornication, 39
genocide, 20, 23, 24, 25, 27, 28, 33, 36, 39, 42, 54, 76, 90–3, 147, 160, 172, 174, 176, 177, 179
highway robbery, 39
hijacking, 40
kidnapping, 88, 111
mail offences, 40
mercenaries, 39
obscene publications offence, 39, 40, 121–5, 176, 177
piracy, 40, 79, 132–4, 177
prohibitions on alcohol, 39, 40, 131
slavery, 39, 79–89, 98, 149, 160
taking of hostages, 40, 113–5
terrorism, 33, 40
theft, 39
torture, 39, 98–106, 160, 174
unlawful acts on the sea, 40
unlawful medical experimentation, 39
unlawful use of Weapons, 25, 39, 74–5
war crimes, 22, 25, 33, 39, 63–73, 93, 155, 156, 161, 174, 177, 178, 179
    list of, 64–5, 72–3,
dar al-'ahd, 7
dar al-Harb, 7
dar al-Islam, 7
dar al-sulh, 7
defensive war, 16, 52, 55, 56
Definition of
International criminal law, 20
Islamic international criminal law, 20–22

Islamic international law, 3–6
European
    community, 10
    conventions, 100
    countries, 79, 129, 136, 143
    Human Rights Court, 37
    international criminal law, 108–9
    international law, 4
Fatawa, 34
Geneva Conventions, 26, 36, 60, 66, 67, 68, 69, 76
Governments
    Chinese, 54
    Turkish, 54
hadith, 7, 31, 127, 129, 162, 165
Hague Peace Conferences, 3
Herzegovina, 42
Humanitarian law of armed conflicts, 3, 8, 9, 22, 26, 33, 64, 83, 140, 148, 157
ibadat (ritual), 9
Ijma, 29, 30, 32–33, 35, 51
Ijtihad, 35, 55–61
International Court of Justice, 27, 147
International Military Tribunal, 22, 27, 42, 63, 65, 66, 76, 93, 172, 179
International   treaties   (conventions, protocols), 14, 46, 63, 66, 67, 68, 69, 74, 76, 77, 80, 81, 90, 94, 95, 99, 100, 101, 107, 108, 110, 113, 116, 121, 122, 123, 133, 154, 155, 160, 172, 179
Intervention, 33, 39
Islamic
    human rights, 3, 6, 8, 9, 33, 93, 148, 149, 162–71
    laws, 3, 9, 30
    principle of jurisdiction, 10, 11
    principles, 31
    subjects, 38
Istislah, 29
Jihad, 7, 50, 52–61
Jus Cogens, 14–5, 20, 100
League of Nations, 17, 46, 70, 142
De Lege Lata, 13–4
Medina, 1
    Covenant of Medina, 1
Middle Ages, 156
mu'amalat, 9
Mukhtar al-Kawnain, 3
Muslim states, 1

de facto, 3
de jure, 3
Names
  Abu-Sufyan, 51, 136
  Ali Ben Abi Taleb, 51, 140
  Arab, 56, 58, 59, 83, 84, 87, 142, 143, 158
  Aristotle, 45
  Augustine, 45
  Ayala, 45
  Balfour, 142
  Banu–Quraizah, 135, 150
  Bynkershoek, 45
  Cicero, 45
  Farqad, 1
  Grotius, 2, 45
  Heraclitus, 45
  Herzl, 142
  Irish, 102
  Jaffa, 143
  Jew, 56, 58, 93, 142, 143, 154
  Kurd, 54
  Langaroody, 34
  Lemkin, 94
  Plato, 45
  Pufendorf, 45
  Rashidin Caliphs, 51
  Serb, 54, 144, 155, 174
  Victoria, 45
  Wolff, 45
  Zionism, 143
Nato, 144
nulla poena sine lege, 21, 179
nullum crimes sine lege, 21, 179
Organization of Islamic Conference, 141
PLO (Palestine Liberation Organization),
  144
Pacta Sunt Servanda, 12–3, 54
Peace Treaty of Versailles, 46
Place of Worship, 60
Purpose of international criminal law, 20–1
Qital, 55, 57
Qiyas, 28, 30, 34–35
Quesas, 92
Sacred Mosque, 12
Second Pledge of Al-`aqaba, 1
self–defence, 16, 50, 52, 55, 58, 59, 60, 61,
  71, 135, 136–8, 140, 146
Self–determination, 33, 108, 110, 141, 143,
  144

Shari'ah, 6, 8, 9, 12, 13, 15, 50, 51, 129,
  164, 167
Al–Shaybain, 1
Shi'a, 140
siyar, 1
Statute of the International Court of
  Justice, 4, 147
Sunnah, 5, 6, 9, 29, 31–32, 35, 51, 115, 157,
  168, 177
Treaty of *Hudaybiyah*, 59
United Nations, 11, 14, 17, 23, 33, 42, 46,
  47, 48, 50, 53, 54, 63, 66, 68, 70, 76, 80,
  99, 108, 122, 133, 138, 141, 144, 147,
  160, 172, 173
  definition of aggression 38
  draft code, 38, 40, 48
  General Assembly, 33, 48, 121, 141, 144,
    161
  International Law Commission, 38, 173
  Security Council, 42, 47, 48, 49, 53, 54,
    138, 141, 143, 144
War
  American Civil War, 79
  Badr, 84, 87
  Gulf War, 54
  Vietnam War, 74
  World War I, 17, 22, 24, 42, 46, 64, 70,
    94, 154
  World War II, 17, 22, 24, 38, 70, 78, 90,
    94, 143, 154, 160, 172
Western, 2, 3, 49, 149, 154
  writers, 11